Charles Benson

on
Board Barque
Glide

This Journal
was
Written For Jenny—
by

Chas. A. Benson
on
Board of Barque Glide
Her Voyage on to the East Coast
of

Africa

1862
—

Charles Benson

MARINER OF COLOR IN
THE AGE OF SAIL

Michael Sokolow

University of Massachusetts Press
Amherst and Boston

LC 2003006416
ISBN 1-55849-409-X

Designed by Dennis Anderson
Set in Bell by Graphic Composition, Inc.
Printed and bound by The Maple-Vail Book Manufacturing Group

Library of Congress Cataloging-in-Publication Data
Sokolow, Michael.
Charles Benson : mariner of color in the age of sail / Michael Sokolow.
p. cm.
Includes bibliographical references and index.
ISBN 1-55849-409-X (alk. paper)
1. Benson, Charles A., 1830–1881. 2. African-American sailors—Massachusetts—
Salem—Biography. 3. Seafaring life. 4. Glide (Bark) I. Title.
G540 .S645 2003
910.4'5'092—dc21
2003006416

British Library Cataloguing in Publication data are available.

All illustrations are courtesy of the Peabody Essex Museum,
Salem, Massachusetts.

FRONTISPIECE: Title page of Charles Benson's 1862 journal.

Ar-Ar is a darling wife
She is My Love, My Joy, My Life

What a miserable life a sea fareing life is.
I will stop it if I live & that soon (that is if I get any thing to do on shore).
you & the children must have things to eat drink & were
& I must get it some were if not on land, on the sea
I am willing live & die on the sea if you are only contented

good night Jenny

CONTENTS

ILLUSTRATIONS

ACKNOWLEDGMENTS

"Thanks to kind friends"

THIS BOOK could not have been written without the support of the following, and I am grateful to them all. Boston University was generous with graduate stipends while I pursued my degree. A Phillips Research Fellowship at the Essex Institute (now the Peabody Essex Museum) and Mystic Seaport Museum's Paul Cuffe Fellowship for the Study of Minorities in Maritime History aided my research. Later I benefited from a Summer Seminar for College Teachers funded by the National Endowment for the Humanities, and also a PSC Research Grant from the City University of New York. The Peabody Essex Museum was kind enough to limit its illustration fees for this volume. The Sokolow Foundation provided two computers, a laser printer, and unlimited free babysitting; I hope their faith and support have been justified.

Many archival staff members and librarians helped me obtain and navigate the sources I needed. Jane Ward at the Essex Institute's Phillips Library was the first to place Charles Benson's journal notebooks in my hands; I thank her along with everyone else at the Peabody Essex Museum, particularly Will LaMoy. My thanks go out to Mystic Seaport Museum's Blunt-White Library and the research staff at the New England and Middle Atlantic branches of the National Archives, the American Antiquarian Society, Brandeis University, and Yale University's Beinecke Library.

I would also like to thank those individuals who stewarded my earliest work on Charles Benson: Marilyn Halter and Nina Silber of Boston University, and Benjamin W. Labaree, Edward W. Sloan, William M. Fowler Jr., and John Hattendorf of the Munson Institute at Mystic Seaport. B. R. Burg and Joseph Reidy provided careful and insightful readings of my work, as did William Fowler and the editorial staff at the *New England Quarterly*. I thank David Thelen and the anonymous readers on the Pelzer Prize Committee at the *Journal of American History* for their suggestion that I submit my work to the *Quarterly*, and for their advisory comments as well.

Three scholars have been particularly important to me. W. Jeffrey

Bolster has been a part of this project from its inception. He made time for me after panel presentations and museum lectures, on the telephone, and at professional meetings large and small; I thank him for his valued criticism and patience. David Katzman chose me as a participant in an NEH summer seminar at the University of Kansas, "The Growth of African-American Urban Communities." He has guided me ever since with gentle kindness and good humor, and has been both a mentor and very good friend to me. Finally, I am grateful to Julie Winch for her boundless support, insight, and good cheer.

I extend my appreciation as well to Lisa Norling, James O. Horton, Lois E. Horton, E. Anthony Rotundo, Nick Salvatore, and Daniel Vickers for going above and beyond the standards of professionalism in their warmth and courtesy. Paul Wright, my editor at the University of Massachusetts Press, has been a marvel of patience and commitment over a period of more than five years. Deborah Smith, my copy editor, and Carol Betsch, managing editor of the Press, were both tremendously important in the preparation of the final manuscript.

Many shipmates have helped me weather the calms and storms of my long voyage with Charles Benson, including Tom Denenberg, Stephanie Taylor, and Glenn Gordinier. Johnny Clegg, Peter Garrett, Mark Knopfler, Andy Partridge, Julia Quinn, and Paul Simon helped motivate me to sit down at the computer, and Alex and Janet Evanovich lent me the soul of a writer. CUNY has been my home for nearly two decades, and I have flourished under the tutelage of Lillian Schlissel, Kenneth Bruffee, Teofilio Ruiz, Bernice Levinson, the late Robert L. Hess, Bernard Klein, and Stuart Suss. Dennis, Faye, Benjo, and Yosef Wilbur provided me with all the affection I could ever need, as have Melanie, Jennifer, and Daniel Sokolow. To my parents, Vera and Peter Sokolow, I owe years of boundless gratitude and love.

My children, Nat, Aviva, and Zahava, have no idea who Charles Benson was. Since there were times when I wasn't too sure myself, I know how they feel. My crew at home deserves a lot of credit for putting up with me throughout this process and for helping me to understand what family dynamics are all about. As for the Captain, my wife Arden, she knows that I will happily sign on as her steward any time, anywhere. This book is dedicated to her.

Charles Benson

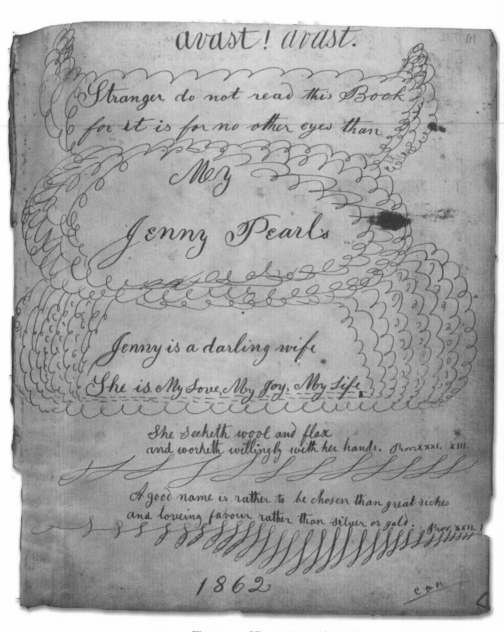

avast! avast.

Stranger do not read this Book
for it is for no other eyes than

My

Jenny Pearl's

Jenny is a darling wife
She is My Love My Joy My Life

She seeketh wool and flax
and worketh willingly with her hands. Prov. XXXI. XIII.

A good name is rather to be chosen than great riches
and loveing favour rather than silver or gold. Prov. XXII. I

1862

FIGURE 1. First page of Benson's 1862 journal.

INTRODUCTION

"Stranger do not read this Book"

"AVAST! *avast*. Stranger do not read this Book for it is for no other eyes than My Jenny Pearl's." Charles Augustus Benson, steward of the merchant bark *Glide*, wrote these words in late April 1862. Heartsick, "home sick, sea sick, & in fact sick all over," the thirty-two-year-old mariner was beginning a lengthy sea voyage from his home port of Salem, Massachusetts, to trading destinations scattered throughout the Indian Ocean and Red Sea. As a deepwater veteran who had spent the better part of the previous decade under sail, Benson had traveled this route before. But his long years of experience did little to mitigate the loneliness he felt at sea, his sense of isolation exacerbated by the racial divide that lay between him, a black man, and the white sailors who constituted the majority of the *Glide*'s complement. Bereft of the company of his beloved wife, Margaret Jenny, he sought solace and comfort in the expression of his personal reflections. For the first time in his seafaring career and perhaps the first time in his life, Charles Augustus Benson began recording his most private thoughts daily in the pages of a journal.[1]

Charles Benson was one of thousands of men who shipped out of New England in the nineteenth century. As he and his contemporaries knew very well, the life of the sailor encompassed long periods of tedium and hardship, punctuated by moments of great excitement and at times life-threatening danger. The testimony to the challenges, difficulties, and rewards of this life exists in the form of sea journals. Hundreds of men took pen to paper and faithfully recorded their seafaring experiences. Some of these men confided their innermost thoughts and feelings to their journals. Others were more reticent about revealing their emotions. Although thousands of black men shipped out in the nineteenth century, almost none left behind any detailed testimony of their lives at sea. Most extant descriptions of black seafarers at sea come from secondhand sources, such as the journals and ships' logs kept by white sailors.[2]

As one of the few existing narratives composed by a black mariner,

Benson's personal diaries provide a window into the hopes, fears, and experiences of one nineteenth-century black man who went to sea. On the surface, there is little to distinguish this sea journal from those kept by thousands of white seafarers during the age of sail. Benson's diary entries describe his constant homesickness and boredom, reveal his fears and the contents of his dreams, and speak of the daily realities of his sea life; these elements are present in journals kept by sailors of all races. Yet Benson was different from other sailors, not only because of his race but also because of his unique shipboard role as a seafaring steward and sometime cook. His tasks, responsibilities, and attitudes differed from those of the men before the mast, and his journal entries reflect this difference. Benson's journals, like those kept by white sailors and officers of his era, record the highs and lows of sea life. But in many ways his journals differ significantly from other diaries, and like their author, a literate, expressive, mixed-race seaman of color, they are unique.

In fact, they are unique because few people of color in any occupational field kept diaries during the nineteenth century. Of those who did, only a small percentage were members of what is conventionally known as the working class (although within the black community definitions of wealth and status differed in some ways from those of contemporary white Americans).[3] The four extant volumes of Benson's sea journal offer a singular opportunity to explore the experiences of an unremarkable nineteenth-century black worker. The two-decade period covered by the journals makes them even more valuable, offering the chance to chart the long-term changes and transformations that took place over the course of an individual black working-class man's experience.

In general terms Benson's life was similar to the lives of most blacks in the nineteenth-century North. Like him many blacks were transient, and over the course of the century many abandoned tiny and scattered black settlements like the Massachusetts town where Benson grew up to join together in larger urban communities. Occupational instability and economic hardship were common throughout northern black communities, where few blacks ever owned any property or could afford to buy a house, and many spent their lives in rented ramshackle houses similar to the ones where Benson lived out his life ashore. His decision to find maritime work was replicated by many black men of his era, who sought to take advantage of the unusually broad job opportunities seafaring offered them. Finally, Benson's death at the relatively young age of fifty-one also reflected the conditions of blacks in the urban North, where black mortality rates outstripped those of whites and black life-spans were substantially shorter. Single-parent female-headed households were prevalent in black communities, and among them were the families reared by Charles's mother, Elizabeth Benson, his abandoned first wife, Martha Ann Benson Boquette, and his eventual widow, Margaret Jenny Benson.

According to many historians, most people of color who grew up in this environment were bound together by shared culture, language, and space. Race became the primary determining factor of identity for nineteenth-century blacks, far more important than outside factors such as work. In their settlements throughout the urban North, black culture and consciousness were formed, nurtured, and preserved by black schools, churches, and social organizations. Black communities devised strategies to cope with the strictures of a racist society, such as flexible living arrangements that accommodated kinfolk, boarders, and foster children. Their leaders, including prominent religious figures, abolitionists, and members of the small but active black elite, further united the people in common causes that affected all black Americans, drawing them into the struggles to end slavery, to win the Civil War, and to end racist maltreatment of blacks by whites.

In this view, a strong sense of racial identity among nineteenth-century blacks is a given. Tied together by communal bonds and strongly influenced by the words and deeds of black leaders, they shared the experience of being black in a white America that was often oppressive and hostile to other races. Their shared space and culture and thus their sense of blackness affected their personal identity formation.[4]

This pattern did not hold true for Charles Benson. At no time in his life did Benson live in a thriving black community rich in black institutions and social organizations. Although he was affiliated with a black church as an adult, the connection between Benson and the church seems to have been brief and of secondary importance to him over the long run. In his journals Benson mentions few other blacks, rarely refers to the black community to which he and his family belonged, and never alludes to any black leaders, elites, or religious figures. Furthermore, Benson's relationship with his race and blackness was complex, ambiguous, and at times uncertain. His journal entries shy away from overt references to race, and even the most careful examination of his diary yields only a few clues that its author was not white, as most sailors were.

In many ways, Benson's determination to define himself for himself represented the apotheosis of the American ideology of individualism. In his era Victorian culture promulgated the concept of the self-constructed identity for all men, not merely the upper classes. As the forces of political, economic, social, and cultural democratization swept through the nation, the ideal of the fully realized individual was exalted. Through self-improvement, one of the fundamental core values of the antebellum period, each man was believed to have the power to sculpt his own sense of self, to develop it further or even create it anew. At a time when the American vision of community was moving toward Walt Whitman's conceptualization of "ensemble-Individuality," there was a great deal of emphasis on one's own agency and self-determinism.[5]

Although this autonomy of the self was intended chiefly for white male Protestant Americans, Charles Benson refused to be excluded from the promise of American culture. Secluded from a larger black America by the circumstances of his rural birth and upbringing, Benson absorbed the mores of the world around him. Throughout his life Benson was steeped in the values of mainstream America. The rhetoric of this ideology suffused the newspaper articles and books he read and resonated in the words and attitudes of the men with whom he lived and worked. The American dream of self-definition became his dream, guiding his behavior and interpretation of the events and decisions that characterized his life. But because the nineteenth-century American compact was not and had never been intended for a working-class black man, Benson would never be able to fully reconcile his borrowed ideals with the realities of his life.

Benson's attempts to construct an identity for himself were also complicated by the fact that he did not have a single identity but several, none of them clear-cut. By the standards of his time Benson was a Negro, a black man in terms of his race, ancestry, and social status, although he was of mixed-race heritage. For an extended time Benson identified himself by his occupation, variously calling himself a mariner, a seafaring cook, and a steward; yet he came to the sea late for a sailor, in his mid-twenties, and he took a long break from seafaring in the middle of his career. Benson firmly held himself to be a true man in the Victorian sense of the term, a devoted father and husband and an economic provider for his family. At times, though, his ability to fulfill the masculine imperatives he held dear was severely curtailed, and his manhood was also compromised by the feminine nature of his occupational tasks.

The components of Benson's self-conception—his racial, gender, and work identities—coexisted, overlapped, and sometimes conflicted with each other.[6] They also were not static but dynamic, gradually changing. His frank and expressive journal entries provide some measure of access to the processes of his identity formation and transformations. As Benson revealed through his writings, the different roles he played throughout his life—individual man of mixed race, member of a black community, resident of Salem, career mariner, and literate nineteenth-century American—all shaped his sense of self.

"Avast! *avast.*" Benson admonished on the first page of his first journal notebook in 1862, "Stranger do not read this Book." That warning has resounded for me ever since the first time I brazenly ignored it, opened up his journal, and began to read his story more than a decade ago. Although I no longer consider myself a complete stranger to the man, I still pause to contemplate that cautionary statement every time I renew my acquaintance with Charles A. Benson. At the time that I first read it, I knew nothing of his background or history; for me, it represented the beginning of his story. I did not know then that the true origins of Benson's tale lay further back in the past, in the eighteenth-century town of Framingham, Massachusetts. As I reveal Benson's full story for the first time, I ask that you do "read this Book," for it has much to tell.

CHAPTER ONE

"My Fathers Birth Day in 1800"

FRAMINGHAM, 1721–1830

CHARLES BENSON was born into the oldest and largest black family in Framingham, Massachusetts. His paternal great-great-grandparents, Nero and Dido Benson, were brought to Framingham from Africa sometime before 1720. Their son William, born into slavery in 1732, attained his freedom shortly before the birth of his son Abel, Charles's grandfather, in 1766. Eighteen years later Abel married a young woman named Rhoda Jahah, and over the next quarter-century the couple had eleven children. Their ninth child, born on July 5, 1802, was Charles Benson's father, George.[1] Charles Benson's century-long heritage, with its roots in slavery and small-town Massachusetts life, was common among black New Englanders of his generation. But in several important ways his tale is unique, not least because so much evidence remains to reconstruct his personal past.

In the days of Nero and Dido Benson, Framingham was an agricultural hamlet with several forges and small mills and fewer than five hundred inhabitants. The town comprised small farming families living in residential settlements loosely arranged around kin relationships. By the end of the eighteenth century the town's population had swelled to more than sixteen hundred, including twenty-six blacks (up from zero when the town was first incorporated in 1700). The tiny proportion of blacks in Framingham was typical of farming communities in Massachusetts, a state where blacks made up less than 2 percent of the general population.[2]

Blacks in colonial Framingham were either slaves or the children of slaves. Identified in official records solely by their forenames, slaves known only as Jane or Cuffe toiled on small farms and in craftsmen's shops, performing domestic service and agricultural work. Much like unbonded laborers, the village's slaves performed the ritual tasks of New England

farming, passing the seasons in the fields alongside their owners. Together master and slave tilled the soil, planting and harvesting their
crops and fulfilling attendant activities such as fertilizing, clearing fields,
chopping wood, repairing fences and furniture, and making bricks. As in
small towns throughout the North, Framingham's "servants for life" were
few in number and geographically scattered among the residences of local
whites. Housed in attic rooms, cellars, and barn lofts, these rural slaves
shared the dwelling spaces of the white farmers with whom they worked
throughout the day. Marked by commonalities of experience and environment, the relationship between master and slave in towns like Framingham took on familial qualities, with the master in a patriarchal role
over the slaves that were owned by him but worked with him.[3]

The cultural values of rural New England society shaped this specialized form of slavery. Centered on the patriarchal model of the family unit,
identified by the historian John Demos as "the little commonwealth," colonial culture stressed lineal values in all things, from religious observance
to kin-based labor structures. In Framingham, like other towns and villages, relatives shared farms and dwelling space, worked with and for one
another tending their holdings, and joined in cooperative economic and
social efforts. The select few who owned slaves patterned their practices
after the prevalent values of their environment, and so they treated their
servants with a semblance of real, if limited, familial feeling.[4]

The first Benson ancestor to experience this kind of bondage was
African-born Nero Benson, brought to Massachusetts possibly by way of
the West Indies around 1720. Nothing is known of his background, cap-
ture, or history as a slave save his own name, whose origins are lost, and
that of the man who bought him when he reached Framingham: the Reverend John Swift, minister of Framingham Church. In Swift's household
Nero Benson met another slave from Africa, Dido Dingo, and the two
were wed in 1721. Not only were the two legally married in the eyes of
both church and state but they were permitted to keep a separate last
name, something that set them apart from the rest of the slaves in Framingham. This distinction may have reflected a special leniency on the part
of their master, who also saw to it that Nero was admitted to Framingham Church as a member "in full communion." Since many northern
slaves actively sought the opportunity to establish legitimate relationships and incorporate themselves into mainstream society, master Swift's
munificence was probably appreciated by the two legally married slaves

who lived under his roof. They may have been less satisfied with his choice of classical Roman forenames for them, a common practice among slave-owners of the day.[5]

Nero Benson's religiosity was likely encouraged by his master. Framingham's sole clergyman since 1701, Swift would have been familiar with the contemporary philosophy embodied in Cotton Mather's work, *The Negro Christianized*. "Teach your *Negroes* the *Truths* of the Glorious Gospel," Mather admonished New England slave owners. "*Who can tell but that this Poor Creature may belong to the Election of God!*" As a member of the Swifts' extended patriarchal household, even a slave was due religious instruction in the ways and means of Christianity. Nero Benson sat in the remote corner pews designated for the "exclusive use of colored people" week after week, his presence in Framingham Church verifying that both he and his master were upholding their obligations to God.[6]

Such religious devotion, however, combined with a streak of self-assertiveness in Nero, could and did lead to trouble. In the early 1730s a squabble broke out in Framingham Church between a group of disaffected lay members and the minister, Reverend Swift. In the end, the disaffected abandoned the church to worship in nearby Hopkinton, some ten miles away. Among the separatist contingent was Nero Benson, the only person of color involved in the schism. He completed his religious break from Framingham Church and his master when he applied for formal admission to Hopkinton Church in 1735.[7]

The slave was never punished for his effrontery, at least not to the extent that he was sold or removed from the Swift household. Still, his actions must have caused some tension for himself and his family, as well as the physical inconvenience each Sunday of an arduous ten-mile trek out to Hopkinton for services. By asserting his independence in this manner, the slave was challenging his master's religious authority, as well as his position as household patriarch. Within the distinctive world of New England slave owning, where slaves were considered not mere chattel but even quasi family members, Nero Benson's act was a betrayal of a father figure. Nevertheless, Nero Benson was willing to endure personal difficulties for the sake of expressing his own agency and autonomy. This act set a powerful standard for his descendants to follow, including his great-great-grandson Charles, born a century later, a legacy of independence in thought and deed.[8]

At the same time, the slave's rejection of his master also revealed the depth of his commitment to the values he had learned in bondage. Nero

Benson's quarrel with his master was confined to matters of religion, and it was for the sake of his spiritual observance that he did what he felt he must. Although the church had been locked around his neck with the chains of his captivity, the slave had taken the religion of his captors and made it his own. For the rest of his life Nero Benson would serve both his earthly masters and his heavenly one, the former with his body and the latter with his soul. This attitude was concordant with the cultural dictates of pre-Revolutionary rural New England, which remained firmly in the grasp of the Congregationalism of its Puritan founders. As a church member and family patriarch living according to the proscriptions of Massachusetts village society, Nero Benson fit the ideal profile of his time and place. But as a black slave he could never achieve full acculturation into the world around him, no matter how hard he tried.

When master John Swift died in 1745, the realities of slavery forced changes upon Nero Benson and his family. Swift's will, composed two years earlier, parceled out the slave family along with the remainder of his possessions among his wife and five children. According to the testament, the "Two Negro's namely Dido and Esther," Nero's wife and daughter, would remain with the widow Swift in the family home in Framingham. But Swift gave to his son-in-law Ebenezer Robie his "Negro-Man Named or called Nero." The separation of the slave family would endure even after the death of the widow Swift, for the will established that a married daughter, Martha Swift Farrar, would then inherit the Benson women. Nero, his proud surname unacknowledged in the legal prose of the Swift probate documents, was carted off by the Robies to the town of Sudbury, at the northeastern border of Framingham, as soon as probate matters were settled. Within a year the slave sought and received admission to Sudbury Church, acknowledging the permanence of his place on the town but also reaffirming his Christian resolve. For the remaining twelve years of his life he remained in Sudbury, where he died in 1757.[9]

Nero Benson, as the chattel of another, though dedicated to the axioms of New England culture, was impotent when it came to the most fundamental one of all: safeguarding one's family. Instead, it was his fate to be used for the security of others, as a portion of the lineal inheritance of John Swift's heirs. His master's will used the slave Nero to accomplish that which he could not do himself: it provided for the economic well-being of the family, subsidizing posterity. Nero Benson had spent his adult life learning and implementing the ideals of the world around him. In the end those selfsame principles sentenced him to a dozen years of solitude and separation from his family, all for the benefit of those whose position within that world far outranked that of a lowly black slave.

ALTHOUGH NERO BENSON spent the last third of his thirty-six-year marriage apart from his wife and family, they may yet have reunited at Swift family gatherings and visits. Eventually Benson's son William, twelve years old when John Swift died in 1745, may have seen his family only at such gatherings. William Benson was not mentioned by name in Swift's will; he evidently remained with his mother and sister for some time before he too was forcibly relocated out of Framingham to become the property of Joseph Collins, a resident of nearby Southborough, Massachusetts. William remained in Southborough, Framingham's next-door neighbor to the west, until the 1760s, when he was in his early thirties.[10]

Most of William Benson's life, like that of most slaves, remains hidden from the historical record. The first major public event of his life took place in the early or mid-1760s when he was married to an equally obscure individual, Sarah Perry, a white woman from Sudbury. Exactly how the couple met is unknown; William's only recorded connection to Sudbury was through his father, Nero, who had been a slave there until his death some years before his son's marriage took place. It is certain that William Benson and Sarah Perry both knew that they could never truly legitimize their union in the eyes of Massachusetts law, which forbade interracial marriage, or in those of their rural neighbors, who shared the law's antagonism toward racial intermingling. Nevertheless, they engaged in a sexual relationship—perhaps even while William was still enslaved—and conceived a daughter, Katy, who was born in April 1763. Around the same time, William managed to attain his freedom through unspecified means (perhaps a testamentary manumission, one common variety of emancipation for slaves of this era) and then formalized his connection to Sarah Perry through an official, if not precisely legal, marriage.[11] The small family then settled in Framingham, William's hometown and in close proximity to any Perry family roots that may have existed in Sudbury. Three years later, in 1766, their son Abel arrived, his light complexion providing obvious testimony to his mixed parentage. Two generations later Charles Benson would inherit similarly light skin, the legacy of a choice made by great-grandparents who died more than thirty years before his birth.[12]

William Benson's decision to marry outside his race was unorthodox but not necessarily surprising, considering the paucity of young black women in colonial Middlesex County. It also reflected his openness to assimilation, a process initiated by his father's adoption of the dominant cultural paradigm decades earlier. William's path to acculturation was smoothed by the groundswell of support for complete emancipation in Massachusetts, which had likely helped effect his own freedom from slavery. As T. H. Breen has observed, the pre-Revolutionary crises of the 1760s sparked a growing consciousness among even the most rusticated New Englanders that liberty and freedom were not merely political concepts. White Massachusetts was not yet ready to embrace the idea of full and unencumbered racial equality, nor would it be in Charles Benson's day a century hence. But the self-described "cradle of liberty" extended to black men like William Benson a welcoming hand-up out of slavery, an offer they eagerly accepted. With a new world of possibilities now open to them, these former slaves sought to find their futures within the culture that had made their emancipation a reality. William Benson would do so in the familiar confines of Framingham, raising a new generation of Bensons in the town where he had once been a slave.[13]

BY THE TIME young Charles got to know his grandfather Abel, the older man was in his late sixties, "lame and infirm." It would have been hard to picture this wizened figure as a boy growing up in Massachusetts during the turbulent era of the American Revolution. The stories told and retold by his father, uncles, aunts, and Abel himself were enthralling, though. As a lad on the threshold of his teens, Abel Benson watched in the 1770s as black men like the Framingham native Peter Salem fought with distinction in the Revolutionary cause. Salem's adventures were especially inspirational. A slave freed so that he could enlist in the American armed forces, Salem gained fame and renown at the battle of Bunker Hill, where he was credited with firing the shot that killed British commander Major John Pitcairn. With dreams of glory—and, perhaps, the hundred dollars a year he was promised by the town of Framingham for enlisting—fourteen-year-old Abel Benson gave his age as sixteen and signed up for a three-year stint in the Continental army in March 1781.[14]

Unlike the heroic Salem, Abel Benson did not serve the Revolutionary cause with a gun. Instead, like his grandfather Nero, a volunteer in one of Framingham's militia companies in the 1720s, Abel was armed with a trumpet. This noncombat assignment was consistent with the military

service of most Negro soldiers of the American Revolution, who worked
as cooks, waiters, body-servants, and musicians. Abel likely accepted his
assigned role with some equanimity. He had a keen musical ear—in
Framingham he later was known for his ability to "draw a fiddle bow
when he was fast asleep in his chair and keep his audience on the full
trot"—and could find reward in the skilled aspect of blowing his horn. So
over the course of the war, through "several skirmishes on the lines" but
"never any battle," Abel toted his instrument around the Hudson River
region of New York. He was proud of his service as a soldier in the Massachusetts Eighth and Third Regiments, regardless of his role. As a poor
landless farmer, son of a former slave, and a black man, he was used to
privation and personal discomfort and would expect no promotion of any
kind. Abel Benson's role in the Revolutionary Army prefigured that of his
grandson Charles in the merchant marine, a noncommissioned black man
concentrating on the specialized tasks and skills that set him apart from
his white compatriots.[15]

When his three-year enlistment ended in December 1783, Benson received his honorable discharge from the army and returned to Framingham. There he tendered his belated congratulations to his sister Katy,
who had become Mrs. Peter Salem several months earlier in his absence.
Now eighteen years old, a proud veteran of the Revolutionary War, and
brother-in-law to a bonafide local hero, Abel cut a fine figure if a diminu-
tive one, all of five feet two inches. At least, one young woman clearly
thought so.

Rhoda Jahah lived in the town of Natick, one of Framingham's neighbors to the east. The daughter of Caesar Jahah, an African-born slave,
Rhoda was eighteen years old when Abel Benson came back home in
1784. With similarities in their ages, family histories, and rural Middlesex County upbringing, the two young people had much in common.
They certainly wasted little time taking their acquaintance to a more intimate level, for by mid-spring of that year Rhoda Jahah was pregnant.
In a pattern that would be replicated later by their grandson Charles, the
couple arranged a hasty wedding in Framingham in September 1784, five
months before their daughter Patty was born the following February.

The family settled on land acquired as a bounty for Benson's military
service during the war. Over the next two decades the small Benson homestead would have to stretch to accommodate numerous family members.
Abel's father, William Benson, living alone three decades after his marriage to Sarah Perry, came to live with his son shortly after he received

his land. So too did Peter and Katy Salem, until their marriage ended unhappily and Salem departed to live on his own in Leicester, Massachusetts. In the meantime, Abel and Rhoda Benson were producing children at the rate of one every two years. By 1810 eleven Benson babies were born (one child, William, died in infancy in the late 1780s). For Rhoda Benson, the enormous physical stress of constant pregnancy and childbearing was torturous, especially when combined with her years of "hard labour" imposed by poverty and necessity. For Abel, farming the land and supplementing the family's meager income as a blacksmith, life was full of toil and harsh pressures that eventually broke his body. With limited means and many mouths to feed, the Bensons of Framingham scraped by as best they could.[16]

Although they were nearly destitute, the Benson family possessed one significant resource: land. Abel Benson's land-warrant bounty, paid him by the town of Framingham in lieu of his $300 enlistment bonus, was central to the family's survival. By the standards of most northern blacks, who were as bad off as the Bensons or even worse so, land ownership was both unimaginable and unattainable. Even the war hero Peter Salem lacked a parcel of his own, having traded away his military service for the price of his freedom at the outset of the Revolution. As a black landowner, Abel Benson was one of only a handful of landed men out of thousands of black New Englanders.[17]

Exclusive of the land, generously valued at $300 in 1820, the Bensons had little else. The remainder of the family's possessions that year consisted of "one old horse" and sundry farming tools and furniture with a combined worth of $20. With a lame knee and a broken shoulder that had never healed properly, Abel Benson was a fifty-four-year-old laborer who could no longer perform work. The family already owed more than $100, with little ability to repay. Although he was awarded a military pension of $8 a month in 1818, Abel still barely eked out a livelihood for himself and his family. When the pension payments were cut off in September 1820, the situation grew desperate.

Lacking any other means of survival, the Bensons began converting their land into cash, selling it off piecemeal or mortgaging it for debts or loans. Indebted to his eldest son Henry for more than half the value of his land, Abel deeded him a quarter of an acre to discharge his debt of $155 in 1822. The following year, debts to the family doctor John Kittridge forced Abel to mortgage the remainder of his holdings, only three and a half acres of land, for a paltry $60. The Bensons continued to stave off complete insolvency for the next several years, subsisting on loans and favors as they had before. Finally, some relief arrived in 1829 when Abel's military pension was reinstated, supplemented by a single lump-sum reimbursement for decade-old payments still in arrears. The pension monies were welcome but still provided only a temporary respite from the grinding poverty that was the family's lot in Framingham.[18]

Throughout these years, the Bensons were acutely conscious of their dependence on others. Abel's pension applications described at length the heartbreaking circumstances that left him penniless. The property assessments that accompanied his personal statements only emphasized the urgency of his family's need. Sustained only by mortgages and credit secured from neighboring landowners and family members, the Bensons were too poor to afford pride or independence.

Such poverty was common among the small farming families in rural Massachusetts. Most yeoman farmers established an interdependent existence out of necessity. They subsisted on the barter of labor and goods with the members of their immediate circle, their kinfolk and neighbors (often one and the same in many farming communities). When necessary they also turned to larger landholders and creditors who aided them through loans or mortgages like the one Abel Benson obtained from John Kittridge. These arrangements also took place under the rubric of what Christopher Clark terms the "local exchange" ethos that guided the agricultural economy.[19] Debt collection was sporadic and flexible, lawsuits or other legal action rare, and familial relationships outranked economic concerns even when debt was involved.

Although rural debtors—and there were many when lean years occurred in the late eighteenth and early nineteenth centuries—held fast to their vision of the rural economy, they also recognized when they held a subordinate position in an economic relationship. Underlying interpersonal interaction was the model of the patriarchal household, an image fostered by the elite creditors who sought ever-increasing political power within their districts. The patriarchal system that had defined a lifetime of slavery for Nero Benson now placed his impoverished grandson in the position of supplicant. Only by appealing to the generosity of those in authority could Abel Benson gain the barest means of survival for his family. After three generations of attempted acculturation in Framingham, the Benson family had little to show but continual and mostly unrewarded dependence on a culture that had little use for poor black farmers. Nero's church attendance, William's interracial marriage, even Abel's military service availed them little in the way of physical comfort or social advancement. Nevertheless, the Bensons continued to follow the dictates of their culture in pursuit of the promise of something better.

FRAMINGHAM, the only home they had ever known, lost its allure for Abel Benson's children as they grew up. Throughout their childhoods they had known few other black children, for none lived in or near Framingham. By the 1820s, nearing adulthood and marriageable age, several of the young Bensons saw little reason to remain trapped on a small homestead with dwindling resources and no opportunity for economic or social advancement. Along with thousands of other restless and ambitious rural New Englanders of their day, they left the countryside to make a life for themselves in the closest available city, Boston.

Compelled by necessity and personal choice, the youngest Bensons made their way out of Framingham. The eldest, Henry, left first for Boston in search of work and a wife. By 1818 he had found both, filling a position as a waiter and marrying a black woman he met there named Hannah Howe. His younger brother Labin followed, and several months later he too married a young woman, Rhoda Gibson. The Benson brothers were soon joined in Boston by another brother, William (Abel and Rhoda's second child of that name), who took a job selling fruit and in late 1823 by George, twenty-one years old and William's junior by two years. Of Abel and Rhoda Benson's surviving children, four now made their home in Boston. Only their two youngest sons, Gardner and Eric, remained at home.[20]

The country-bred Benson men now found themselves in a bustling city that dwarfed the tiny agrarian town of their birth. Boston was the second-largest port in the United States, a major hub of trade and mercantile activity. Swollen with migrants, the city's population grew to nearly forty-five thousand in 1820, and more than fifty-eight thousand by 1825. Crowding the narrow cobblestoned streets and alleys, thousands of poor blacks joined the steady stream of aspirants seeking employment and lodgings. Many found opportunities in the wharves, anchorsmithies, and ropewalks of Boston's North End as laborers or mariners. Other black migrants, like the Bensons, found homes in Boston's West End, close to the downtown hotels and eateries where they found low-level, low-paying jobs. Many West Enders made their homes along the lower slopes of posh Beacon Hill, making the steep climb to perform domestic service for wealthy Boston Brahmins. In all, two thousand blacks packed Boston's crime and vice-ridden "New Guinea" waterfronts and shabby residences along "Nigger Hill," composing the largest black community in all of nineteenth-century New England.[21]

Upon arriving in Boston, each of the Benson men found living quarters on Belknap Street, a four-block lane that snaked upward from Nigger Hill into Beacon Hill proper. More than one hundred black households were situated along Belknap Street and in its tiny courtyards and alleys in 1825.[22] Boston's first black house of worship was there as well, the African Baptist Church. In the basement of the church's African Meeting House was the city's African School, a grammar school for black children established in the late eighteenth century by black community leaders. In 1820, a second Belknap Street grammar school opened to ease the overcrowded conditions at the African School. These institutions filled vital needs for Boston's blacks, who were segregated from white institutions by law and custom.[23]

Temptation as well as salvation beckoned young men in the West End. The lower section of the neighborhood, Mount Vernon, was known by some as "Mount Whoredom," after what contemporary Bostonian Charles Bulfinch termed the "torrent of vice at the Hill in West Boston." A major anti-vice campaign was mounted in the Bensons' Boston, spearheaded by community leaders and ministers such as James Davis. For the West End, which Davis described as "Satan's seat," he had little but outrage.

> Five and twenty or thirty shops are opened on Lord's days from morning to evening and ardent spirits are retailed without restraint, while hundreds are intoxicated and spend the holy sabbath in frolicking and gambling, in fighting and blaspheming; and in many cases of iniquity and debauchery too dreadful to be named. . . . Here in one compact section of the town, it is confidently affirmed and fully believed, there are *three hundred* females wholly devoid of shame and modesty. . . . Multitudes of coloured people, by these examples, are influenced into habits of indolence.

The four Bensons, who did not marry until they were in their mid- to late-twenties, may have passed some time among the sinful multitudes before settling down. Whether or not they personally sampled the earthly delights the West End had to offer, the young men certainly found their new surroundings rather eye-opening after placid Framingham.[24]

Affording the pleasures of the flesh was another matter, especially for

George Benson, the youngest and least-skilled of the brothers in Boston. While Henry prospered enough as a waiter to lend money to his destitute father, Labin joined the relatively lucrative world of black seafarers, and William tried his hand at entrepreneurship, George eked out a living as a laborer, performing unskilled work along the docks or in Boston's commercial areas. Day labor was a perilous and insecure way of life. The average daily wage for laborers was less than one dollar, and the sporadic nature of employment meant that most were out of work for three months or more each year. According to one contemporary estimate, a family of four living in 1830 Massachusetts needed at least $430 to afford basic necessities; the annual salary for day laborers, who averaged but 260 working days a year, came to only half that figure. As a laborer, George Benson was one of the many black men trying to survive in Boston and not quite making it.[25]

George Benson was no stranger to poverty and hardship and so he struggled on, determined to find success, at least in his personal life. It did not take him long. On December 10, 1823, not long after his arrival in Boston, George married twenty-two-year-old Elizabeth Simpson. A year older than her new husband, Elizabeth hailed from the Plymouth County town of Pembroke, whose black population was as miniscule as Framingham's.[26] She too was a recent migrant to black Boston, one of the many young single blacks pouring into the growing city. The couple spent the first five years of their marriage together on Belknap Street.[27] From there they moved to nearby May Street, where they would live for two years. They brought with them their possessions and their one-year-old son George L. W., born in 1827.[28]

With only George Benson's inadequate earnings to depend on, the small family faced heavy odds against its survival. Like the majority of Boston's impoverished blacks, crowded into a warren of filthy back alleys thick with refuse and without access to clean water, the Bensons feared the constant outbreaks of infectious diseases. Poor and unhealthful living conditions bred abnormally high mortality rates—higher than those of Boston's whites—especially among black infants, who died in far greater proportions than white infants. In addition to the threat of death at an early age, Boston's black children, barred from the city's whites-only public schools, also labored under serious educational deficiencies. The separate schools for blacks provided a woefully inadequate education, omitting even the basic grammar that white students learned. After

years of schooling on Belknap Street, the best that could be hoped for
little George L. W. Benson was a bare modicum of literacy, if he survived
his childhood at all.[29]

Like other northern cities throughout the 1820s, Boston had segregated railroad cars, stagecoaches, and places of entertainment, as well as
schools and churches.[30] Further indignities were commonplace, as Prince
Hall observed in a 1797 address at Boston's African Lodge, a black Masonic organization. "Patience," he counseled his listeners, "for were we
not possessed of a great measure of it, you could not bear up under the
daily insults you meet with in the streets of Boston." Black public festivities, such as abolition parades commemorating the Constitution's ban of
slave importation, brought out the worst in white onlookers. "How are
you shamefully abus'd," Hall continued, "and that at such a degree, that
you may truly be said to carry your lives in your hands; and the arrows of
death are flying about your heads." Confronted with whites' vituperative
scorn and ridicule of "Bobalition," and beset by verbal and physical harassment as they marched, black Bostonians were quite familiar with the
hostility and "shameful abuse" described to them by one of their own.[31]

After spending nearly six years under these conditions, George and
Elizabeth Benson left Boston. Although George's day labor provided
enough money to keep the family alive, it offered no security or prospects
for the future. With one small child and another on the way, the challenges of raising a healthy family in their circumstances may have been
too great to overcome. It would also be difficult for the Bensons to replicate their own small-town upbringing, whose slower pace and emphasis
on kin ties were overwhelmed by Boston's clamor and crowdedness. Like
many nineteenth-century migrants, Elizabeth Simpson and George Benson had abandoned rural homes for the attractions of a growing metropolis. And like thousands of their fellows they returned to the countryside
within only a few years.[32]

So in late 1829 or early 1830 the Bensons turned their backs on the big
city, trundled their few belongings down the turnpike, and made their
way to Framingham, George's childhood home. There they may have
moved back in with his aged parents Abel and Rhoda Benson, who lived
alone with a granddaughter they had raised. It is also possible that the
small family came to some arrangement with George's eldest brother,
Henry, and arranged to occupy his Framingham holding, the quarter-
acre of land deeded him by his father years before. Wherever they settled
in, the Bensons had barely enough time to unpack before Elizabeth went

into labor and delivered her second son, Charles Augustus, on January 26, 1830.[33]

EVEN AS the newborn infant took his first gasping breaths of frigid Massachusetts air, momentous events were taking place on the floor of the United States Senate. Massachusetts senator Daniel Webster, enmeshed in a lengthy and contentious debate with secessionist Robert Hayne of South Carolina, was poised to deliver his "Second Reply to Hayne." Throughout the first two days of Charles Augustus Benson's life, Webster staged an impassioned performance that would bring him to national prominence. In his rumbling, resonant voice Webster championed the sovereignty of the federal government over individual states. His speech, ostensibly intended to defend a bill curtailing cheap western land sales, articulated a broad vision of the Union that opposed the nullificationist arguments of Hayne and his fellow South Carolinian John C. Calhoun. In his greatest moments of oratorical bravura Webster invoked the heroic legacy of the American Revolution, the supremacy of the Constitution, and apocalyptic images of a nation rent by the bloody carnage of Civil War. Emphatically rejecting Hayne's philosophy of states' right to set aside or "nullify" federal laws, Webster argued that this "South Carolina doctrine" violated the fundamental principles of the republic. "Liberty *and* Union," he thundered, "now and for ever, one and inseparable!"[34]

Many different facets of Webster's speech would resonate in the life of Charles Augustus Benson, then the youngest and least consequential of the Senator's Massachusetts constituents. Among those who participated in the "great struggle for Independence," as Webster called the American Revolution, were Charles's grandfather Abel Benson and greatuncle Peter Salem, two of the proudest exemplars of his family heritage. Dedicated to the cultural ideals and dictates of his day, Charles Benson would instinctively understand Webster's meaning when he spoke of the spirit of the nation and the "strength of its manhood," concepts that encompassed gender definitions as well as political ones. As a loyal son of New England and supporter of national "harmony, both of principle and feeling," Benson would have approved of Webster's nationalist sentiments. Unlike Webster, who died in the 1850s, Benson would live to see the war that embodied Webster's fears of the "broken and dishonored fragments of a once glorious Union . . . a land rent with civil feuds" and "drenched . . . in fraternal blood." Perhaps the most affecting image of all was the one Webster used to begin his address, that of a "mariner . . . tossed for many days in thick weather, and on an unknown sea." The role of mariner would come to define Benson's life in ways that no one could imagine on the day of his birth.

Like most Americans, the Bensons knew nothing of Senator Webster's speech as it was being delivered. Far to the north in ramshackle quarters in the rural town of Framingham, the poor black family was more concerned with the immediate needs of food, shelter, and sleep than they were with the bombastic posturing of Washington politicians. Perhaps the adults did discuss the reports of the "Reply to Hayne" as they filtered in over the ensuing weeks, especially George and Elizabeth Benson, now in their late twenties and more cosmopolitan after their years in Boston; Abel and Rhoda Benson, decades older, functionally illiterate, and closeted in Framingham for forty years or more, were less aware of the larger world around them.

Charles Benson spent his childhood in an insular environment of kinfolk and neighbors, separated by distance and culture from the wider world and by race from many others around him. In his isolation, Benson learned to function alone. And as his communal world shrank further throughout his adolescence and young adulthood, he came to depend upon his own inner resources for strength and motivation. At the same time, he was driven to look around him for guiding principles that would give his life direction and purpose. He found these in the same cultural milieu that had produced Daniel Webster, in the dominant New England ethos that, in an earlier form, had once attracted his great-great-grandfather Nero Benson. Although his wanderings would take him far from the small town where he was born, Charles Benson always carried with him the ideals and values he had learned there.

CHAPTER TWO

"You ocupy a place in my heart which none never did"

FRAMINGHAM AND SALEM, 1830–1853

DURING HIS formative years, the young Charles Benson was different from everyone around him because of his race. That difference affected his relationships with others in his small town, shaping their expectations of him and the way they defined him. Society consigned him to the role of Negro from birth, and it was his lot to live his life within the confines of that role. Yet in the absence of a larger black community or role models he would have to define the parameters of black manhood for himself. Isolated from white local networks but lacking the support and guidance of any black institutional structures, the boy formulated his own conceptions of a man's responsibilities. Taking his cues from the dictates of the New England culture that surrounded him, Charles Benson began to adopt the values and middle-class outlook of that mid-nineteenth-century cultural landscape. This process began when he was too young to appreciate the barriers that would prevent someone socially pigeonholed as a black man from fulfilling his dreams of respectability and manly achievement. By the time he was old enough to perceive the inherent tensions of his dilemma, it would be too late for him to reorient his views and life goals. Engaged in the fruitless pursuit of middle-class success, Benson would never fully reconcile his aspirations with his preordained status as a working-class black man. He would also find it difficult to come to terms with issues of race, which remained unsettled in his own mind throughout his life.

Charles Benson might have developed a clearer sense of his own position on the racial spectrum had he grown up in Boston. The largest and most prominent of New England's black settlements, black Boston had many resources that helped center the community and its youth. Two black churches, one Baptist and the other African Methodist Episcopal (A.M.E.), ministered not only to the spirit of the community but also its social needs, hosting entertainments and get-togethers. The churches also aided indigent blacks with direct financial contributions and employment assistance. Black schools were housed and maintained by the churches, which also provided platforms for leadership, both religious and political, within the black community. The church anchored black Boston and centered it, nurturing racial pride, activism, and solidarity among the city's two thousand blacks.[1]

Black Boston's communal resources also included other organizations, such as the African Society and a black Masonic lodge, one of the first of its kind. The all-black Massachusetts General Colored Association promoted the abolition of slavery, established as an alternative organization for blacks uncomfortable or unwelcome in the predominantly white antislavery societies of New England. These groups provided opportunities for black Bostonians to speak up and assert themselves, as David Walker did in 1829 in his militant *Appeal to the Coloured Citizens of the World*, a strident proclamation of black manhood and liberty. They also organized demonstrations and parades, uniting the black community in celebration and demanding an end to slavery.[2]

The efficacy of these efforts in unifying Boston's sprawling and unstable black population is undeniable, but the extent of their success is less clear. Black abolitionists such as David Walker and the Reverend Thomas Paul of the African Baptist Church did achieve some degree of prominence in Boston in the 1820s and 1830s. But the actual number of black members of abolitionist organizations was small. At the American Anti-Slavery Society's first convention in 1833, only three of sixty-two delegates were black, and one of those was from Boston. Furthermore, if the later experiences of black abolitionist Charlotte Forten are any example, these constituted a small elite clique of prominent and relatively well-to-do individuals who spent most of their time in the company of white abolitionists, rather than the common folk who constituted the majority of black Bostonians.[3] For all their vitality and importance, Boston's black churches had relatively few members. Only two hundred or so of Boston's two thousand blacks joined either the African Baptist or A.M.E. churches during the 1820s and 1830s. According to at least one contemporary observer, William Lloyd Garrison, the vast majority attended white churches where they remained segregated in the balcony "pigeon holes" and "Nigger Heavens." Nevertheless, the stabilizing influences of Boston's black institutions gave young black children a strong sense of belonging and purpose at a time when mainstream America denied them both.

Charles's parents, Elizabeth and George Benson, as products of their isolated rural upbringing in small-town Massachusetts, showed little inclination to participate in the public activities of the black community while they lived there in the 1820s. Neither was a member of a black church. A white Unitarian minister, John G. Palfrey of the Brattle Square Church, performed their marriage, joining the two "people of colour" together in matrimony. When they left Boston at the decade's end, they likely knew they would miss the friends and kinfolk they left behind on crowded Belknap Street in the West End. But the Bensons, who had grown up in small towns that offered no black communal resources, belonged to no abolitionist groups or black churches, did not march in public parades, and had only long years of poverty and insecurity to show for their time in Boston. Just as they had grown up without a strong black community in their lives, so too would their children.[4]

Only a handful of black families lived in agrarian Middlesex County. Thus, there was no black church in Framingham when Charles Benson was a boy, nor were there any black parades to instill a sense of racial pride or even a single black role model outside his immediate family for him to emulate. He did not play with black children other then his siblings, for the rest of the town's hundreds of children were white. If he attended school at all, and it is unlikely that he did, then he did so in all-white classrooms, for there were too few black children in the area to merit a separate institution of their own. Surrounding towns hardly offered more in the way of black playmates, with fewer than a dozen black children in each.[5]

In the limited social setting of Framingham, kin ties loomed large. But throughout Benson's childhood his family circle shrank steadily year after year as tragedy struck. Charles lost several of his uncles while they were young. The first, Levi, died at age thirty-one before Charles was even born. In April 1831, while Charles was still an infant, Gardner Benson contracted smallpox and died at Boston's Hospital Island when he was only twenty-four. Six weeks later forty-one-year-old Henry, the eldest of Charles's uncles, also died. In 1840 another uncle, Eric, died. Dying young as they did, few of the Bensons left families behind, and those who remained fared little better. Charles's one-year-old cousin Abel died of whooping cough in Boston when Charles was four, and shortly afterward the baby's mother, Maria Heywood Benson, succumbed to alcoholism and died, leaving Charles's uncle William a widower. Thus, throughout his boyhood the Benson family celebrated no weddings and few births. Instead, life passages were marked not by festivities but by a succession of funerals, as death claimed his relatives, one by one.[6]

One of the last to die during Charles's youth was his aged grandfather Abel Benson, whose broken, brittle body continued to endure until he neared his eightieth birthday. After decades of poverty and hardship, years of physical agony, and the anguish of outliving most of his children, Abel Benson died in September 1843. He left little more than the dilapidated old home that had housed dozens of family members and on land awarded him for the service of his country. The land was fully mortgaged, to the local doctor John Kittridge. Unpaid debts were augmented by funeral and legal expenses. And Abel Benson had left no will to clear up the disposition of his estate.

Six weeks later, "George Benson of Framingham, yeoman" presented himself to the Middlesex County Court of Probate held in Framingham. In a written statement, he explained to the judge that Abel Benson had recently died intestate, "leaving a widow who has declined the administration" of his affairs. As the dead man's son, the petitioner asserted that he was "entitled to the administration of [Abel's] estate." The request was approved by Judge Samuel P. P. Fay, who promptly confirmed George Benson as the administrator of the estate of Abel Benson, "late said Framingham."[7]

George Benson's quick actions precipitated a major conflict within his extended family. The widowed Rhoda Benson was first to respond, filing a petition of her own shortly thereafter. Written by Josiah Adams, the attorney who was representing her in an attempt to secure the continuation of Abel's Revolutionary War Pension benefits, her "claim of appeal" was unambiguously hostile.[8] Rhoda demanded that her son George be removed from his position as administrator of the estate and replaced by his older brother William, "the eldest son of said deceased." In a stinging rebuke to her son, Rhoda Benson charged that "said George Benson obtained said appointment, by false representations, & by fraudulently concealing material facts from the knowledge of said Judge." "Said George Benson," the appeal stated, "is not a suitable person to discharge the duties of his said office." After due deliberation the judge apparently concurred, for subsequent probate records pertaining to the estate make no further references to George Benson in any capacity, as either administrator or beneficiary.

The estate was settled the following year. Rhoda Benson received a "widow's allowance," her son William fifty dollars and her married daughter Mary Patterson twenty dollars to compensate her for the time she spent nursing her dying father in 1843. But George Benson inherited nothing. He had made one impulsive attempt to stake his claim, to wrest away something from his years in Framingham for himself, his wife, and his children. In the end he would have come away with little; Abel Benson's entire personal estate consisted of "1 old horse" worth a mere ten dollars and another seven dollars' worth of miscellaneous metal implements. For this meager bequest George Benson had driven away his kin. It is impossible to know if they ever forgave him.

After Abel's death the family disintegrated at a rapid rate. Within five years George Benson was gone, dead or disappeared. So too were his siblings and his mother, who vanished from Framingham's public record without a trace. The Benson land was gone as well. Two-thirds of the holding had to be sold in 1844 to cover the claims against the estate. The remainder, a "homestead consisting of half of a dwelling house, a barn, and about one-fourth of an acre of land," was too small and poor to support anyone. As the extended Benson family faded away, Charles Benson spent his teen years in Framingham with his mother, Elizabeth, his older brother, George L. W., and his younger sister, Susan. Never part of a larger community, the boy was forced to watch as his family, the only social network he had, splintered and finally broke apart. Fatherless, with no kin and few peers, Charles Benson was growing up virtually alone. Without a male role model to teach him to be a man, he was forced to extrapolate his definition of manhood from the world around him. Perhaps because of this, his manly self-image would always form one of the central aspects of his adult sense of self, shaping his vision of himself and who he wished to be.

ONE PRIMARY obligation for a man was securing a steady job, something Benson's father had never managed to do. By the time he turned eighteen Benson had surpassed his father in this regard, finding a position as a cordwainer, or shoemaker. He may have been one of the eighty-five employees of Framingham's one shoe manufactory, which produced nearly eighty thousand pairs of shoes and boots each year. Shoemaking jobs were also plentiful in the neighboring town of Natick, whose five factories employed hundreds of workers during the late 1840s. Whether he

worked in a factory or did piecework at home, Benson earned meager
wages and had little job security. Still, steady employment of any kind
was extremely rare for most black men, especially in the shoe industry.[9]

Benson's work allowed him to exercise some independence for the first
time in his life. Before his eighteenth birthday he left his mother's house
and moved to Natick, perhaps to live closer to his workplace. In Natick
he met and courted one of the town's few eligible black girls his age,
Martha Ann Thompson. His suit met with success, at least partially because of his engaging nature. Especially as a young man, Charles Benson
had a strong streak of romance in his soul. He also had a healthy dose of
sexual drive and a way with words. Expressive and sincere, he also had a
distinctive sense of humor. Between his compelling presence and his
economic stability, Charles Benson was a hard suitor to resist. Martha
Ann Thompson, eighteen years old and all alone in town, encouraged his
attentions.

In February 1848, two weeks after Charles's birthday, the two teen-
agers were married in Natick by a justice of the peace. In the eyes of society Benson was now an adult, a full-grown man supporting his new
family through his labor. He had left the town of his birth to establish
himself elsewhere, though only a few miles away. Thus his passage to
manhood was marked by independence and self-reliance, two qualities
that had characterized and sustained his family for generations.

Unfortunately, for Charles Benson, as for most blacks in nineteenth-
century America, such security was impossible to maintain for long.
Within a short time he lost his cordwaining job amid the fluctuations of
the shoe market and had to fall back on his father's old standby occupation of day labor. Now depending on spotty employment opportunities, he was forced to abandon dreams of independent living in Natick
and move back in with his mother in Framingham. Also living in the
small house were his sister Susan, then eighteen; his twenty-two-year-old
brother, George L. W., a laborer as well; James Patterson, nineteen, a
cousin on his father's side; and Elizabeth Thomas, a young black women
from neighboring Natick. The seven black members of Elizabeth Benson's household represented nearly half of Framingham's black population in 1850. As for the five Bensons, they represented the last straggling
remnant of a family that had lived in Framingham for over a century.

Crowded living conditions bred tensions within the impoverished
family. Charles Benson, who later in life valued self-reliant wage-earning
over nearly everything else, would have hated the helplessness of not

knowing day by day whether he would find work. His unwilling return to his childhood home would have chafed as well. Benson would always find it difficult to remain home for any extended period of time, and it would have been especially irksome in the overly familiar confines of Framingham. The tension rose further when two of the women in the household became pregnant within a year. The announcement of Martha Benson's pregnancy after three years of marriage would not have been wholly unexpected. But that of Charles's younger sister Susan, whose baby son was conceived and eventually born into illegitimacy, only aggravated the tension and promised to increase the physical and economic burdens of providing for everyone in the household.

Unable to stay in the packed Benson house any longer, Charles and Martha Benson returned to Natick shortly before their daughter Henrietta was born in March 1852. Charles again found work as a cordwainer, fully aware that the erratic fortunes of New England shoe manufactories translated into poor wages and scant job security for workers, especially the few black ones fortunate enough to find positions in the first place. Only a few short months later, Martha Benson was pregnant for the second time.

At this point, with an infant daughter and a baby on the way, the Bensons' marriage deteriorated. Charles Benson would never refer openly to his first marriage in the personal writings he composed later in life—not once in two decades of diary-keeping—so it is difficult to reconstruct precisely how his marriage to Martha Ann Thompson ended. Benson's inability to retain a steady job, as well as the couple's back-and-forth movement between Framingham and Natick during their marriage, hint at the financial difficulties that afflicted them. Penniless and insecure, they could not seem to live peacefully with Charles' family for long. After four years together the young couple had only poverty, struggle, and discord to show for their years of marriage, and the future held little chance for improvement. With his small family cracking under the tremendous pressure of their circumstances Benson departed, never to return.

Although the possibility exists that his wife threw him out, Benson likely made his own decision to leave. Following the example of his father and his uncles, who left Framingham in the 1820s when circumstances at home grew too strained, Benson solved his present conflicts by leaving home and starting over elsewhere. The bitter years following his grandfather's death had demonstrated to him the pain that family members could inflict upon one another even when they stayed together. As Benson

watched his kinfolk die or disappear one by one throughout his childhood, it became apparent that it was rare for the men of his family to
linger in Framingham long enough to deal directly with the crises of
daily life.

Benson's decision to leave home fit broader patterns of his emotional
behavior. Forever after Benson dreaded discord, a trait that may have
developed during the years of divisive family quarrels during his teens.
Fighting of any kind continued to upset him throughout his adulthood,
especially when he was directly involved. Emotionally sensitive and
slight of build besides, Charles Benson was ill-equipped to handle strife
with equanimity. To minimize his own suffering and discomfort, Benson
would spend most of his adult life indulging his aversion to contention
by withdrawing from it. He may have done so in late 1852, when he abandoned his pregnant wife and infant daughter to fend for themselves in his
absence.

And so Charles Benson left his family and all of Middlesex County behind him. It is impossible to know where he originally intended to go, or
if he initially expected to return home. A black man in his position would
have had several clear choices of places to go next. A turnpike and a railroad offered fast and convenient transport from Natick to two major
cities with sizable black communities, Boston to the east and Worcester
to the west. Boston also provided the additional incentive of a harbor full
of ships bound for ports around the world and the promise of adventure
or merely escape from a small-town life grown constrictive. But Benson
bypassed both of these destinations. For reasons that he never revealed in
his journal, in late 1852 Charles Benson abandoned familiar towns and
cities and headed toward the north and east, further, possibly, than he had
yet been in his life. By stage or by the Eastern Railroad—though the latter was unlikely, since the one-dollar train fare even to Boston would
have been too steep for a cash-poor black man—Benson wound his way
to the coast and then upward along the North Shore. Unencumbered by
marriage, family responsibilities, or the ghosts of his past, Benson was
poised on the threshold of an entirely new life.

The family he left behind had little choice but to carry on. Mary Benson, the daughter Charles would never know, was born several months
after his departure, in early 1853. Shortly thereafter his former wife and
her girls found temporary lodgings with the Cobb family, who maintained one of Natick's few black households; there is no evidence that
she ever attempted to rejoin the Benson relatives in Framingham. The

struggle to support her family eventually forced her to foster her older daughter, Henrietta, not yet eight years old, to a black family in Boston. There the abandoned Mrs. Martha Benson married New York–born mariner John Boquette in 1864, twelve years after the unofficial dissolution of the marriage of her youth. By the time her daughter Mary married a decade later, everything about Martha Benson Boquette's first husband had been forgotten, including his name. On Mary Benson's marriage record in 1874, she inscribed the name of the father she had never met as "Henry Benson," permanently obscuring any evidence of a relationship that was dead and buried long before.

As for Charles Benson, he would conceal his past marriage from nearly everyone who knew him in his new life. In practical terms he had little choice since, in the absence of a legal divorce from Martha Benson, he committed bigamy by remarrying in early 1853. But Benson sought not merely to hide his past but also to forget it completely. In his desire to cast himself as a loyal husband and father to the family he reared subsequently, Benson stifled any guilt, bitterness, and regret along with all memory of his first marriage. In doing so he not only inured himself from suffering for his past mistakes but managed to recreate an idealized version of himself without recalling the ugly flaw of his failed relationship. Benson's fresh start commenced with his arrival in the place that, for the remainder of his days, he considered his home: Salem, Massachusetts.

SALEM WAS first among the towns along the North Shore of Massachusetts Bay. Originally settled in 1626 and incorporated three years later, Salem was a natural seaport offering easy access to ships traveling northward along the coast. The town was initially settled by immigrant planters in search of arable land for farming in their accustomed English style. Within a century, ever-increasing numbers of settlers methodically plowed further into the wilderness that encircled the region, clearing the land and constructing towns and villages. As Essex County burgeoned with people and mercantile activity, Salem remained active at the forefront of commerce. Salem's merchants hastened the eighteenth-century transition to commercialized farming and dominated the business end of the profitable cod fisheries along the coast. Overseas trade blossomed as the region's surplus farm products and fishing catches passed through the busy Salem seaport en route to southern Europe or the West Indies. By the dawn of the nineteenth century Salem's fleet of merchant schooners bulged with silks and spices from the East Indies, bound for European ports across the Atlantic. The maritime trades enriched Salem and crowded it. Over 3,000 people lived in Salem a century after its formation by a handful of settlers; by the mid-nineteenth century the town was a city of more than 22,000.[10]

As Salem prospered, a growing number of blacks settled there. The first were slaves, brought to colonial Salem in small numbers as "servants for life" for their farmer and merchant masters. By the revolutionary era, about 120 blacks lived in a town of 4,469, a proportion similar to that of towns and cities throughout Massachusetts. Over the next half-century more blacks settled in Salem, forming a small but visible community. In the 1820s the local diarist Francis Lee wrote of two groups of blacks that lived on either side of the Salem Turnpike, the first "a colony of ten to twelve negro families" and the second "some four or five houses, containing probably altogether some fifty or sixty inmates." A third settlement was identified by the Salem minister William Bentley in a lower-class neighborhood known as Roast Meat Hill, where he observed "about 100 huts & houses for Blacks from the most decent to the most humble appearance." A fourth nineteenth-century black enclave was identified by Nathaniel Hawthorne, who made reference to a "New Guinea" neighborhood in western Salem in his introduction to *The Scarlet Letter*.[11]

The 412 blacks living in Salem when Charles Benson arrived in the early 1850s comprised the third-largest black population in Massachusetts after Boston and New Bedford and the largest black community in Essex County. Still, in a city of over 22,000, black Salem represented only a tiny presence in a city made up predominantly of native-born whites. This was consistent with the black experience throughout Massachusetts, where blacks constituted less than 1 percent of the state's overall population. It was also consistent with the experience of Charles Benson, who had grown up one of the only blacks in Framingham.[12]

By the time Benson came to live in Salem, the town's black families were scattered throughout the city, no longer living in small clusters isolated from whites. Most black households were small, with under ten inhabitants, and shared dwellings with white families. Unlike the larger northeastern cities, such as New York and Boston, Salem lacked a single visibly black neighborhood.[13]

Several black households were concentrated in two sections of town (fig. 2). The first, at the eastern edge of Salem near Salem Neck, consisted of a few homes along Essex and English Streets and nearby on East Webb

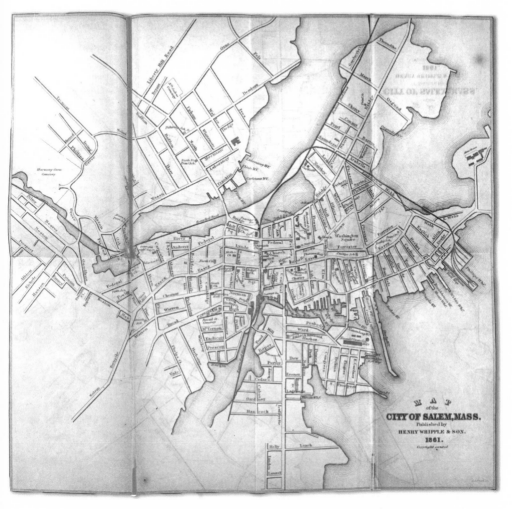

FIGURE 2. Salem, Mass., 1861. Black residents clustered near Salem Neck
(center right) and the Mill Pond (bottom center).

Street. This part of east Salem, reputed to be seedy and unsafe, was close
to Phillips Wharf, the terminus for the busy Essex Railroad.[14] Also at
Salem Neck was the brick structure that housed the local almshouse and
insane asylum, placed there to keep undesirables at a remove from Salem's
more affluent residents. The empty dockside warehouses, noisy smoking
locomotives, and drab institutions for the poor and the mad were all un-
attractive features of black life on Salem's geographical margins.[15]

A second set of black residences surrounded the town's Mill Pond, a pool of stagnant water in southwestern Salem that lay parallel to the Salem Turnpike. At least seventeen of the area's multiple-family dwellings housed blacks, who lived on either side of the pond's northern tip. On the eastern bank, blacks lived on Cedar, Porter, Ropes, and Pond Streets; to the west they lived on Endicott, Summer, Pratt, High, and Creek Streets. Although more blacks lived around the Mill Pond than anywhere else in Salem, they still constituted a minority in the neighborhood of mostly working-class whites.

As in Salem Neck, the Mill Pond area rumbled with the constant passage of steam locomotives making their way to and from Boston. Blacks living on Creek and High Streets experienced even more disruption from heavy traffic at the Eastern Railroad's Salem depot, a ten-track juncture located right behind their homes. At various times during the summer, people living near the Mill Pond also had to endure the reek that emanated from the pond at irregular intervals. As the *Salem Gazette* reported at the time:

> The Mill Pond sends forth a most outrageous stench, often spoiling people's dinners, and causing others to nearly roast to death nights in consequence of keeping the windows closed.... This state of things is not only very uncomfortable, but we have no doubt equally unwholesome.
>
> What immediate cause produces this state of things, we do not profess to know.... Some say the bad smell is produced by the dead fish; but it seems to us more probable that it is produced by the same cause that occasions the death of the fish. Others say that the flood-gates at the City Mills are not of sufficient capacity to ensure a proper change of water by the tides.... Another cause of the trouble is said to be the insufficiency of the culverts under the Eastern railroad. These culverts ... are said to be too high to admit of a proper drainage of the stagnant water above. Whether this is a correct theory or not we do not profess to know. We are informed, however, that the Mill Pond produced similar effluvia, with similar effects, thirty-six years ago, before the Eastern Railroad was built.[16]

Safety was also a concern. Shortly after Charles Benson came to Salem, a local newspaper warned residents to avoid traversing the narrow wooden planks of the railroad bridge across the pond, a common thoroughfare for most blacks living in the area, because of the risk of drowning. Of course, the local hazards and unpleasantries reduced land and rent prices around the Mill Pond, allowing poor blacks to afford the area's low rents, much like the recent immigrants from Canada and Ireland who made up the bulk of the local white population.[17]

Benson probably had never been to Salem before his arrival there in the waning months of 1852 and had little idea where the town's blacks lived. His sole indirect acquaintance with this city more than fifty miles from his home was his familiarity with a Framingham neighborhood nicknamed "Salem End," after its seventeenth-century establishment by a group of refugees from the Salem witchcraft trials. As a wayfarer making his way to Salem a century and a half later, Benson had no knowledge of the ways the town had changed in the interim. In coming years he would get to know the black residents of Salem Neck and the Mill Pond for himself and establish his own home in their neighborhoods. At the moment, though, he was just one of many penniless emigrants to a growing city, without resources or connections and in search of a new life.

Benson wasted little time establishing himself in Salem. Soon after his arrival he secured a job with a black oyster dealer and restaurateur, James Sherman (sometimes spelled "Shearman"). Sherman was a member of a small but identifiable dynasty of successful food-trade entrepreneurs. His wife, Nancy, was the daughter of Curacao-born John Remond, one of Salem's best-known black waiters and owner of a thriving import and export dealership in oysters and wines (fig. 3). James's brother George Sherman, who had accompanied him from their native Rhode Island to Salem in the 1840s, was his business partner until he opened his own restaurant some years later. When Benson came to town, the brothers were still together at James Sherman's busy downtown location in Derby Square. Although Benson was still new to Salem, he evidently impressed the Shermans enough to hire him and let him live at the restaurant. Shortly thereafter, Benson even merited his own name and address listing in Salem's annual *City Directory*.

For Benson, his nascent life in Salem represented everything he once lacked. Although his family had lived in Framingham for over a century, the town had offered little of substance to Charles Benson beyond penury, racial and social isolation, and familial strife. From the ruins of this life Benson emerged craving security and respectability, neither of which had ever been his in Framingham. But in Salem, where he worked for one of the first families of the black world, Benson could tap into a network that linked more than four hundred individuals into a collective black community. With his own listing in the *City Directory* he further

FIGURE 3. John Remond, Salem's most prominent black entrepreneur.

established himself as a member of that community, distinct from the many dozens of young single black laborers who regularly came and went in Salem without setting down permanent roots. Thanks to his steady job and positive attitude, Benson's confidence rose as his memories of failure receded into the past.

BENSON'S EFFORTS to establish himself in Salem were bolstered by the relative health of the black community at that time. More blacks lived in Salem by the early 1850s than ever before. The growth of the black population spurred communal institution-building, beginning with the establishment of a black meeting-house. The introduction of weekly meetings at the black church was accompanied by a rise in community activism. During the years leading up to midcentury Salem's blacks agitated for the integration of the town's public schools, a goal they achieved a decade before schools were finally integrated in Boston, despite the larger community's history of combating racial discrimination. Although most of Salem's whites had little regard for the few blacks living in their midst, at least one predominantly white church developed a reputation as an "abolition church," attracting blacks to worship there and fostering goodwill among the town's black inhabitants. And while racial discrimination persisted in Salem, racist incidents were generally confined to petty harassment and never flared into open conflict as they did in other northern cities during the antebellum era.[18]

The empowerment of black Salem coincided with heightened racial consciousness in black communities throughout the urban North. As the issue of slavery came to dominate national politics during the 1840s and 1850s, northern blacks were growing restive and more militant. They joined abolitionist organizations and attended public lectures and mass meetings in great numbers, sometimes by the thousands. With the passage of the Fugitive Slave Act in 1850, black enclaves grew especially agitated. Designed as part of the Compromise of 1850, this law entitled Southern slaveowners or their representatives to retrieve runaway slaves from anywhere in the United States, armed only with a court affidavit describing the slave's physical characteristics. It further mandated that federal marshals assist the slave catchers, even by compelling the assistance of bystanders or by punishing anyone who obstructed recovery efforts. Once captured, the alleged fugitives were hauled before federally appointed special commissioners, who would adjudge their status without resorting to a jury trial or extending the accused any right to testify. For their service, the commissioners were paid five dollars for blacks found innocent of being fugitives and ten dollars for those pronounced guilty and returned to slavery, virtually insuring rulings in favor of aggrieved slaveholders. Infuriated by the blatant unfairness of the Fugitive Slave Law and fearful of the threat it represented to their rights and liberties, blacks in urban communities throughout the North determined that they would battle the law in any way they could.[19]

In Boston, home to more than two thousand blacks, antipathy toward the Fugitive Slave Act led to several widely reported incidents. When, for example, slave catchers from Georgia arrived in late 1850 to apprehend William and Ellen Craft, a pair of escaped slaves turned abolitionist lecturers, they were met by the organized resistance of a "vigilance committee" of over one hundred members and threatened with explosives. Several months later, in February 1851, a black waiter named Shadrach Minkins was arrested as a fugitive slave from Virginia. In the middle of his hearing before the commissioner, a large group of black Bostonians led by the attorney Robert Morris burst in and freed Minkins, spiriting him away from Boston and dispatching him to safety in Canada. During the ensuing months there were several more disruptions of fugitive slave proceedings, some culminating in rescues, others prompting black protests and threats of civil disobedience. These stories made headlines in newspapers throughout the country and garnered special attention in nearby Salem.

Too far off the beaten path to attract many southern migrants, Salem experienced only one major fugitive slave incident during the uproar following the act's passage. On February 21, 1851, six days after the dramatic arrest and escape of Shadrach Minkins in Boston, a young black barber named Alexander P. Burton was arrested in Salem. Boston newspapers reported that Burton's arrest was accomplished only "with much difficulty," and that "nearly three thousand persons . . . expressed their determination to rescue him from the officers." It turned out that no such activism would be necessary. Alexander Burton was not a fugitive at all, and a closer examination of the warrant revealed that it was for one Andrew J. Burton, a black man living in Boston at the time. Furthermore, Salem's newspapers angrily contradicted the inflammatory version of Burton's arrest concocted by Boston's anti-abolitionist press. According to the *Salem Register* and the *Salem Gazette*, the people of Salem had always cooperated with authorities, and there had never been any danger of a near-riot over the erroneous arrest of a single black youth. Such suggestions, huffed the local press, were "ridiculous."[20]

The truth of the Burton incident likely resembled the more phlegmatic version presented by Salem's newspapers. In contrast to the fierce Garrisonian abolitionism of some Bostonians, antislavery attitudes were rarely expressed loudly in Salem, if at all. The town's newspapers, published by conservative middle-class entrepreneurs, were loath to criticize southerners. Instead they promoted the colonization of blacks in Liberia and other African countries as a solution to "the Negro question." Although the growing political import of the slavery issue had some impact on the flavor and content of news reporting, the *Salem Register* and *Salem Gazette* sought conciliation rather than conflict with the South. In a town where the most popular form of entertainment was the traveling minstrel shows mounted by touring troupes such as Perham's, Peckham's, and the Christie Minstrels, the prevailing attitude toward abolitionism was apathy. Like most white northerners, the residents of Salem enjoyed their Negro shows and the "darkey" jokes that appeared with regularity in the papers. Otherwise, they remained essentially unaffected by the pressures and tensions that were building around the issue of slavery.

While Salem's blacks were more anxious than whites over the fate of Alexander P. Burton, they were too few in number to form the angry crowd of three thousand conjured up by the Boston press. There was, however, a distinct black abolitionist presence in Salem, led by Charles Lenox Remond. An internationally known speaker and mentor to Frederick Douglass, he was the son of John and Nancy Remond, who were dedicated abolitionists. Accompanied by his sister Sarah Parker Remond, Charles Lenox became a stalwart of the abolitionist lecture circuit throughout New England, fundraising and organizing antislavery societies. Listing himself as a "lecturer" in the 1850 federal census, Remond was entirely dependent on his activism for his income. His parents and siblings, who formed his support base in Salem, made their living through more conventional means in the black-dominated fields of catering and "hair work." It is a near-certainty that the unfortunate Alexander P. Burton was in the employ of a Remond when he was seized by authorities, since every black-owned hair-cutting establishment in town was owned by a member of that family.[21]

Charles Benson started his job in a Remond family business eighteen months after the town's brush with the Fugitive Slave Act. From his vantage point in Sherman's oyster-house he could only marvel at the public spirit of his employer's family. His years in Middlesex County had left him with no experience in black communal life or organization. Now he lived at the periphery of the first family of the local black community, one of the most prominent and wealthy black families in New England. His daily world was suffused with references to the Remonds' abolitionist activities or the efforts they spearheaded to integrate Salem's public school system. For many black New Englanders, the descendants of slaves with the same unenlightened rural New England upbringing Charles Benson had, such efforts drew their sympathy for the cause of black racial uplift.

Benson seems to have felt no such sympathy. His name appears nowhere in the rolls of local antislavery societies or activist organizations. Furthermore, the journal he kept at sea during the 1860s and 1870s is notably barren of any abolitionist sentiment or overt expression of racial consciousness. Throughout his years in Salem, Benson's communal participation was limited to his attending weekly church services in the town's black meeting house, and he did so out of a sense of religious and social obligation rather than communal responsibility.

Benson's lack of enthusiasm for institutional reform was matched by his fellow black townsfolk, most of whom likewise avoided participation in large-scale undertakings. Unlike larger black communities in New England, black Salem had no fraternal organizations and no grammar school for black children. The church meeting constituted virtually the only black communal institution in Salem, and that continued only on the sufferance of John Remond, who owned the brick structure that served as a part-time meeting-house. More ominous was the absence of even a basic leadership core among the town's working-class blacks. Other black enclaves with a comparable population, such as the one in Worcester, Massachusetts, fostered a collective identity and sense of purpose through the participation of an identifiable group of public-minded, politically active individuals. In Salem the preponderance of blacks were content to leave such matters in the capable hands of the Remonds.[22]

For their part, the Remond family preferred to lead by example, maintaining a dignified distance from the other blacks in town. Charles Lenox Remond, putative leader of the local abolitionist movement, established his home on Dean Street in northwest Salem, a neighborhood removed from the Mill Pond and Salem Neck areas where most other blacks lived. His married sister Caroline Remond Putnam, a hairdresser and active member of the New England Anti-Slavery Society, lived nearby on Oak Street in a house also situated solely among white homes. The only Remonds to dwell near other blacks were those who maintained living quarters at their places of business, such James Sherman, the restaurateur, Maritche Juan Remond, a hairdresser, and old John Remond himself. Their downtown residences, chosen solely by the demands of the marketplace, signified no particular desire for solidarity with the rest of black Salem. This worrisome pattern was most unusual, for with the exception of the Remonds, Salem's other nineteenth-century black entrepreneurs and business owners maintained homes in the midst of the black community.[23]

Since they were primarily concerned with their own businesses and social circles, the Remonds interacted with few other blacks besides their employees. Charlotte Forten, a teenaged girl who came to Salem around the same time that Charles Benson arrived there, provided unwitting documentation of this phenomenon in her diary. The granddaughter of the black sailmaking tycoon James Forten, Charlotte had grown up in Philadelphia amid wealth and prestige. In a quest to provide their daughter with the best education available to a young woman of color, her parents sent her to Salem to receive secondary schooling still unavailable to blacks in racially exclusionary Pennsylvania. As a scion of the black elite, Charlotte Forten would stay with the most prominent black family Salem had to offer, the Remonds. Since the back rooms of restaurants or barbershops were ill-suited for a guest of such quality, Forten was placed in the care of those Remonds who had private homes. Over the course of seven years in Salem she lived with two different members of the wealthy clan, Charles Lenox Remond and Caroline Remond Putnam.[24]

Charlotte Forten kept a daily journal of her experiences, and throughout her time in Salem she described her participation in a wide array of social and cultural activities. In the company of various female Remonds, Babcocks, and Putnams, Forten read Alfred, Lord Tennyson, John Greenleaf Whittier, and Elizabeth Browning. Together the women played chess and whist, took walks in the picturesque parts of Salem, visited other wealthy blacks in Boston, Philadelphia, New York, and Newport, and promoted abolitionism by hosting and attending antislavery meetings. Forten also joined her hostesses in their working responsibilities, "keeping store" in the hairdressing establishments owned and operated by her companions "Miss S.P.R." (Sarah Parker Remond) and "Mrs. Caroline P." (Caroline Remond Putnam).

Conspicuously absent from Charlotte Forten's diary are the other four hundred or so blacks who lived in Salem. Her faithful reports of Sundays include descriptions of abolitionist meetings but lack even a single reference to church services at Salem's black meeting-house, which neither she nor her hosts appear to have attended.[25] Although she recorded numerous meetings in Boston with such prominent abolitionists as William Lloyd Garrison, William Cooper Nell, and William Wells Brown, not once did Forten refer by name to any of Salem's working-class black inhabitants. On the few occasions that she did mention the common folk, she showed little respect for the people of whom she knew little. "Would that there were far more intelligent colored people!" she wrote in November 1856. "And yet we could hardly expect more of those, who have so many unsurmountable difficulties to contend with." She was equally dismissive of the "generality of colored young men that one sees," a group that included Charles Benson, although she understood that "the unhappy circumstances in which these are placed, are often more to blame than they themselves."[26]

Charlotte Forten was encouraged by her sheltered existence among the Remonds to consider working-class black Salemites only in the aggregate, never as individuals. Charles Benson was part of that working class, looking in at the Remonds and their ilk from the outside. It is small wonder that he absorbed little of the racial uplift philosophy articulated by the Remonds and other black leaders who did not live and worship among those they purported to lead. Instead Benson made himself comfortable in black Salem, learning for the first time in his life to identify himself as part of a community of blacks. For the remainder of his life Benson would associate his sense of home with Salem. At the heart of this identification were the people of Salem, the assortment of neighbors, friends, and family that differentiated his life in Salem so sharply from his lonesome existence in Framingham and Natick.

One person above all others was central to Benson's view of Salem as his true home. Her name was Margaret Jenny Francis, and he met her within a matter of weeks after he arrived in Salem in late 1852.

He called her "Jenny Pearl."

CHAPTER THREE

"Jenny kissed me"

SALEM AND AT SEA, 1853–1861

MARGARET JENNY FRANCIS, Charles Benson's second wife, was born in
Salem on March 13, 1837. Her father, Joseph Francis, was a mariner. So
too was her grandfather, also named Joseph Francis, who had come to
America from his native Africa in the early 1800s. Nothing is known of
her mother or her mother's family. By 1850 neither of Margaret's parents
lived with her in Salem, if they still lived at all. Her father disappeared
from Salem crew lists, where he had formerly appeared with regularity,
before 1840; like many sailors, he may have died at sea. Her mother, whose
name never appears in any of Salem's official records, was apparently not
in Salem either.[1]

The young girl may have had other relatives in Salem, for several black
families named Francis lived there in 1850. Among these were two day laborers, forty-nine-year-old Edmund Francis and twenty-seven-year-old
Augustus Francis, a father of one. A third black Francis, Ephraim F., also
dwelled in Salem, where he ran a successful stove-polishing business. Unlike most of Salem's blacks, "Black Frank" was a man of some means who
possessed property valued at six hundred dollars. Kin or not, none of these
men took young Margaret into their household.[2]

Instead, the 1850 census indicates that by the time she reached her
teens, "Margarett J. Francis" was a foster child in the Porter Street home
of Robert and Hannah Dailey, near the Mill Pond. The Daileys, then in
their late forties, may have taken the girl in because of earlier connections
to her father. Like Joseph Francis, Robert Dailey went to sea during the
1830s, making several voyages aboard Salem trading vessels before abandoning seafaring for shore pursuits. The two men may have encountered
each other professionally, their relationship enduring enough for Dailey
to offer Joseph's daughter Margaret a place in his home a decade later. For
whatever reason, by 1850 the girl had found a place at the Daileys' along

with fellow foster child Charles King, age five, and the Daileys' adult housemates, a newly married couple, Thomas and Sephronia Williams.[3]

Porter Street, a block-long lane that ended at the western edge of the Mill Pond, was fairly typical of mid-nineteenth-century "black" streets in Salem and throughout the urban Northeast. Most dwellings housed one or more black boarders in addition to primary family members; still, most of the block's residents were white, chiefly immigrants and their families. Two dozen blacks lived along the street, occupying four individual buildings. The Daileys' neighbors included the Colman family two doors down. Next door to the Colmans were the Drews, whose house abutted that of the growing family of David and Salome Fuller at "rear 16 Porter Street." As a member of the working class, Robert Dailey, a porter, had much in common with Fuller, a shoemaker; Williams, a laborer; Thomas Drew, a waiter; and William Colman, a mariner. Like most black men in Salem, these men frequently changed jobs and occupations; only William Colman kept one job, as a mariner, for a long and uninterrupted stretch of time. Thomas Drew was also a clothes-cleaner and, briefly, a "trader." Robert Dailey was also a porter and for a short time a trader, perhaps in partnership with his neighbor, Drew.[4] David Fuller became a shoemaker after a failed attempt at restaurant work in the 1840s, and later he worked as a laborer and a porter. Certainly many of Porter Street's black women worked, although only four of them reported their work as seamstresses and washerwomen to city officials and census takers.[5]

Although Margaret Francis was only thirteen, she may have been a laboring woman as well. Many black girls her age or younger were often "sent out," performing domestic service for paltry pay with little time off and suffering through innumerable indignities from their mistresses.[6] But whether Margaret Francis worked as a servant or not, she still possessed a significant level of independence. Living in the Daileys' foster home with adults who worked longer hours than she at intensive manual labor, she likely had plenty of unchaperoned time during which she could choose her own activities and acquaintances. During the last months before her sixteenth birthday, she developed a *tendre* for a newcomer to Salem, a man with a troubled past more than seven years her senior. The relationship quickly turned intimate, and passionate. Before long, Margaret Francis and Charles Benson were lovers.

Because Benson never discussed their initial meeting in the journal he kept a decade later, no details remain to describe how Charles first met his "Jenny Pearl." During his years as a diarist he made only one brief reference to the young girl he knew in Salem, recalling on her birthday in 1878 the "girl of 16" (actually, she was only fifteen) that he had met twenty-five years earlier. But he did record the fateful day the young lovers "begat" their first child, January 9, 1853. Tucked away on a scrap of an old almanac page glued into his journal, Benson committed to paper his memory of the amorous encounter that changed his life. He did so not out of shame but out of pride in the tangible evidence that testified to the love he shared with Jenny Francis, who would be with him for the rest of his days.[7]

Exactly seven weeks after they conceived their baby, Charles Augustus Benson and Margaret Jenny Francis were married. The wedding took place in late February, a month after Charles's twenty-third birthday and two weeks before Jenny turned sixteen. For the second time in his life Benson was married in a nondenominational civic ceremony, this one performed in the nearby town of Danvers by Joseph Shed, Esq., the town clerk. An announcement of the marriage was published in the *Salem Register* almost immediately; Benson, who treasured the memento, would later paste a clipped copy of the short paragraph into one of the journal notebooks he kept at sea.[8] For him, those three lines of newsprint conferred legitimacy on his new marriage, demonstrating in a most public way that he had come to Salem to stay. His seeming carelessness about the prospect of discovery by his undivorced first wife would indicate that he had put his old life behind him for good. Also, he may have banked on the long odds against her ever seeing the small item printed in a faraway local newspaper.[9]

Despite Benson's troubled past and broken first marriage, and despite the necessarily rushed scheduling of their hasty wedding, the marriage of Charles and Jenny Benson would prove to be an enduring and deeply emotional commitment. Like the marriage of Charles's paternal grandparents, Abel and Rhoda, who also came into their nuptials with a baby already on the way, this would be a union that would last a lifetime.

Both husband and wife certainly appeared to love each other very much. In 1862, nine years into their marriage, the couple regularly sent love letters to each other when Charles was away on his long sea voyages. The diary entries he wrote a decade after his wedding day were replete with emotional intimacy and undiminished desire. Clearly his second marriage brought him a kind of fulfillment that his first had not. Young and inexperienced, Charles Benson had wed the first and only marriageable black girl he could find in his small town. When he created a second chance for himself five years later, he was unwilling to settle merely for proximity and availability. His life in Salem was based on security and respectability. A companionate marriage, the romantic partnership that constituted the ideal relationship in nineteenth-century culture, would insure both.

Whether Jenny shared Charles's vision or not, she still seemed to need some reassurances of her husband's constancy and fidelity. Almost a decade later, Benson avowed his undying love almost daily in the journals he wrote for her to read. He also peppered his writings with impassioned declarations so fervent, they might have seemed unintentionally defensive. On shore leaves in tropical ports he made sure to emphasize that he did not "see a woman," a loaded statement from a man who referred to his sexual urge to "see Jenny" when away from home. It is unlikely that such comments signified his hidden guilt over some past indiscretion or affair. Adultery would have been out of character for Benson, who regarded even occasional masturbation as a betrayal of his values and his relationship with his wife. Instead, Benson sought to reassure his wife that she would always be first in his heart, even if she had not been the first in his bed. Benson was concerned that Jenny suspected him of lingering feelings for his previous partner, and possibly a roving eye toward attracting new ones. In response to this jealousy, real or imagined, he wrote: "None nor nothing never need think trying to fill your place. You ocupy a place in my heart which none never did nor can. That place is for you alone."[10]

As always, the stark financial realities of urban black life soon intruded on the security Benson hoped to achieve. His job at Sherman's oyster-house did not pay enough to support a growing family, especially after the birth of Fransisca G. Benson in October 1853, seven months after the wedding. Unfortunately, even a city as large as Salem offered black men few opportunities to find lucrative or even merely steady employment. Many found temporary work as day laborers, an unreliable occupation that Benson had already tried unsuccessfully in Framingham. The few blacks who held semi-skilled or skilled jobs were mostly members of the well-to-do Remond family that dominated the traditionally black fields of food service and barbering in Salem.[11] Others found employment as seafarers aboard merchant vessels bound for South America or the Indian Ocean. The remainder of Salem's black working men included several small-business entrepreneurs and those who performed assorted odd jobs; 23 of the 159 black men in Salem, or about 15 percent, listed no occupation.[12] Most of the men changed jobs frequently as they tried to make the most of the limited opportunities available to them in Salem. These figures so common to black communities throughout the urban North offered little hope to Charles Benson, one of many working-class black men with no capital for starting a business, few marketable skills, and rising expenses.

In many black families the woman's earning power helped make up the shortfall in their husband's wages, as Jenny Benson knew from her years living with the Daileys on Porter Street. At least four black women operated businesses in Salem, including Hannah W. Williams, a "fancy cake baker" who worked out of her home, and three hairdressers from the Remond family who operated their own shops.[13] At least eight black women were employed as live-in servants, working and living in the homes of white Salemites, while others, such as Hannah Blossom, a laundress, performed various domestic services as piece work or day labor.[14] Like black women in other northern cities, many more of Salem's black women worked as washerwomen, seamstresses, and domestics, although their efforts went unrecorded in official accounts.[15] But as Jenny Benson recovered from childbirth and tended her newborn in early 1854, it was impossible for her to supplement her family's income in this manner, at least for a while.

Charles Benson's first marriage had crumbled under the twin pressures of economic need and rising domestic tensions. Given his past history, his second marriage might well have ended much the same way. But Benson approached this relationship with a deep commitment absent from his previous one and was equally dedicated to maintaining his life in Salem, his adoptive home. Prepared to find any job that would allow him to support his wife and child, Benson seized an opportunity that had not existed for him in the landlocked farming village of Framingham. Shortly after the birth of his daughter in Salem, he took the fateful step that would determine the course of the rest of his life. In early 1854, he accepted the berth of cook and steward aboard a merchant brig bound for Canada. For what was likely the first time in his life, Charles Benson would go to sea.

NORTHERN BLACK men had played an active role in American seafaring for over a century, first as slaves and later as free men. The attractions of seafaring for black men included relatively high wages, stable employment, and personal fulfillment; the constant arrival and departure of merchant ships also provided a wealth of short-term menial jobs along the docks of the large port cities, further contributing to the economic well-being of local blacks.[16] By the early nineteenth century, the black presence in the Atlantic maritime world had expanded to the point that the large number of berths held by black mariners was disproportionate to their tiny presence in the overall population of northern cities. By 1825, blacks occupied nearly one-fifth of all berths aboard foreign-bound vessels leaving Philadelphia and New York, and blacks composed roughly one-quarter of all mariners departing from Providence, Rhode Island. Although few records remain, the same would have been true of Boston, then the second-largest port in the United States. In the large port cities of the Northeast, black men offered to meet a seemingly limitless demand for seafarers. One of these black mariners was Charles Benson's uncle Labin, who shipped out of Boston on one or more voyages in the late 1820s.[17]

Because few Boston crew lists exist, the exact dates of Labin Benson's seafaring career are unknown beyond a single listing in the 1828 edition of Boston's *City Directory*. Thus it is impossible to determine the names of the vessels on which Labin Benson served, or his shipboard rank. Like his nephew Charles decades later, he may have found a berth as a cook or steward, positions commonly filled by black mariners. At the same time, many black men of the early nineteenth century took advantage of the egalitarian nature and comparative racial flexibility of the Atlantic maritime culture of that era. Black seamen could attain a high degree of equality with whites aboard deep-water vessels, in terms of their crew positions and ranks, their wages, and even (in some rare cases) the potential for occupational mobility. Many black mariners worked and lived in relative parity with whites aboard ship, serving as ordinary seamen, able-bodied seamen, or officers, and, in a very few instances, as the masters of oceangoing vessels. Some black mariners even found their opportunities aboard vessels with predominantly black crews and officers. The range of seafaring opportunity available to black men in a large port like Boston may have enabled Labin Benson to attain salary and status otherwise unavailable to him in the alleys and courts of Belknap Street in his "Nigger Hill" neighborhood.[18]

Born in 1830, Charles Benson may have arrived too late to hear firsthand reports of his uncle's maritime experiences. Still, as a boy living in Framingham with his parents and grandparents, he may have read some of Labin's letters from abroad, or at least spoken of him with his relatives.

Though the only bodies of water in Framingham were the town's tiny ponds, the boy could still imagine the great seas his uncle traversed. As an adult, Benson, once he tried the seafaring life for himself, would be forever drawn by the allure of the sea. The pull he felt may have had its roots in his childhood imaginings, and in stories of his uncle Labin's exploits.

But Charles Benson never acted on any youthful impulse to seek his fortune at sea. Unlike thousands of his adventure-seeking contemporaries in New England, he did not ship out in his late teens, choosing instead to marry young and toil in low-paying jobs ashore. When he reached the bustling seaport of Salem in 1852, having left Framingham, his marriage in shambles, Benson's first impulse was to find employment in town. Only when financial privation truly threatened him and his new family did Benson turn to the sea, as he would later put it, to "ern [his] bread."[19]

Black mariners had maintained a significant presence aboard Salem's merchant vessels since the early nineteenth century. Too few in number to make a noticeable impact in earlier years, black mariners shipped out regularly by 1810. As in the larger ports of the Northeast, Salem's black men were welcome in an industry that suffered chronic labor shortages, but the types of job open to them were restricted from the outset. Only four out of the dozens of black men who shipped out of Salem in 1810 were listed as seamen aboard their vessels, and none was an officer. The remainder were identified as cooks or stewards. White servants indentured to ships' officers were the only other seafaring population to be limited in this manner. They too left Salem as the cooks and stewards of merchant vessels, added to the crew specifically to provide for their masters' needs at sea.[20]

Over the next several decades Salem's black men continued to find opportunities in seafaring, but only under the same conditions. In 1830, the year of Charles Benson's birth, eighty-seven merchant ships left Salem with black crewmembers. Only one or two black men were aboard each of these vessels, serving as ship's cook, steward, or both. In all ninety-seven black mariners shipped out of Salem that year, forming a larger cohort of workers than any other single occupational category in Salem, including day labor. Despite the lack of occupational mobility for these men, seafaring was still the most popular form of black male employment in Salem a decade later. In 1840, eighty-seven black mariners departed the wharfs of Salem in the galleys and pantries of merchant vessels, bound for ports in the South Atlantic and Indian Oceans.[21]

Only seven of the eighty-seven black mariners who sailed out of Salem in 1840, however, had sailed in 1830, demonstrating that few of the city's black men chose to remain in seafaring for the long term. Furthermore, maritime opportunities were rapidly disappearing. In 1850 only fifty-six black mariners sailed out of Salem, and by 1854 their number had dwindled to forty-three, less than half the number in 1840. Seafaring was still the largest employer of black men in the city, but the outlook for the future was dim.[22]

Ports throughout the Northeast were experiencing the same decline in demand for seafarers. This trend boded ill not just for the mariners themselves but for entire black communities, which had relied on the regularity and wages of seafaring work for decades. By the 1840s fewer and fewer black men in Philadelphia, New York, Providence, and presumably Boston looked to the sea for regular employment. The number of black career mariners dropped precipitously, and most black mariners shipped out only once or twice before abandoning the sea. As demand dropped, so did the range of options available to black sailors, forcing them to sign on as stewards and cooks in port cities where once they had served as able seamen, officers, and even masters. Little changed for Salem's black seafarers, who had always been relegated to these positions. But the rippling effects of a larger decline in black maritime work were felt in Salem, as the number of black seamen diminished.

Most men who depended on the sea for their livelihood, whether black or white, were feeling the bite of hard times by the midpoint of the nineteenth century. The global position of U.S. maritime trading was eroding markedly, and there was little anyone in the seafaring world could do about it. Throughout New England, once a stronghold of the Atlantic trade, the maritime industries deteriorated. Along the docks and wharfs, in the mercantile houses, shipyards, sailmakers' shops, ropewalks, and smithies, belts were tightened. Harbors once thickly forested with the masts of arriving and departing vessels were now thinned, denuded of the tall ships that had brought such prosperity to the region. Shipowners no longer saw the sense in building newer and larger vessels, since their holds would never bulge with sufficient cargo to justify their construction. And shipmasters had greater difficulty finding experienced and willing crews for their aging brigs and barks, as the sons of Yankee farmers turned up their noses at the poor conditions and wages of sea life.[23]

With only small ports and few resources to compete with larger rivals, Essex County, Massachusetts, was especially ill-equipped to ride out the bad days ahead. The first serious dip in the county's maritime fortunes in 1845 heralded a quarter-century of bad news, reflected by a nearly 50 percent drop in tonnage registered for foreign trade. In Salem, the county seat and crown jewel of Essex County prosperity, that figure suffered an even steeper cut as foreign-bound trade tonnage plummeted from 18,700 tons in 1845 to a miserable 3,700 tons by 1870. Unable to muster the wherewithal to continue operating under the worsening trade conditions of the late nineteenth century, Salem's shipping magnates divested themselves of their trade interests. Their departure had drastic effects on the careers of the many masters, officers, seamen, and other personnel who had once looked to the sea for sustenance.[24]

This pattern of declension had little impact on Charles Benson in 1854, if it were apparent to him at all. With no seafaring background and little knowledge of the old days in Salem, Benson had no sense of the city's declining maritime fortunes when he decided to go to sea. He also had no reason to concern himself with anything but his immediate future, with securing a steady job with a good salary. Seafaring work offered these, along with a respite from the more hectic aspects of raising an infant. Over the course of his lifetime Benson would prove especially adept at avoiding this stage of his children's lives. In later years he would ask his wife "Am I not in the way some times?" Although he was sincere, his query was also disingenuous. Mixed in his own heart were guilt and insecurity, as well as a very real sense of relief, and the way he phrased his question rather adroitly removed any blame for his behavior from his own shoulders.[25]

It may have been Jenny Benson who sent her husband away on his first voyage. As both the daughter and granddaughter of seafaring men, she knew as well as anyone in black Salem the opportunities available to those willing to undertake the rigors of life at sea.[26] If not his wife, then perhaps patrons or fellow workers at Sherman's oyster-house guided Benson into maritime work. Although his employer, James Sherman, had never been a sailor, other members of the black restaurant fraternity, such as the oyster-saloon proprietor Joseph Morris, had been cooks or stewards aboard Salem vessels at one time or another. It could have been Morris or Jenny Benson's foster parent Robert Dailey or any of a number of experienced black men in town who gave Benson the idea to look for work as a mariner. He may have also done so independently. Spending so much time at Derby Square, not far from the wharfs where sailing vessels still came and went with some regularity in the early 1850s,

Benson may have spun his own fantasies of sailing away on one of the vessels gliding by the shore each day.[27]

So it was that on July 12, 1854, Charles Benson shoved off a Salem wharf aboard the tiny merchant brig *Gem*. The *Gem* was a coaster, a small vessel following a route that hugged the coastline of the Atlantic seaboard throughout its relatively brief journey. Coasters were ubiquitous in Salem, as five or six of them came and went in the harbor each day. Benson's maiden voyage was a coal-hauling mission to Pictou, Nova Scotia, at the southeastern tip of Canada. For six weeks he served the needs of the seven men aboard, including himself. He cooked and prepared all meals, keeping a weather eye on the remaining food supplies. The galley and pantry were his domain and solely his responsibility. The short voyage was a good initiation, allowing him to assimilate the ways of the sea cook, all the time drawing on what he had learned at Sherman's oysterhouse. The novelty of cooking in a kitchen that bounced and rolled beneath him did not alter his basic tasks of preparing simple fare for working men.[28]

Benson's short trip to Canada aboard the *Gem* passed without incident. After his return home on August 22, he wasted little time before signing on his next voyage. About two weeks later, Benson loaded his gear aboard the trading bark *Miquelon*. This time out, the vessel was bigger, the crew larger, and the voyage longer. Charles Benson was bound for Buenos Ayres, an exotic destination as far from home as he had ever imagined.

WHEN BENSON shipped out aboard the *Miquelon* on September 11, 1854, he joined the Brazil trade, one of the most profitable commercial ventures in nineteenth-century Salem.[29] The town had established its Brazilian trade connections in 1801, when a tiny Salem schooner tried its luck in Brazil rather than crossing the Atlantic to continue on to the Far East and Indian Ocean. Over the next half-century, Salem sent hundreds of ships to South American ports-of-call in Brazil, French Guiana, and Argentina. Merchant brigs and barks dropped anchor in Para, Maranham, and Pernambuco in the north, or Rio Grande, Montevideo, and Buenos Ayres along the Rio de la Plata, at the border between Brazil and Argentina, its southern neighbor.[30]

Two former ship captains named John Bertram and Benjamin Upton led Salem's charge into the markets of South America. Familiar with the region from the days when they sailed there as masters of other men's

ships, the two entrepreneurs set up competing firms that grew and prospered during the 1830s and 1840s. Fleets of small trading vessels, generally under three hundred tons, bombarded South American merchants
with New England's manufactured goods: barrel staves, gunpowder,
flour, glass, and yards and yards of machine-woven cotton sheeting from
the region's ubiquitous mills. In exchange, the ship captains employed by
Bertram and Upton filled their holds with raw materials to provide to the
factories back home, including tallow for making candles, gum copal to
be processed into varnish, and crude rubber to be "vulcanized" by Yankee
acolytes of Charles Goodyear. Salem's trade barons were especially interested in cattle hides from Maranham and Rio Grande for the bur-
geoning leather industry, which would supplant the faded maritime trades
as one of the town's chief money-makers by century's end.[31]

Unconcerned with the larger forces at work, Charles Benson played
his role in the Brazil trade as cook and steward of the *Miquelon*, preparing and serving meals all the way to Montevideo and Buenos Ayres and
back. The *Miquelon* was a merchant bark with ten men aboard, including
the captain and officers, which meant more work for Benson in the galley. Also, since this voyage was more than twice as long as his previous
voyage to Canada on the tiny brig *Gem*, he had to learn to ration the
vessel's food supplies so they would last out the trip. With repeated trips
down the Atlantic coast to South America Benson developed habits of
economy and efficiency that he would need later, on voyages to East
Africa, the Indian Ocean, and the Red Sea that lasted three to four times
longer than the voyages in the Brazil trade.

Even a seafaring novice like Benson may have realized that Salem's
South American trade was dying by the time he joined it in 1854. John
Bertram, who became one of the premier Salem traders active in Brazil,
would later reflect that "the Para trade . . . continued good until [the
1850s] when I found that the New York merchants had an unsurmountable advantage over us." Competition from large and affluent commercial
interests in New York, New Jersey, and Boston made quick work of the
small Salem trade. All of the American traders faced the additional ob-
stacle of Great Britain, the true master of foreign commerce in Brazil and
Guiana at this time. Without any real incentive to continue fighting a
battle he could never win, Bertram curtailed his operations in South
America. By 1858 he no longer did business there at all, effectively ending more than a half-century of trade. As Bertram wrote in his memoir
twenty years after the fact, "We gave it up."[32]

FIGURE 4. *M. Shepard*, brig. Benson was cook and steward aboard the *M. Shepard* to South America in 1855.

While John Bertram was on the verge of giving up, Charles Benson was just getting started. Benson spent the three years between 1854 and 1857 shuttling up and down the Atlantic coast to and from South America. After his return from Buenos Ayres aboard the *Miquelon* in early 1855, Benson signed on the brig *M. Shepard* bound for Para at the end of March (fig. 4).[33] Eleven days after the *M. Shepard* unloaded a full cargo of rubber in Salem in early June, Benson departed on the bark *Wyman* for "Rio Grande & a market." After a second voyage on the *Wyman* to South America, Benson next embarked upon what would prove his final voyage to Brazil on the merchant bark *Swallow*.

By the time the *Swallow* returned to Salem on March 17, 1857, Benson was a deepwater veteran, having made six voyages in less than three years. He had sailed under five different shipmasters in the employ of both John Bertram and Benjamin Upton, once under the command of Upton's brother Edwin. The ease with which he found berths suggests that Benson developed a reputation as a willing mariner who could be counted on to do his job. As the ranks of Salem seafarers thinned, a man like Benson could expect a fairly hearty welcome to any crew he cared to join. In fact, a man like Benson did exactly that. A black man with a similar physical description who used Benson's name traveled to Africa aboard two more Salem vessels, the brig *Ann Maria* and bark *Costarelli*, while the real Benson was on various South American trips in 1855 and 1856. Carrying forged or borrowed seaman's papers, the imposter took advantage of the liberal hiring practices along the wharfs to find his own berths. Even a third individual, this one a man five feet, eight inches tall with light skin and hair color, took to calling himself "Charles Benson" when he boarded a Salem vessel at Rio Grande "to proceed on a voyage to Salem." With time running out on Salem's maritime fortunes, no one apparently cared to examine a sailor's paperwork too closely. Far more important were reliability and a willingness to accept a seafarer's berth, two qualities that several "Charles Benson's" demonstrated in the mid-1850s.

THE GENUINE Charles Benson was one of a small cadre of black men who earned their livelihood from the sea in the 1850s. These men were generally in their thirties; Benson, then in his mid-twenties, was among the youngest. Several were family men, with listings in Salem's city directories and regularly enumerated by Salem's census-takers. Like Benson, who spent barely four months at home in Salem over the course of three years of seafaring, these men shipped out regularly as cooks and stewards with only a rare few weeks ashore between voyages.[34]

Benson's contact with his peers began at the docks, where they shared drinks and meals, relaxed, and swapped stories while loading personal effects and supplies on board before they set sail. Small-craft cooks like Benson did not make their voyages in the company of other blacks, for the ship's complement was too small to require both a cook and steward. Still, they might meet during a voyage when ships passed at sea, or when docked simultaneously at a wharf in Maranham or Para. Benson and his compatriots also regularly traded berths, filling slots other Salem blacks had just vacated; because of the small size of the hiring pool of black mariners, this exchange was inevitable. Thus in 1854 Benson stowed his gear in a space formerly occupied by his predecessor aboard the *Miquelon*, James R. Brown. The following year Benson was one of three cooks who served on separate voyages aboard the *M. Shepard*. The other two were Isaac Hallock and William Ready. Another cook, who spent a full voyage in the company of the spurious Charles Benson in 1856, John B. Stout of the *Costarelli*, would eventually find himself replacing the true Benson as steward on board the bark *Glide* in the mid-1860s. Salem's black mariners certainly knew of each other and met once in a while, forming a small and exclusive community. But it was a community in spirit only, for each of Salem's black seafarers spent his long months at sea alone in the company of whites.

By the end of the 1850s, even this small community of black mariners was disintegrating with the collapse of Salem's shipping fortunes and the ignominious end of the Brazil trade. Still in the early stages of his seafaring career, Charles Benson was unwilling to give up so easily. But the end of Brazil shipping made it difficult for him to return repeatedly to familiar berths on vessels with short routes. By the time Benson arrived home aboard the *Swallow* from Buenos Ayres in 1857, the changes were already apparent. Virtually all of Benson's prior vessels were disappearing from active duty in overseas shipping. Benson had first gone to sea aboard the brig *Gem* when he went to Canada in 1854; after that voyage ended, not a single black crewmember ever left a Salem dock aboard that vessel again.[35] The same was true for Benson's next vessel, the *Miquelon*, which vanished from Salem's customs records after the completion of Benson's September 1855 voyage to Montevideo and Buenos Ayres.[36] Benson had served as cook of the *Wyman* on two successive voyages to South America, but after his departure no black man would take over the galley of the trading bark, which had only a very few years of usefulness left. Even the *Swallow*, on which he took his last voyage to Brazil, would sail out of Salem only one more time.[37]

Only the indefatigable *M. Shepard* continued to offer Salem's black seamen regular berths. Black cooks shipped out aboard the vessel as long as it continued operating out of Salem, which it did through 1861. But once the owner, John Bertram, withdrew from Brazil in 1858, the *M. Shepard* was forced to change course. After over a decade of South American activity, the brig now took a southeasterly heading and steered around the Cape of Good Hope and into the Indian Ocean. With no remaining commercial interests in the Americas, it began to follow a route Charles Benson first traveled a year earlier in 1857, when he left the *Swallow* to join the crew of the trading bark *Elizabeth Hall*. The *M. Shepard* was now one of the many deepwater vessels from Salem that sought profits in the city's last great foreign trade partner, Zanzibar.[38]

ZANZIBAR IS a small island, fifty-four miles long and twenty-three miles broad at its widest point. It is situated off the eastern coast of mainland Africa, from which it is separated by a channel about twenty miles wide. Along with much of East Africa, Zanzibar was controlled by Portugal during the sixteenth and seventeenth centuries. With the waning of the Portuguese empire Zanzibar fell under the dominion of Muscat, a key port at the mouth of the Persian Gulf and the most important port city in the Arab state of Oman. By the end of the eighteenth century, Zanzibar was ruled by an Arab governor appointed in Muscat to represent the interests of the Omani ruling class. Then the British arrived in the form of a naval squadron en route to the Red Sea. Their timing was fortuitous, for the small island was about to become a focal point for the entire region.[39]

In 1804, shortly after Britain's first visit to Zanzibar, Said bin Sultan ascended to the throne of Muscat, becoming its "sayyid," or Lord (rather than its "sultan" or "imaum," two titles misapplied to the sayyid by the British and Americans who came to Zanzibar). Said's rule brought great change to much of East Africa, and especially to Zanzibar. During his early decades on the throne the sayyid was forced to deal with a series of rebellions in the East African country of Mombasa, where fractious Swahili chiefs resisted his authority until 1837. Concurrently he strengthened his position along the East African coast and further bolstered his rule by welcoming friendships and treaties with the British. Once his Mombasan troubles ended, Said shifted his seat of power from Muscat to Zanzibar. He now dominated the entire East African coast from his palace in Zanzibar, leaving his eldest son, Thuwaini, to govern Muscat in his absence. Sayyid Said remained in Zanzibar until his death in 1856, one year before Charles Benson first visited the island.[40]

Said's removal to Zanzibar signified the growing importance of the island in the larger scheme of East African and Indian Ocean trade. The island's principal role was that of middleman, brokering the sale of raw materials from the African mainland to foreign consumers. African ivory, soft and easily polished, was traded to merchants from India, Europe, and America. Gum copal, an essential ingredient of varnish manufactured in New England, also garnered significant profits for Zanzibar's mercantile interests. So, too, did the flourishing East African slave trade. Despite British efforts to stem the tide of slaves flowing through the island, tens of thousands of mainland Africans went up for sale in Zanzibar's open-air slave markets each year. A significant number of these slaves were exported to the Middle East aboard small Arab dhows manned by slave crews.[41]

Most slaves remained in Zanzibar. They were bought there by wealthy Arab planters for the cultivation of cloves, the island's primary crop and only homegrown trade commodity. Cloves were first introduced to the island's agriculture around 1810 and soon dominated Zanzibar's economy; by the time Sayyid Said moved his headquarters there in 1840, major portions of the island were blanketed with clove plantations owned by the Arab ruling class. Toiling in the clove trees were hundreds of thousands of East African slaves. As the clove trade boomed, Zanzibar's society expanded and diversified under the influence of Indian merchants eager to reap their share of the bountiful profits. Soon hundreds of expatriate Indians moved to the island and carved out places for themselves as traders, moneylenders, and eventually landowners.[42]

The first Americans to arrive at Zanzibar were merchant traders from Salem, who saw an opportunity to expand their existing commercial activities in the Indian Ocean region. Among them was the ship captain and aspiring entrepreneur John Bertram, who, having made a few contacts in the 1820s, arrived at the island aboard his *Black Warrior* in 1831 bearing gunpowder for trade and an additional thirty thousand dollars in cash and notes to invest. Bertram returned home loaded with gum copal and with a firm commitment to expanding Salem's business interests in Zanzibar. In short order savvy Salem merchants successfully negotiated international trade agreements between the U.S. government and Sayyid Said, which included official appointments for themselves as U.S. consuls to Zanzibar. These appointments enabled them to devote their full attention to generating tremendous profits from the island's various sources of income. The success of their ventures sparked a fierce trade war among Salem merchants and traders. Although John Bertram eventually bested most of his competitors, he had little time to savor his victory, for the imminent collapse of his efforts in Brazil heightened his need for success in Zanzibar.

Zanzibar was now one of Salem's only remaining trade partners overseas, and the town's merchants struggled to get as much out of the island as they could. By the end of the 1850s the United States accounted for over one-quarter of Zanzibar's foreign trade; virtually all of that trade took place aboard merchant ships from Salem.[43] Replicating John Bertram's voyage aboard the *Black Warrior* some three decades earlier, these hardy barks sailed from Massachusetts down to the Cape of Good Hope at Africa's southernmost tip, then up through East African waters into the Indian Ocean. The entire round-trip journey could last from eight or nine months to thirteen months or more, depending upon winds, weather, and trading conditions. For such a long, arduous journey experienced officers and men were at a premium. Accurate navigation was essential, rounding the Cape perilous, and finding men willing to spend a year away at sea—and then repeat the journey a second or third time—was nearly impossible. Thus, with a little seasoning in the tropics of the eastern hemisphere, Charles Benson would be an asset to any of John Bertram's shipmasters, for such a capable, experienced, and hardworking crewman with his solid reputation was becoming hard to find.

Benson's first foray into the Indian Ocean aboard the Bertram bark *Elizabeth Hall* commenced on May 23, 1857, two months after his return from Buenos Ayres on the *Swallow*. At thirteen months, this would be the longest voyage of his seafaring career so far. It would also be the first voyage with another black crewman. That crewman was George Lee, the seventeen-year-old son of a widowed domestic servant, going to sea for the first time in his life. Although Benson had never made a journey of this magnitude before, he was ten years older and vastly more experienced than Lee, who became his apprentice in the daily management and preparation of food supplies for more than a dozen men.[44]

To secure a full cargo for the homebound voyage, outbound Salem barks like the *Elizabeth Hall*, after rounding the Cape of Good Hope, would make several stops before reaching Zanzibar. After trading for ivory, ebony, and cattle hides, they continued on to Zanzibar for gum copal, cloves, and more ivory. If a merchant ship still lacked a full cargo to take home, as it usually did, it proceeded northward into the Red Sea to Aden for coffee, then to Muscat for hides and the port's specialty crop of dates. In return, the American traders offered cotton cloth, guns and gunpowder, and manufactures. After distributing the last of the outbound cargo at Muscat, vessels like the *Elizabeth Hall* retraced their paths back to Aden, Zanzibar, Mozambique, and Madagascar to retrieve cargo purchased outbound and left there in the care of American commercial agents. Only after making all of these stops, each one lasting for days or even weeks of negotiation, loading and unloading, and shifting cargo around the hold, was the vessel ready to head for home. Although the longest and most halting part of the journey was over, the crew still had months of laborious sailing ahead of them before their return to their own shores.[45]

The *Elizabeth Hall* finally brought Charles Benson back to Salem in June 1858, reuniting him with Jenny and his daughter Fransisca, who had turned four while he was gone. He spent the next four months at home with his family, their longest time together since he first went to sea in 1854. He did not linger until Fransisca's fifth birthday, however. Benson's commander aboard the *Elizabeth Hall* and two prior voyages on the *Wyman*, John Ashby, was now given the bark *Nubia* by his employer, John Bertram. When Captain Ashby cleared Salem Harbor on October 8 aboard the *Nubia*, he took his old shipmate Charles Benson back to the Indian Ocean with him.

Benson's stint as steward of the *Nubia* was his second consecutive voyage with Captain Ashby, and the first of three in the company of the cook John L. Jones. Jones was five years younger than Benson and originally from Virginia. Like Benson, he was short, five feet four inches to Benson's five feet three and a half inches, an asset in a man who would spend months at a time ducking low ceilings and bulkheads belowdecks. The two black seamen struck up a companionable relationship that served them well over their next three years together. Benson spent the remainder of 1858 and most of 1859 with shipmaster Ashby and cook Jones aboard the *Nubia*, and then transferred with Jones to the *Dorchester* for two voyages in 1860 and 1861. The team then shifted in 1862 to the bark *Glide*, the vessel that would be Benson's home at sea for decades to come. Throughout this period, neither Benson nor Jones had more than two months at home each year. For all intents and purposes, they were each other's family, sharing their work, their dreams, and their lives.

Earlier in Benson's career it was rare for two black men to serve together even once, let alone several times as he did with John L. Jones. But when Salem's markets in South America began to disappear, opportunities were severely limited. Fewer vessels meant fewer berths for blacks, as did the longer trade routes followed by East Indian merchantmen. A single crew would now suffice for a voyage of more than a year, eliminating the turnover in manpower that used to take place between trips. In 1855, for example, black cooks and stewards left Salem aboard more than twenty vessels bound for Brazil and other South American ports; the ensuing shift away from South America limited that number to only five vessels by 1860. In 1855 ten black sailors, including Charles Benson, made multiple voyages; only three did so in 1860, and Benson was not one of them. In 1855, more than fifty of Salem's black men went to sea; five years later that number had been cut in half and was dwindling rapidly. The reduction of Salem's commercial flotilla was destroying the livelihood of the city's black mariners, even as the remaining few passed more time in each others' company on their long journeys together.

IN APRIL 1862, on his second voyage as steward of the bark *Glide* and his eleventh overall, Charles Benson began to keep a diary. He originally intended his "'high old' log book" as a gift for his wife, Jenny. "Stranger do not read this Book," he inscribed on the first page of his first notebook, "for it is for no other eyes than My Jenny Pearl's." He would address each daily entry to his absent wife: "It is Monday Jenny Pearl," "To day is Sunday Jenny Pearl," and the like. Each day of the voyage was counted as another day away "from my Jenny Pearl," and each night Benson ended his day's journal entry with an affectionate "good night Jenny." This first journal was essentially epistolary, an extended love letter he addressed to "the girl I left behind" and filled with poems, declarations of love, and remembrances of days and nights spent together at home.[46]

It was common for literate seafarers of Benson's era to keep personal diaries aboard ship. Throughout long days and nights at sea, the faint scratching of quills on paper marked the slow passage of time for sailors of the American Age of Sail. Aboard merchant barks and whalers, passenger ships and naval vessels, mariners kept sea journals, recording virtually everything that occurred on ship. Diarists included cabin boys and captains, fo'c'sle hands before the mast and officers in their cabins aft, crewmen and passengers, and, aboard the *Glide*, at least one ship's steward. Whether they wrote to dispel the tedium of a seemingly endless voyage or, like Benson, to provide an accounting of sea life for those left behind, these journalists took note of the intimate details of their shipboard world. Balancing their notebooks and inkpots on surfaces that rocked with the rolling motion of their vessel, maritime writers inscribed every shift of the wind, every slight change of course, and each "snapping & creaking of ropes & timbers."[47] In the pages of their journals they were adventurers and homesick lovers, resentful subordinates, amateur naturalists, wide-eyed tourists, and a great deal more. These slim volumes, so painstakingly inscribed over months and years spent under sail away from home, provide a wealth of information and insight into the men who went to sea and the times in which they lived.[48]

Although Charles Benson's diary generally resembles other seafarers' journals in both style and content, it is unique in several ways. Few black seafarers kept journals, so Benson's offers a different racial perspective from the thousands kept by white New Englanders. The period covered by Benson's journal entries, from 1862 until his death in 1881, provides a rare, extended chronicle of the declining era of American seafaring in the late nineteenth century. The unusual combination of frankness and reticence in Benson's writings allows insights into his identity and relationships and the ways he saw the world around him. Finally, Benson's sea journal is one of the only ones to originate in the galley or pantry of a sailing-vessel.

Never a proper officer or even a foremast hand, Benson was either a cook or a steward on every voyage he made during more than fifteen years at sea. Benson's profession came to define him in his adult life, affecting the choices he made, the self-image he maintained, the way he died, and ultimately the way he was remembered. It also provided the forum and form for his personal observations in the pages of his sea journals, a specialized type of diary keeping that did not carry over to his life ashore. His role as a seafaring steward provided the impetus for Charles Benson to keep his diary, and so that is a fitting place to begin.

CHAPTER FOUR

"*This sea life is hard*"

AT SEA, 1862

"I HAVE LITTLE to do with a sailor," Charles Benson wrote in his diary in May 1862 as he traversed the South Atlantic Ocean aboard the Salem merchant bark *Glide* (fig. 5). As the ship's steward Benson could indeed claim that he had "little to do with a sailor," for he was to some degree alienated from nearly everyone else on board the vessel. Benson had his own cabin, which was physically separated from the fo'c'sle and which afforded him a far higher degree of privacy than the *Glide*'s dozen sailors had. His tasks revolved around the pantry and ship's storage areas, and he never had to join the ship's hands aloft or in their hated tasks of scraping, painting, hauling sails, slushing the spars, or picking oakum. When "the people," as Benson called sailors, were "doing ordinary ship duty" or "varnishing water casks," he might find himself entirely at loose ends. Benson's idling could not have endeared him to hot, sweaty, hard-laboring crewmen on sweltering June days like the one when he reported "the people are scrapeing decks. . . . I aint doing any thing in particular."[1]

As steward, Benson was in constant contact with the officers as he served their meals and tended to many of their personal needs. This further distanced him from fo'c'sle hands, who often regarded stewards as members of the officer's camp and possibly as enemies (of course, the officers did not treat the steward as a peer either, for his rank and status aboard ship was lower than theirs). Shipboard personnel also blamed the steward for the inadequacies of their fare, or for keeping too tight a rein on the vessel's limited food supplies.[2] Additional resentment stemmed from the relatively high wages stewards received in Benson's era. Aboard merchant vessels like the *Glide* the steward was paid as much as some officers, a fact that might anger officers as well as the lower-paid seamen.[3] Of course, racial differences further widened the separation between black stewards and nearly everyone else on board. When white mariners

FIGURE 5. *Glide*, bark. The "Bonie *Glide*" was Charles Benson's home at sea during the 1860s and 1870s.

condescended toward black mariners or refused to socialize with them at all, there was little for black men to do but retreat to their own space. Thus Benson spent most of his time in his cabin or in the galley. There he passed time in the company of the cook (the only other black man aboard), who shared the steward's isolation from the other men of the *Glide*.[4]

Benson had personal reasons for keeping his distance from the rest of the crew as well. Shortly after leaving home in 1862 he wrote:

> I have not spoken of our officers yet. I like them very well so far, as to the men I have hardly seen them I suppose I shall find them the same as most all sailors these days a pack of fault finding ignorant men. But it is all the same to me, for I have little to do with a sailor.[5]

Benson rarely referred to any of the *Glide*'s crewmen by name, grouping them together instead as "the people" or "the men." Although he spent months at sea closeted with only a dozen others aboard his vessel, Benson often blocked the men out of his experience. The possible lack of regard the men felt toward the steward was matched only by his disdain for common sailors, predicated on a decade spent in extremely close quarters with them and their ilk. Even when the men were on their best behavior, Benson could only damn them with faint praise, as in the port of Zanzibar: "at sundown the liberty men came on board, all sober & what is more remarkable. This is the 3d time the men have had liberty & not one has been drunk or the worse for liquor yet."[6]

At sea, Benson filled much of his solitary time with his shipboard duties. His first written allusion to his role as ship's steward came on April 30, 1862, when the *Glide* was a week out to sea. "Our fresh meat is all gone," Benson reported, "now for salt junk." As keeper of the ship's stores, Benson was responsible for doling out food in appropriate quantities. Because the bark would spend over three months at sea before reaching its first stop at the island of Majunga, this was an important and necessary function. The steward had to keep his supplies organized and clean, for it would be some time before they could be replenished. He also had to beware of spoilage or infestation by rodents and insects, which could cause the unforeseen loss of vital food stock. Benson's sporadic references to the performance of these duties are simple and unadorned. His journal notes read, "4 Pm opened a tierce of pilot bread," or "1 Pm opened a bbl of hams took 2 out & headed it up again." Yet when he wrote "I am shifting around my small stores," "I commenced cleaning my pantry," or "cleaned up my store *hole*," Benson's journal entries reflected not only the quiet way he went about his business but also his proprietary interest in the ship's stores. He kept a meticulous eye on "his" supplies, and took his responsibilities seriously.[7]

Benson's other responsibilities involved tending to the needs of the officers, especially the captain. He was charged with cleaning and scrubbing the captain's cabin and staterooms, painting and varnishing the walls and wooden trim about the entryways, and scrubbing the floors. He also took care of personal supplies, such as the captain's cigars and dirty laundry. Although the cook prepared and served meals for everyone aboard, Benson took a hand in cooking for the officers, often taking a turn in the galley to bake them apple pies or his personal favorite, "Sugar Cakes" (also a pet name he sometimes adopted for his wife, Jenny, in his journals).[8]

The nature of his duties meant that Benson followed the same daily schedule as the captain, not the men. While crewmen typically toiled on watches throughout the day and night on shifts of four or as little as two hours, Benson slept through the night. At sea he usually awoke between four and five o'clock in the morning in the aft cabin he had to himself, a far cry from the crowded and noisy fo'c'sle occupied by the crew. Although Benson never detailed his early-morning routine in his journal, he likely spent some time helping the captain prepare for the day, perhaps helping him dress and shave, or giving the cook a hand in the galley when the officers sat down to breakfast. After he and the cook had eaten their own meal and everything was cleared away, Benson turned to the stewarding tasks that usually occupied the remainder of the morning and part of the early afternoon, presumably with a midday break for dinner. After a third mealtime in the late afternoon or early evening, Benson was done for the day by seven o'clock. He usually spent the next hour reading and writing, wishing Jenny a good night in his journal before turning in at "8 Bells Pm."[9]

Throughout the day, when Benson was not busy "getting things straight and clean" in his steward's role, he had ample time to see to his personal needs. Since his presence was never required aloft or on deck when "'All hands' [were called] to get up chains, anchors off the bow &c.," he could devote time to "making a pair or wristlets for cold weather," or "making over a pair of new wollen pants." All sailors needed to learn how to patch their own clothes and turn "Knight of the Needle" when necessary, often during the Sunday afternoon "sailors' pleasures," when work routines were relaxed enough for them to attend to their own needs rather than those of the ship. But with his unique status and responsibilities aboard ship, Benson had much greater control over his own schedule. Virtually any afternoon of any day of the week, Benson could indulge himself in "making some elasticks for under sleeves, out of some Arab horse hair." He passed entire days "carpentering [and] ... fixing my berth more convenient, making a shelf, &c." After many years of fulfilling his own domestic needs at sea, Benson counted needlework, carpentry, haberdashery, coopering, and even ink-making among his skills.[10]

After about three months of this daily routine, the vessel approached its first port-of-call, the island of Majunga off the eastern coast of Africa, and the crew would make ready for port. This arduous procedure would be repeated with greater frequency now that they were in the waters of the Indian Ocean. At Majunga and again at Mozambique, Zanzibar, Aden, Muscat, and then for a second time at Zanzibar and Mozambique, the sailors hauled away at the anchors and lines and resigned themselves to even more "painting scrapeing varnishing &c." And if they dreaded port for the drudgery of heaving and stowing away hundreds of bags of cargo under the tropical sun, the men could still console themselves with thoughts of what awaited them on shore. A sailor on liberty, freed from the enclosed confines of his bunk in the fo'c'sle, could look forward to as much time in the grog shops and "nacking shanties" of the waterfront as he could afford.

This was no less true for the officers, who anticipated the native singing and dancing "notches" they would attend as guests of local potentates, trading partners, and business associates. But because they had yet to guide the vessel to its destination, the officers worked even harder than the men as they approached landfall. Captain John McMullan (fig. 6) was only thirty years old—two years younger than Benson, his steward—when he brought the *Glide* halfway across the world to Majunga in 1862, yet he was wholly responsible for correctly judging winds, currents, and navigation on a journey of thousands of miles. The sighting of land, which all aboard hoped was the *Glide*'s proper destination and not one of the myriad of smaller islands or outcroppings that obstructed the waters off the East African coast, only compounded his responsibilities. Once a local pilot came on board to see the bark safely into the harbor, McMullan exchanged the role of sea captain for the multiple guises of trader, diplomat, and engineer. In port and aboard other visiting ships in the harbor he would haggle over prices for trade goods. He also had business to transact with island governors, local entrepreneurs, and agents of his Salem employer, John Bertram. The *Glide* required rations for the months ahead, often in the form of livestock and poultry that would live on deck in pens and coops painstakingly constructed by a captain doubling as ship's carpenter. Even as he was still settling his accounts and tallying the sacks of goods arriving on his ship, the stowing of cargo in the hold and distribution of the ballast demanded his attention. In the sweltering, crowded, hectic days in port, the captain and his mates would face the busiest part of their voyage, and the most important as well.

For more than three months the *Glide* would work its way up the East African coast, traveling north to the port of Muscat on the Arabian Peninsula before turning back. In addition to the trade goods that occupied most of the cargo hold, the *Glide* carried freight between ports on consignment. The *Glide*'s officers also brought aboard goods of their own to sell later in the voyage or in Salem, after their return home; thus the first mate found room for two thousand oranges he purchased at Zanzibar to sell at Aden, and the captain stowed away various "curiosities" to peddle to neighbors and acquaintances.[11] With all of the sundry items strewn about the decks and cabins of the *Glide*, sailors had a busy time

FIGURE 6. Captain John McMullan (1832–1865) of the *Glide* relied on his steward in a variety of ways.

dodging the clutter. At various points during the voyage the crew shared the maindeck with a large "safte" filled with "a lot of money" and "6 Pigs, 120 Chickens, 49 Ducks, 1 goat," a restless horse, and a cow given to the captain as a present by the governor of Majunga.[12] The crowded conditions could lead to peril, as Captain McMullan learned to his dismay. "Of a sudden," wrote Benson, who witnessed the incident, the ship's cow "made a dart at him with her horns & came very near killing him, her sharp horns piercing his clothes through & tearing them upwards from below his ribs as far as his right breast, two inches farther," Benson observed, "& it would have torn his bowels out. it was a narrow escape."[13]

As the frenetic business of making port took hold of the *Glide*, the steward, like everyone else aboard, had much to do. Because the captain would be entertaining company aboard the ship, Benson had to clean the cabins and staterooms thoroughly. Floor rugs that had been stowed away back in Salem had to be aired out and beaten clean, then laid out on the floors. Benson's port duties also included serving guests, such as the "4 English men" who paid a social call on Captain McMullan when the *Glide* was anchored in Aden. Benson brought them "coffee cake Oranges & thin tea," which he likely prepared himself.[14] Other duties sometimes also fell to the steward. In July 1862, for example, shortly after the *Glide* arrived at its first scheduled stop at Majunga, "a English Man of War Steamer came to anchor in the harbor." Taking immediate advantage of his fortunate encounter with an American merchantman, the British captain "boarded us & made a bargain for some flour chease Butter &c." The following day, Benson described the scene:

> Noon the steamers cutter came alongside full of customers. The Captain Mate & myself had a busy time of it for an hour or so in selling Hams Butter Flour cheese &c. Took about 3 to 4 hundred dollars.[15]

As keeper of the stores, Benson took part in the exchange of goods with buyers from other vessels, whether English men of war, "Portogues Barques," or Native "dows."[16] He also was entrusted with handling the money that exchanged hands, and even with disbursing some of the captain's personal funds from the "bag of dollars in his under draw."[17]

With all of the trading and loading and unloading of goods and freight, his regular schedule was disrupted, and he often "worked late" into hours when he ordinarily slept or relaxed. But he kept a meticulous record in his journal of the provisions that came on board, including yams, sweet potatoes, oranges, eggs, milk, poultry, greens, mutton, and beef, and all the cargo that was moved. He recorded, for example, the loading of 1,600 hides at Majunga, another 4,908 hides at Zanzibar, and 79 bags of far dates at Muscat, along with copious quantities of foodstuffs, senna, and even opium.[18]

Benson was not only busier in port but was also more alone than ever. The rhythms of the *Glide* at anchor exacerbated his sense of separation from the rest of the crew. When the men went ashore on liberty, Benson did not join them but remained on the *Glide* instead. He remained apart from the men even one 94-degree night in Aden when Benson reported "we have a table rigged on the quarter deck & do not use the cabin neither to Eat or sleep in" because of the unbearable stuffiness below. Nevertheless, he added, "all hands sleep on the deck but me." One day in Muscat, when "the thermometer was 102 in the shade & 135 in the sun," most of the *Glide*'s complement went ashore. "The Mate & most of the people go in swimming every night in a little cove at Muscat Island," Benson wrote. But he did not accompany them. Instead, he explained, "2d mate & myself take a bath on board of the ship (so also does the captain)."[19]

When he did leave the ship to go ashore, Benson always did so alone. Sometimes he had business to conduct, purchasing cloth or medicine for his stewarding duties.[20] Other times he sightseeing and souvenir shopping, picking up some small items to bring back for his family or the *Glide*'s cook. He also visited with local friends he had met over the years. In Zanzibar he received a warm welcome from an Arab named Saide, one of the local merchants charged with provisioning the *Glide*, before proceeding on to the house of Sallie, another local contact. Still, Benson went ashore only a handful of times throughout the long voyage. Most of the time, Benson spent his days "working Reading loafing" aboard the *Glide*, just as he did at sea.[21]

Benson's solitary existence in port reflected his special status in the hierarchy of the vessel. Benson did not toil alongside the men in the blistering tropical heat, loading, unloading, and shifting of cargo. Instead he performed his tasks by himself or in collaboration with the officers, who entrusted him with supplies and cash to an extent far beyond the *Glide*'s other crewmen. Bathing alone on shipboard with only the captain and a mate for company, Benson reinforced his image as an officer's man, separate from the crew. Even outsiders recognized this distinction. When three of the *Glide*'s local interpreters in Muscat came aboard for a final visit before the bark's departure, they brought gifts for the captain and officers. They also brought several "handsome presants" for Benson, the only non-officer so honored. Captain McMullan supplemented their generosity with his own, adding a "jar of Rose water & a basket of hallower" to Benson's bounty. Touched by the gesture and the affection it conveyed, Benson stowed his "presants" in his cabin, that most tangible reminder of his distance from the men of the *Glide*. There they remained until the vessel reached Zanzibar a month later and Benson sold off his jar of Rose water for two dollars and fifty cents, sentimentality notwithstanding.[22]

Benson's solitude was also in part his choice. His antipathy for sailors, already expressed in his journal earlier in the voyage, contributed to his unwillingness to join them swimming at night or sleeping on the deck. Even the first mate, a "mean man" who clashed often with nearly everyone aboard the *Glide*, and, apparently, the cook, a black man like Benson, swam and relaxed with the others in the hundred-degree heat of Muscat.

Benson did at times let his guard down with other crewmen. Once in Aden he approached a white crewman named Peter for a loan of three dollars, which he repaid soon afterward. Two days later, while shopping ashore, Benson made sure to purchase some trinkets for "the people" as well as the cook. In November 1864, when the *Glide* was completing the homeward leg of a yearlong voyage, the steward loosened up even further. He indicated through a cryptic entry in his diary—"lost a good pair of Pants overboard, through carelessness, served me right"—that he had fallen victim to a shipboard prankster. Benson waited a week before exacting his revenge. "Somebody threw one of the mates shoes overboard," he wrote, chortling, "ha ha." His Thanksgiving gift to his shipmates, an unexpected treat of date pudding and mince pies, was another departure from his usual reserve. Weary after long months at sea and relieved to be on his way home at last, Benson finally relaxed enough to join in the camaraderie of men at sea. Like everyone else aboard, the steward craved a respite from the sea and the seafaring life, and the giddiness of homecoming fever was irresistible.[23]

In fact, Benson had much more in common with other sailors than he was willing to admit. Whether at sea, leaning over the taffrails to peer at the "mighty deep," or in port, watching an Arab dancing troupe stage a "grand performance" aboard the *Glide*, Charles Benson was an American mariner abroad, gawking at exotic sights. Crammed along with the rest of the crew into the *Glide* for months at a time, Benson made the same tedious voyage, ate the same odious food, endured the same discomforts, and experienced the same feelings of homesickness and restlessness as every one of his shipmates. And like them, he also came to define himself

by his work. This phenomenon, central to the gender ideology of Benson's era, was common among career sailors and seafaring communities
ashore. It was much less typical of black workers, whose values and identities were usually determined by other factors than their jobs. But then,
Charles Benson had never been a typical black worker.

As Margaret Creighton and Lisa Norling point out, nineteenth-
century mariners inhabited a "single-sex masculine space, in contrast to
a feminized and domesticated society on land."[24] In some respects, the
sailor's life was a model for the male role in the dominant gender ideology of the time. During this period the cultural ideal of masculinity was
the self-made man. When a young man reached his twenties, he left the
protective arms of his mother and the feminine environment of home to
make his way in the world of men. He entered the workplace, an all-male
domain where he would be tested and hardened, ultimately succeeding
or failing according to his personal achievements. The man's work role
was expected to form the essence of his adult identity. The dictates of
nineteenth-century American culture held that when a man devoted himself almost entirely to his work (and cultivated self-discipline, which
would guard him against harmful excesses and vices), he insured his own
economic and social prosperity.[25] In this context, the sailor's life was
widely seen as an archetype of independent manhood. When a teenaged
boy went to sea, he entered an all-male world of work.[26] The dangers and
adventures of seafaring life toughened him, teaching him the aggres-
siveness and self-reliance that would make him into a true man. Even
Richard Henry Dana's *Two Years Before the Mast*, which forcefully condemned the brutality, violence, and danger of sea life, still confirmed that
Dana emerged from the fo'c'sle older, tougher, and more hardy than
when he entered it as a youth. He was now, in fact, a man.[27]

Although the nineteenth-century ideology of gender and work was
created by and for middle-class men ashore, seafarers adopted it for
themselves. Officers, who were the closest thing to middle class in the
maritime world, were especially dedicated to the principles of providership and occupational pride. So were the remainder of the men, although
they lacked the financial resources or social status of captains or mates.
Mariners linked their manhood to their seafaring skills, demonstrating
masculinity to themselves and to others through their prowess in the
sailor's art. Mastery of the arcana of sailing denoted higher levels of

manliness in a society that especially prized that quality. The sailor's life was circumscribed by the conditions of his workplace. Everything he did, whether working, eating, sleeping, or socializing, took place within the confines of his working space, the ship. For months or even years at sea he was foremost a worker, spending his entire life among men who shared every aspect of his experience. The sailing ship was the Victorian ideology of manly work stripped to its core, a purely male, wholly un-feminine environment whose raison d'etre was work. Consequently, a man's performance of that work would greatly affect his perception of himself as a man, as well as others' perception of him.[28]

Although Charles Benson's duties did not include overt acts of sea-manship such as reefing sails or manning the rigging, he too imbued his seafaring labor with masculine overtones. He did so explicitly in his jour-nals, often when describing the work he did most often, some variety of cleaning or scrubbing. While many sailors disdained such work, Benson bent to his task with a will and even with pride. He wrote on May 3, 1862:

> I have been quite Busy to day in cleaning my cabin, we have taken up the carpets So I have a large cabin floor, & 4 smaller rooms that have white floors to scrub, it took me 2 hours to day, on my hands & knees, but I can do them quicker by & by.

Four days later Benson scrubbed his floor again and then stated proudly, "it looks pretty well now." On another such occasion Benson remarked to his absent wife, "I should like to have you try your hand at it to day I think you would rather scrub your kitchen floor."[29] Despite the pride Benson took in this work, he called it "the hardest job I have."[30] In late 1864, with less than six weeks of an eight-month voyage remaining, Benson wrote: "I scrubbed up my cabin floor. I hope that I shall not have to scrub it more than six times more this voyage, & I would be glad if it was much less than six."[31]

Benson's pride in his work and the efforts he made show that his role as steward of the *Glide* was important to his sense of self and his personal ideals of manhood. Benson's occupation paid him well—better, in fact, than any other non-officer aboard the *Glide*—and so his hard work and suffering on long sea voyages paid off financially. Simultaneously, Benson fulfilled a vital cultural imperative of masculinity: his earning power es-tablished him as the primary financial provider for his family. Yet he faced a major paradox. When he acted as a provider, Benson affirmed his own manhood. By nineteenth-century standards, though, the work he did on boardship was much like the work women did on shore: he cleaned and scrubbed, shopped for provisions, prepared food for the other men on the vessel, and nursed them back to health when they were ill.

In the hyper-masculine world of the ship, cooks and stewards fulfilled anomalous roles. Men like Benson worked as "homelike attendants" aboard ship, primarily for officers. Their primary functions of food preparation and cleaning were seen as overtly feminine, and under normal circumstances they were not involved in the actual sailing of their ships. In the 1830s a young white passenger aboard the brig *Palestine* named Thomas Larkin Turner even went so far as to refer to "our Steward— alias, Kitchen Maid" in his journal. Few sailors matched this level of sarcasm in their references to cooks or stewards, but it is clear that the men occupying these positions were regarded as separate by their shipmates.[32] Their separation from the other seamen was physical (stewards and cooks lived aft, or below in steerage) and psychological (they were often considered to be allied with the aftercabin and not the fo'c'sle in shipboard society). They were also isolated by their feminine tasks, which marked them as lesser men.[33]

This identification with femininity was especially true for black men. Nineteenth-century American culture frequently ascribed femininity to nonwhite men, further emasculating the black cooks and stewards whose tasks already feminized them in others' eyes.[34] The caustic Turner underscored this perceived lack of manliness in his sea journal with the comment, "[W]e here, in our house, have a kitchen-girl—Oh! but this said personage is a black man!"[35]

On shore, black men who were limited to unskilled labor or what was considered women's work found means to affirm their manhood despite this imagery. In the antebellum era, black Americans equated manliness with freedom, and black male abolitionists often linked freedom from slavery with the independence and personal power reserved for men in nineteenth-century American culture.[36] This linkage carried through into the Civil War, when black men demonstrated their manhood as soldiers in the Union army.[37] Also, throughout the nineteenth century black men found validated their manhood through black fraternal organizations, which they formed and maintained separately from white groups (from which they were generally barred), but in much the same manner and for similar purposes. In male environments of their own creation, black men affirmed their masculinity and manliness.[38] So although their attempts to exercise their public rights as citizens and men were increasingly frustrated in the post–Civil War era, black men still found outlets to express their masculine identities.[39]

Such outlets were not available to black seafarers. Yet the experiences of Charles Benson show that although the roles of black seafarers in shipboard society were primarily domestic or feminine, the man still found numerous ways to affirm their own manhood. Benson did so by describing the six hours he spent scrubbing floors on his hands and knees as intense physical labor. He comes across, in his own account, as a hardworking seafaring man who, just like other sailors, was toughened by his experiences. Benson further validated his manliness by expressing pride in the quality of his work and in where he performed it: in a floating workplace at sea, as opposed to the kitchen floors his wife tended ashore. He also dwelt on the details of how he managed "his" pantry and supplies, emphasizing the responsibility and authority granted him by his shipboard role. The other men of the *Glide* may have viewed his tasks as feminine ones, and even shunned him as a result. Benson's own interpretation of his shipboard role differed from theirs.[40]

THE MASCULINE challenges of living aboard the *Glide* were apparent even when the vessel was at rest. Benson intimated these challenges in a journal entry he addressed to his wife in June 1862:

> every thing is quiet, the captain & mates are reading, the sailors are either reading, sewing, or asleep, you can hear nothing but the rush of water past the vessel & the snapping & creaking of ropes & timbers, but them noises I am so used to that I do not notice them. I can say now it is so still I could hear a pin drop. I suppose you would say there was such a noise you could not hear your self think, what a difference.[41]

Whether scrubbing floors or resting in his bunk, the steward was a seafaring man far from the comforts of home. He was never more conscious of this distance than in bad weather, when heavy seas tossed the vessel about without surcease. "Thank god we are alived this morning" wrote Benson, only five days after his earlier description of a peaceful evening on the *Glide*. "[D]id not sleep last night for there was no staying put in any position. . . . I should liked to have had you in some safte place to have seen us toss about, it would of made you open your eyes, I can tell you." After more than a week of "heavy squalls" punctuated by "wind, rain, hail, thunder, & lightning," the "fearful storm" passed. Once again a thankful

Benson could appreciate the beauty of a life at sea: "[T]he sea is like glass, birds are flying around us, it seems as though we & the birds were all alone in the world, every thing is so still and lonely."[42] At sea, Benson saw a side of nature that did not exist in the crowded city streets of home, a "safte place" where danger rarely threatened. The solitude he described so evocatively was that of the pioneer; some of his entries are much like contemporary depictions by pioneers of the American West.

In the absence of the fraternal organizations available to men, black or white, on shore and excluded from the common society of the foc's'le, Benson nonetheless shared in the fraternal values of the working men around him, but in his own way. He passed his time in the company of the *Glide*'s cook, the only other black man aboard.

Benson and the cook spent the majority of their voyages in the same space, the galley. The galley of the *Glide* was a distinctly male workplace and social club for the two men. There they prepared and served food and cleaned up after meals ended. They also socialized there, passing the time smoking their pipes, reading, and conducting endless discussions on a variety of subjects. In the galley of the *Glide* Benson fulfilled the masculine ideals of shore society, as well as of the fo'c'sle world from which he was excluded by his position and race. Together, cook and steward formed a solely male family of sorts; in fact, they spent more time in each other's company than they did with their respective wives ashore over the course of a calendar year. As much as fo'c'sle society, the masculine world of the galley exemplified Victorian ideals of male fraternity and nurturing.

But try as he might, Benson found it difficult to shake loose of his sense of solitude. Despite his close relationship with the cook and the hours they spent working side by side, Benson always seemed to keep a vital part of himself locked away, maintaining a certain distance even from his closest companion. In 1862 that man was John L. Jones, a long-time Salem cook making his third consecutive yearlong voyage in Benson's company. During the first few weeks of the journey the two men shared their space, company, and reminiscences about people and places at home in Salem, conversations Benson mentioned in his journal entries. But as the voyage progressed their relationship seemed to level off, and their intimate discussions ceased. Although they still dwelt and worked in close proximity to each other below decks, the two men apparently spoke only infrequently, at least according to Benson's journal. Unlike others aboard, who cemented friendships by sharing adventures ashore on liberty, the *Glide*'s two black men never went on shore together. Benson's rare allusions in his diary to the cook were spare and distant. Once he mentioned that his black shipmate he baked pies and several times that he suffered from recurring joint pain in his hands. This pattern repeated itself in 1864, when the *Glide*'s cook was Canadian-born Aaron Moses, later a close friend and business associate of Benson's on shore. Benson never mentioned Moses by name in his journal and made only one extended comment about him in over three months at sea: "the Cook goes to sleep every night now as soon as he gets through work." In a critical aside Benson added, "I never could sleep so much."[43]

CHARLES BENSON had the same cultural background as the rest of the men of the *Glide*, his working-class rural New England upbringing similar to the ones that spawned many a young sailor of his era. The beliefs inculcated in him during his youth found expression in his career as a seafarer. In his devotion to his work and his dedication to Victorian principles of masculinity, Benson was attempting to be the kind of sailor and man that his culture valued. His struggle to reconcile nineteenth-century ideals with the realities of his life at sea was one faced by many mariners of the Age of Sail.

This reconciliation was not easy. Most sailors, like virtually all men who were not a part of the bourgeois class, found it difficult if not impossible to fit their life into the idealized manly code. Elliott J. Gorn has shown that the brutalities of working-class industrial urban life precluded self-definition through labor for most men, whose unskilled jobs were likelier to lead to broken bodies and broken spirits than economic success or class mobility. "Daily labor," Gorn writes, "undermined rather than buttressed masculinity" for nineteenth-century working men.[44] This would have been especially true for sailors, who lived on the economic margins and risked sickness, injury, and death throughout their professional lives.

Married sailors like Charles Benson faced additional obstacles to their living up to societal definitions of masculinity. While they were at sea for months or years at a stretch, their wives assumed their roles in their absence. These women managed their family's financial affairs and performed physical labor to support their families. When the perpetual financial shortfalls of a mariner's family became too onerous, they might be forced to resort to some form of public or charitable aid. It was a central paradox of the sailor's life that by leaving home to fulfill the manly duty of a provider he accomplished the reverse, leaving his wife to find alternative means of support on her own. In terms of providership, a seafaring life could undermine the perception of manhood and the sailor's position as the head of his own household.[45]

Charles Benson, at sea for most of the decade between 1854 and 1865 and a black man, was especially vulnerable to crises over the nature of his work. Most black men were well aware of the perils of identifying too closely with their unskilled, unfulfilling occupations. Their solution was to distance themselves from their work identities and define masculinity by other means. Benson took a harder way out. When he chose to fit his seafaring life into the mold of the manly sailor, he also had to accept the dysfunctions inherent in that ideology.

His choice was complicated further by the additional complexities of his singular existence aboard the *Glide*. By hierarchy of rank, roles, and responsibilities and by shipboard protocol, Benson's position as ship's steward set him apart from the others aboard. His close connection to the officers, who also did not accept him as one of their own, further isolated him. His race, which played such a vital part in determining his seafaring occupation, served as an additional means of separation between him and the crew. Moreover, Benson's alienation from the rest of the men of the *Glide* was not limited to external factors. He kept his own distance from his companions, even his most intimate fellow, the ship's black cook, for his own reasons.

Issues like these formed the core of Charles Benson's identity. From his earliest days Benson had become accustomed to a life of solitude, a state that was inextricably linked to his experiences as a man of color in a white environment. Still, his race was but one of several elements in his detachment. A youth marked by broken families and deteriorated relationships left him an adult legacy of self-determinism. Charles Benson was comfortable with the idea of being alone for lengthy periods, even in the midst of a crowded ship that offered only limited privacy. In many ways he was at his best under such circumstances, taking pleasure and satisfaction in the performance of his required tasks. Unencumbered by many of the demands of close interpersonal contact, he could act and think as he saw fit, establishing and fulfilling the tenets that he used to define himself and guide his behavior. Within his world he controlled his own destiny, to an extent rarely realized by nineteenth-century working-class men laboring at increasingly dehumanized jobs.

At the same time, the paradoxes of Benson's situation bred fears and insecurities. Far removed at sea from the emotional turmoils of family life, he spent a great deal of time and energy obsessing over the wife and children he left behind at home. Ensconced in the solely masculine world of a sailing vessel, he fulfilled tasks and roles usually considered feminine, forcing him to reevaluate his definitions of manhood at sea. Identified as black by everyone around him, Benson still struggled with his conception of race and his own place in the racial spectrum. Isolated from his wife and unwilling to find comfort in another's arms, he was also tortured by aspects of his own sexuality during the long, lonely months. Night after night, in the pages of his journal, Charles Benson unburdened himself of these and other concerns. Alone in his cabin with pen in hand, Benson attempted to define the man he was and the man he wanted to be.

CHAPTER FIVE

"Jenny I want to see you bad"

AT SEA, 1862–1864

ALTHOUGH CHARLES BENSON found his work rewarding, he had a harder time coping with the consequences of his shipboard isolation. For most sailors, life aboard ship was communal in the extreme. Trapped in a small wooden vessel with only fourteen other men for months at a time, the men of the *Glide* were forced to share their space in both physical and emotional terms. They became intimates, forging a kinship over the long weeks they passed at sea with only each other for company. The men grew familiar with each other's habits, the behavioral idiosyncrasies that distinguished them from each other. They confided their most private memories and dreams, displaying cherished mementoes from home during weekly "sailor's pleasures" each Sunday. Even the most private thoughts were laid bare in endless hours of "yarning" or when personal journals were read aloud to the amusement of all. By the time the *Glide* returned to Salem after nearly a year away, the men of the fo'c'sle knew each other better than the families they had left at home long before.

But Benson's experience of seafaring was an interior one, both by necessity and by choice. Lacking the opportunity and the inclination to mix with the shipmates he considered a "pack of fault-finding men," he preferred the solitude of the steward's cabin to the crowded bunkroom before the mast. In his isolation, Benson retreated further into himself as the voyage progressed, to the point that he even shut out his closest companion, the *Glide*'s black cook. While such self-sufficiency fulfilled the manly ideals he held dear, Benson was left without a single intimate to dispel the loneliness that often threatened to overcome him. His solution to this dilemma was to focus exclusively on the most important relationship of his adult life. Whenever he was not actively engaged in his duties, and oftentimes when he was, he thought about his wife, Margaret Jenny

Benson. As Benson wrote less than three weeks into his 1862 voyage, "my whole soul yearnes for my Jenny Pearl."[1]

"This Journal was Written for Jenny," he inscribed on the title page of his first journal notebook, "by Chas. A. Benson on Board of Barque Glide on Her Voyage to the East Coast of Africa 1862." Like many seafarers, Benson wrote in his journal not merely to keep busy but to record his thoughts and experiences for future readers. Some addressed their writings to those at home. Others hoped to reach a wider readership, and some even dreamed of the day their journals would be printed or published. Often sailors came to regard their journals as confidants and trusted friends, their intimate companions on long voyages; in his later years Benson would behave this way himself. The sailor's journal was private, intensely so, as Benson made clear with the stern warning "avast! *avast*. Stranger do not read this Book, for it is for no other eyes than My Jenny Pearl's."[2]

In his thoughts and the daily journal entries he used to express them Charles Benson crafted a world of all-encompassing marital intimacy. "Morning, noon, & evening" his wife remained at the center of his attention, "and at midnight to[o]." Across the Atlantic and Indian Oceans and back again Benson yearned for his Jenny, dreamed of her, held imagined conversations with her, wrote to her, and gazed at her picture, an "anbrotype hung up clost to my writing shelf so you are looking at me every time I write, or wash, or comb my hair." In his imagination, he and Jenny had long romantic interludes together, murmuring sweet endearments, strolling arm in arm, and making love. He saw himself as the most dedicated of husbands, alternately longing for his wife's presence and "fretting" over her well-being. He depicted her in words and illustrations as an ideal of a devoted wife who missed him as much as he missed her. Wrapped up in his fantasies, Benson scarcely felt the lack of close interpersonal relationships with the other men on his vessel. The scrap of doggerel that introduced his first journal volume was aptly chosen: "Jenny is a darling wife/She is My Love, My Joy, My Life."

Two pages of fulsome quotations and illustrations followed as he continued to emphasize his journal's central theme. Verses from Proverbs extolled his personal woman of valor, who "seeketh wool and flax and worketh willingly with her hands." Pasted-in depictions of beauteous women adorned the early pages of his first journal volume, the largest one showing a pining female draped in pearls and captioned "Devotion," relabeled "Jenny Pearl" in Benson's painstaking hand (fig. 7). There was also a faded newspaper clipping from the marriage column of the *Salem Register*: "[Married] In Danvers, by Joseph Shed, Esq, Mr. CHARLES A. BENSON to Miss MARGARET J. FRANCIS, both of Salem." Just above the scrap of newsprint he again added the words "Jenny Pearl."

Each day in early 1862 Benson began his journal entries with a greeting to his absent wife. "Now Jenny Pearl we will have another chat," he wrote on April 30, and on the following day, "Come Jenny Pearl this is

FIGURE 7. Jenny Pearl/Devotion. Charles Benson envisioned his marriage in idealized terms of companionate romanticism.

May morning jump up & be away to the hills." He took to logging the number of days he had spent "from my Jenny Pearl" along with the calendar date, temperature reading, and the position of the vessel at sea. At the end of each day he made sure to end his diary entry with the phrase "good night Jenny" before shutting his notebook and turning into his bunk. He was joined in his nightly signoff by numerous other sailors, the oceans of the world resounding with a chorus of good night wishes to the Jennys, Annies, and Sarahs who awaited their return home from the sea.[3]

If his journal entries are to be taken literally, then Benson dedicated nearly every waking moment of April and May 1862 to Jenny. "O how I wish I was with you in body as I am in mind," he wrote on a warm May day. "At 6 Am a steamer in sight. . . . I almost wished it was a privateer to come & take us so we might get the sooner home." He passed a great deal of time in front of the small picture he had of her. "I have just been gaseing in your eyes," he confessed on one such occasion, adding "I have been thinking dear dear Jenny of you."[4] In some ways this habit helped dispel his loneliness at sea, especially when he imagined her presence with him.

> This is the time I should like to have you with me. you would enjoy it now. there is something sublime in looking around, all you can see is the deep blue sea below & the deep blue sky above, it seams as though we were alone in the world. but now I look up from my book and there is Jenny looking me right in the face. (stop I must have one kiss) there I feal better. now don't think me foolish will you for you know I love to kiss you.[5]

Benson often turned to his small hanging picture of Jenny to "feal better." One afternoon when he was "stiff & sore, & home sick," his two-dimensional traveling companion offered much-needed succor. "As I turn my head there is your ambrotype looking me right in the face & seems to say 'how can you be home sick when I am here with you[?]'" But Benson remained morose. "I answer I know it is a comfort to have your picture by my side but it aint Jenny after all." Still, the few physical artifacts of Jenny's that he kept were his most precious possessions. When he kissed her portrait, caressed a lock of her hair, or read and reread her letters "o'er & o'er," his talismans served as a tangible connection to the only person with whom he felt true intimacy while he was aboard the *Glide*.[6]

Although he sometimes wished Jenny could be with him at sea, more often he wished he were with her back in Salem. "Oh! how I should like to be with you," he sighed one evening, "to go & gather flowers & hear the birds sing." At least once a week he expressed his desire to be at home with a terse, "my mind wanders home to Salem." Memories of Jenny loomed large for Benson when he had free time, as he related on an otherwise unremarkable Saturday night in November 1862. "I have been thinking how Jenny & I used to go to Market Saturday nights, last time I was at home," he wrote. "how I like to get out in the street with her. it is my delight.... I hope we may live to have many pleasant walks together."[7] His homesickness intensified each Sunday, when sailors paused to reminisce about their homes and families.

> I Remember Jenny Pearl that this is the sabbath day & I cannot go to church with you I spent some very pleasant sabbaths with you this time at home. I shall think of them every Sunday while I am away. I hope we shall have many more pleasant days together by & by....
> the sailors are having a "sailors pleasure" overhaul their "donkeys" (chests) & spining yarns about home. I always feal the most sad when Sunday comes. but then I love to have it come for then I can think of home more undisturbed. I wonder how Jenny is today is she at church, & does she think of me. I hope so.[8]

On each subsequent Sunday of 1862 Benson remarked, "I wonder if Jenny has been to meeting," usually adding "I hope so."[9]

Alternately worshipful, worried, and wistful about his wife, Benson exhibited many of the characteristics of mid-nineteenth century romantic lovers. Anchoring the doctrine of the spheres that guided male and female behavior, the ideal of romantic love advocated a bond of extreme emotional intensity and near-total intimacy between couples. This bond was necessary to overcome the inherent distance between men and women, whose lives were separated by nature, function, and purpose. Men were expected to be autonomous and able, their inner qualities demonstrated in the public settings of the workplace and the outside world. Women were consigned to the private spheres of home and hearth in deference to the innate domesticity of their character. The emotional and spiritual essences of women reputedly predisposed them to a life that was directed inward, away from the more profane elements of the public arena. The romantic link between women and men provided fulfillment for both, each incomplete without the other.

Because it would have been inconceivable for women to meet men on their own public terms, it was incumbent upon nineteenth-century men to emulate the female model in their intimate relationships. This meant that they had to subsume the personae they had assumed outside and take on a more civilized demeanor appropriate to private interaction. Personal qualities that had no place in the putative world of men, such as emotional expressiveness and vulnerability, were requisite in the parlors where lovers met. In the place of stoicism and ambition men were urged to exhibit tenderness and caring, the hallmarks of a loving union. Deep sentiment ruled matters of the heart; the depth of one's love was measured by the extent to which personal feelings were expressed and reaffirmed, over and over. The strict hierarchy of the eighteenth-century patriarchal household, which cast the husband as ruler and wife as subordinate helpmeet, had been superseded by a romantic vision of marriage that stressed the sanctity of conjugal love.[10]

Charles Benson, determined to cast himself in the idealized role of the loving husband, hewed closely to what Lisa Norling calls "the romantic blueprint." He wrote in his era's language of love, using the literary devices common to Victorian romanticism. His tributes to Jenny in verse and extravagant avowals of undying love were typical. So was his association of their love with nearly every aspect of his daily life, his thoughts of Jenny Pearl triggered by everything from creaking timbers to beautiful sunsets, even scrubbing floors. He thought of her when he "read in Psalms," or during the long, peaceful evenings at sea when he contemplated "nature [and] Nature's God." The spiritual connection he felt to Jenny was as important as the tangible reminders of her that he cherished. In the Bensons' marriage, physical contact was fleeting, lasting only a short time between Charles's yearlong voyages. What nurtured the relationship over long periods of separation was the culture of sentimentality and its portrayal of love as a sacred bond between hearts and minds, not merely bodies.[11]

For couples like the Bensons, the idealization of the marital relationship was abetted by the physical separation many nineteenth-century couples were forced to endure. While women were expected to remain at home, the demands of work often sent men far from their families, sometimes for months or even years at a time. In an effort to stem the loneliness and foreboding that accompanied their long-distance relationships, couples came to rely even more heavily on the formulae of sentimentalism to reassure themselves and each other. They reasoned that if their love were to endure over a separation of hundreds of days and thousands of miles, then it must be strong, durable, and without flaw. In the private writings they used to construct these relationships, the correspondence and diaries where they revealed their innermost feelings, lonely lovers idealized the love that bound them together across time and space. With pen and paper they attempted to craft a union that reached for romantic perfection. All the while they were alone, bereft of the company of the singular individuals they held most dear.

In a sense, insecurity was the basis for romantic love. Out of contact with each other for long periods of time, couples worried endlessly about each other's welfare. Fears of illness, injury, or death could be borne out with alarming suddenness, a situation worsened by the unavoidable delay before bad news would be relayed to those still ignorant of what had occurred. Lovers fretted constantly over infidelities, real or imagined, that undermined their faith in the bond they thought they shared. The travails of daily life intruded as well, as individuals struggled through their lives without the solace of loving arms to hold them. Faced with a surfeit of dread and aware of their own powerlessness, lovers did their best to cope with a situation that was out of their control. Their private writings reflected the enormity of their efforts. Beneath the conscious expressions of love and longing lurked layers of doubt and worry, only partially hidden and sometimes not at all.

It did not take long before Charles Benson's insecurities began to surface in his personal journal. In his first journal entry, composed within days of leaving home in April 1862, he wrote:

> we have now been out 5 days. . . . I have been home sick, sea sick, & in fact sick all over I never felt so down heartedny in my life at the first of a voyage. poor Dear Jenny how she will "miss me at home" & how I will miss her . . . Oh! dear ———.

He would remain homesick for some time: after eighteen days at sea he moaned, "Oh! how long the time has been to me," and this feeling continued to worsen.[12] As the months slowly passed, his homesickness prompted uneasiness and doubt. In June he mused, "my mind wanders home to Salem. Do they think of me to night? Oh how lonesome & unhappy I feal. This is a miserable life to lead."[13]

Despite his reassurances to himself, Benson's confidence in the strength of his relationship with his wife began to ebb. He took to "fretting" about his wife, and about his importance to her. "Does she think of me," he asked, more than once. "Yes," he answered himself in May, "I know she does she thinks too much of her charles to forget him so soon no she is too good & true god bless her[.]" But as time wore on he was less sure. In October he again asked, "does Jenny think of me or am I for-

gotts?" He did not have a ready response this time. His silence underscored his uncertainty.[14]

Jenny Benson had faithfully endured her husband's long absences for
eight years by this time, but still he worried that she would forget him
while he was away from home. He knew, however, that Jenny sometimes
felt the same way. In a note full of "prose & poetry" that she composed for
her husband before he left home, Benson reported, she made sure to "ask
me not to forget you." Touched by a vulnerability that matched his own,
he responded, "No Never will I forget my Jenny Pearl. it asks me to think
of you at morning, noon, & evening. yes, I will, and at midnight to."[15]

Benson's unease grew as the weeks turned into months and his feelings of isolation from his wife and family worsened. Sometimes his dread
was inchoate and unfocused: "I have been fretting about you to day. I
don't know what makes me so down at times." More frequently he worried about specific issues, foremost among them his fear of being "for-
gotts" by those he had left behind. With little else to occupy his mind during the long passages across the ocean he thought constantly of home.
The lack of contact with his family tormented him, and at night his subconscious conjured up dark dreams of death and destruction. "Last night
I dreamed I was at home & Mrs. Henry told me that Jenny was dead," he
related in September 1862. "Oh! How bad I did feel." The following night
Benson dreamed that it was he rather than his wife who died, this time a
steamboat wreckage in Salem Harbor. "I awoke crying out All lost, All
lost! —"[16]

Benson's inability to "hear from home" lay at the root of many of his
anxieties.[17] Trapped aboard the *Glide* thousands of miles from Salem, he
had no idea how his family was "getting on" in his absence. While he was
away his wife might become ill (as she did in mid-1862) or even die, with
Benson knowing nothing until his eventual return. In the meantime his
daughter Fransisca was growing from a toddler into a young girl without her father's presence in her life. On October 3, 1862, Fransisca's ninth
birthday, Charles hinted at his feelings on the subject of fatherhood:

> to day it is Fransisca's birthday. 9 years old 'is it possible'? how time flyes
> it seems only the other day that Sis was born & yet 9 years have rolled
> around. I wonder if they think of to day at home if so then they will think
> of me. how is it jenny do you think of Charles to day[?][18]

Like many men of his era, Charles Benson's work drew him away from
the confines of home, and consequently his children looked to their

mother or the outside world to learn life's lessons. But social imperatives also urged working fathers to involve themselves in bringing up their offspring. It was part of a father's responsibility to display warmth toward his children and to cherish them, even as circumstances separated him from them. Caught by the conflicting demands of work and fatherhood, Benson's solution was avoidance.[19]

Children were an abstraction to Charles Benson, father to at least three children he saw rarely or not at all. His two daughters from his previous marriage to Martha Ann Thompson, Henrietta and Mary, were completely out of his life, and his daughter Fransisca might as well be for all that he knew her. While he loved his "dear children" and expressed concern for their well-being, his attitude toward them was far less consequential to him than his all-consuming attachment to his "dear beloved little wife." The children he had with Jenny were evidence of the great passion the couple shared, tokens of their love for each other. But they remained strangers to their father, taller and gawkier each year than when he had last seen them, their daily lives and friendships in Salem a mystery to him. It is significant that Benson summed up his feelings about Fransisca with a wistful "how time flyes" before moving on to his primary concern on his daughter's birthday, or any day for that matter: "how is it Jenny do you think of Charles to day?"[20]

ALTHOUGH HE preferred to idealize his marriage, on a few rare occasions Benson was more forthcoming about some of the flaws he perceived in the relationship and in his wife. Foremost among them was his concern about her religiosity. Each Sunday, Benson took pains to mention his own weekly Bible readings, which ranged from Psalms to "matthew corrinthians & revelations." He contrasted his own behavior and his wife's one November Sunday, en route from Muscat to Zanzibar:

> to day is Sunday. I wonder if Jenny has been to meeting. I hope so. my mind has been dwelling on Salem. it makes me feel lonely & sad when Sunday comes & the weather is light for everything is so quiet that it seems as though we were the only liveing beings in the world. I have been reading the bible have you dear Jenny? it is a blessed book that god has given to show our souls the way to heaven. I hope you will try to read it more. dear Jenny good night.[21]

In this context his weekly queries about Jenny's churchgoing take on a more critical light. The repeated "I wonder if Jenny has been to meeting,

I hope so" stands out from his usual obsession with his wife's activities, suggesting an old argument honed over years of Sunday church meetings. A reconstruction of the scene would show Charles, home for only a short time between voyages, enjoying the company of the "Salem people" he missed so at sea in the convivial setting of the meeting-house, and Jenny, exhausted from a week of sewing and laundering for others to make ends meet, with little interest in attending a storefront church in the company of the same faces she saw every day.

Charles could not fully appreciate his wife's point of view. Eight years at sea, alone with only his thoughts and a few letters and keepsakes to remind him of his wife, made him myopic about the relationship. The "Jenny" of his journals was the woman he wanted her to be: devoted, romantic, yearning for his return. The real Jenny Benson did feel this way—Charles refers to a letter from her, "w[h]ere you say that your love for me growes stronger the older you grow." But her life in Salem often did not include her husband. She alone was responsible for raising her children and providing them with food, clothes, and shelter in Charles's absence. Jenny also had to make decisions about the family's living arrangements with little or no help from her husband. She had moved house three times since her marriage, all while Charles was away at sea. Her first move was to a small dwelling on Pond Street, two blocks north of her foster parents, Robert and Hannah Dailey, which she shared with the families of two other black mariners, William Capela and Joseph Curtis. In 1857, while Charles was on his first voyage to Zanzibar, Jenny Benson relocated to Pratt Street, on the western side of the Mill Pond. Two years later she again gathered all her possessions and carted them around the Mill Pond to a small Cedar Street home occupied by a Maryland-born barber, John Cassell, and a widow, Susan Seymour, and her daughter Mary. With her Jenny brought her daughter, Fransisca, and two children Charles barely knew: Emma Benson, whose relationship to Charles and Jenny was never specified, and Joshua Owens, a boy who was fostered with the Bensons between 1860 and 1865. Charles had little time to accustom himself to the bewildering changes awaiting him in Salem, so seldom was he there. Considering his near-total focus on his relationship with Jenny, he likely took them in stride.[22]

Jenny, whose concerns were more pressing and immediate, had little time to spare to acclimate her husband during his rare stops in Salem. The small pleasures of home life that Charles found so comforting on visits home were without romance for Jenny, who saw merely added responsibility where Charles saw tranquility. It is unsurprising that Charles' attachment to going "to Market Saturday nights" held little appeal for his spouse. When Jenny went to Salem Market she was forced to balance the need for thrift against the needs of her family; Charles saw only his own "delight" at the chance "to get out in the street with her." Faced with her inexplicable lack of enthusiasm for food shopping, Charles could only sigh "I wish she liked it as well as I do." His complaint revealed the extent of his tunnel vision when it came to his wife.[23]

As Charles well knew, the biggest problem in his marriage was the strain caused by his own seafaring career. His job demanded that he spend nearly fifty weeks each year away from his home and family. Aside from the personal misery this caused him, the long stretches of separation also created tension in his household even when he was home. As he once remarked to his journal in a moment of unusual candor, "how home sick I feel. how I want to get home & yet I some times dread the thoughts of going home, for it seems to me at times as though I was not wanted there. is it so? am I not in the way some times?" In his reading of this passage, W. Jeffrey Bolster comments, "of course he was 'in the way sometimes.' Benson's wife and children had their world and routines without him. . . . Charles Benson became an intruder in his own house."[24]

As a sailor—and this was also true for many Victorian men in general—Benson was torn by the tension between his need to provide for his family and his need to be with them. His responses to this internal conflict were typical, and at times typically contradictory. By constantly affirming his love for his family Benson showed that he recognized the polarity between business and love, and that he clearly put love over business in his own heart. But sometimes he felt he had to rationalize his separation from his family. He argued that his work had to take priority in his life now, until some future time when he would be able to choose love over business. Thus Benson complained, "what a miserable life a sea fareing life is. I will stop it if I live & that soon." In other journal entries he tried to brush over the tensions he felt between his work and love relationships. Claiming that his work absences actually proved his love for his wife and concern for her well-being, he continued, "you & the children must have things to eat drink & were & I must get it some were if not on the land on the sea. I am willing live & die on the sea if you are only contented."[25] Although his comments were not always consistent, they show that he saw many sides to his role and responsibility as a man, and that his conceptions of his home, family, and responsibilities played a large part in his definitions of manhood.[26]

In an adroit bit of misdirection, he had also managed to deflect some of the blame for his plight onto his wife. His comment that Jenny's contentment was his motivation implied that she shared responsibility for his leaving home, just as his plaintive comments about being "in the way some times" reproved her for what he saw as a lack of appreciation when he was home. Romantic lovers frequently took each other to task, their chiding a spillover from the wellspring of their insecurity. But Benson's need to implicate his wife was motivated by something more, his desire for absolution.

At this stage in his life, Charles Benson was extremely susceptible to guilt. Whether or not this pattern had its roots in childhood (since Benson never wrote about his youth there is no real way to tell), there was likely some residual guilt connected to the failure of his first marriage. Benson made only one reference to that early relationship, an oblique but emphatic declaration to Jenny that "None nor nothing never need think trying to fill your place. You ocupy a place in my heart which none never did nor can. That place is for you alone."[27] As he did so often in his journal, Benson sought to persuade himself as much as his wife. The dissolution of his marriage to Martha Ann Thompson, he told himself, was not his fault. It was the lack of true love that doomed their union, not his abandonment of his pregnant wife and infant daughter when he fled to Salem. The parallels to his current situation made it crucial for him to reconcile this issue. At sea, far from his new wife and family and uncertain about his place in their lives and in his own home, Benson was desperate for reassurance that this relationship would succeed.

His salvation was the ideology of companionate marriage. The tenets of romance provided Benson with the framework for his marriage to Jenny, and with an outlet for expressing his desires and concerns. It also offered a ready-made explanation for the failure of his previous marriage. As a young man in rural Middlesex County, Massachusetts, Charles had patterned his decision to marry on the only examples available to him, his parents and grandparents. Like his father and grandfather before him, he assumed that he could craft a viable match by choosing a girl around his age whose race and farming background were the same as his own. In emulating his elders he also made the unconscious choice to copy their patriarchal household model, which cast the husband chiefly as provider and authority figure. But a young black man in his time and place had little opportunity to succeed in providing enough for a wife and growing family, especially without the extra benefit of property that had once

helped earlier generations of Bensons to survive. Unable to secure steady
work or financial stability, he had been a failure as an old-style patriarch.

As a romantic lover to Jenny Pearl he could see himself as a success,
however. Even in patriarchal terms he had achieved respectability through
his occupational achievements and regular wages. But his true accomplishment was finding his life's mate, the woman who reciprocated the
deep spiritual love he felt for her. To this way of thinking, it was not Benson's failings as a provider that doomed his first marriage but the absence
of true love. Only by leaving his first wife to start over with Jenny could
Charles Benson become a better man, the man he felt he was meant to be.

ALTHOUGH HE usually described his relationship with his wife in the
idealized spiritual terms of nineteenth-century lovers, Benson did not
shy away from expressing his physical needs and desires for his beloved
Jenny Pearl. In his first journal entry in 1862 he lamented:

> poor Dear Jenny how she will "miss me at home" & how I miss her. How
> she will miss "that Arm" & how I shall & do miss that dear head. Oh!
> Dear —

One quiet night several months later he repeated his wish, sighing "what
would I not give to hold that head to night." Like many nineteenth-
century lovers he spoke rapturously about kisses; on occasion his kissing
fantasies were stimulated by his gazing at Jenny's picture, which then
served as a stand-in of sorts for his wife. In one such episode Benson be-
stowed a flurry of kisses upon his ambrotype of Jenny Pearl, writing afterward, "there I feal better. now dont think me foolish will you for you
know I love to kiss you. Ha Ha."[28]

His physical needs were not limited to a desire for comforting em-
braces or affectionate kisses. His first written references to more powerful physical urges came two weeks after leaving port in 1862, when a
homesick Charles wrote, "Jenny I want to see you bad." The following
day he elaborated by commenting, "I am getting in a bad way I am beginning soon. never mind. I gess I can stand it . . . no more to night." The
underlining of key words and phrases and self-censorship of stopping
abruptly mid-sentence reveals the sensitive nature of what he meant to
say. In an indirect way, Benson was confessing to his wife that his sexual
desires were increasing the farther he got from home.

Charles was most direct in his reference to sex in late May, when he had been at sea for about a month. On May 26 he wrote: "8 pm I done a bad deed I will try not to be guilty again. & your picture was looking at me to forgive me wont you I think you will." After a night's sleep he grew even more uncomfortable about his "bad deed," and the next morning he added, "I don't feal very well & I know why, what a fool I am. I will do better." But that night his subconscious undermined his effort to purge himself of sexual thoughts by conjuring up "a funny dream" to torture him. Benson was so disturbed by this trend that he took drastic action late that week:

> I feal stupid & down to heel to day, this morning took caustic & burnt "John" he dont behave, thinking of "molly", I suppose. well let want be his master.

During the ensuing months Benson reiterated his desire to "see" his wife, experienced several more "funny dreams," and made numerous references to the "trouble" he continually experienced.[29] While he reported no further use of "caustic" to tame his desires, he continued to feel guilty about his feelings and actions. In October 1862, after several months of infrequent occurrences of this sort, his sexual desires surged again in the tropical climes of the Indian Ocean. "I have ———— to day," he wrote on October 10, and the following day's entry noted, "to day I have again ———— I will do so no more. I was in trouble & was tempted. . . . O! dear." On October 12 Benson attempted to bolster his self-control by "reading several chapters in the bible," but this only provided temporary relief from the "trouble" and "funny dreams" that returned in force only days later. After nearly two weeks of this, Charles gave his clearest description yet of the nature of his distressing behavior. His journal entry for that evening describes his activities in the form of a picture—a tiny illustration of a penis—followed by the words "enough of that" (fig. 8). As it turned out, he did not have "enough" after all; over the next several weeks, three more miniature penises made their way into his journal, to Benson's great dismay.[30]

The "bad deed" that so concerned Charles Benson was masturbation. As a healthy man in his early thirties, isolated not only from the presence of women but from any type of interpersonal intimacy (with the single exception of his relationship with the black cooks of the *Glide*), his behavior was understandable. Over the course of his year-long voyages he formed no sexual relationships with other individuals. The females he met on his voyages were off-limits, for his commitment to mainstream

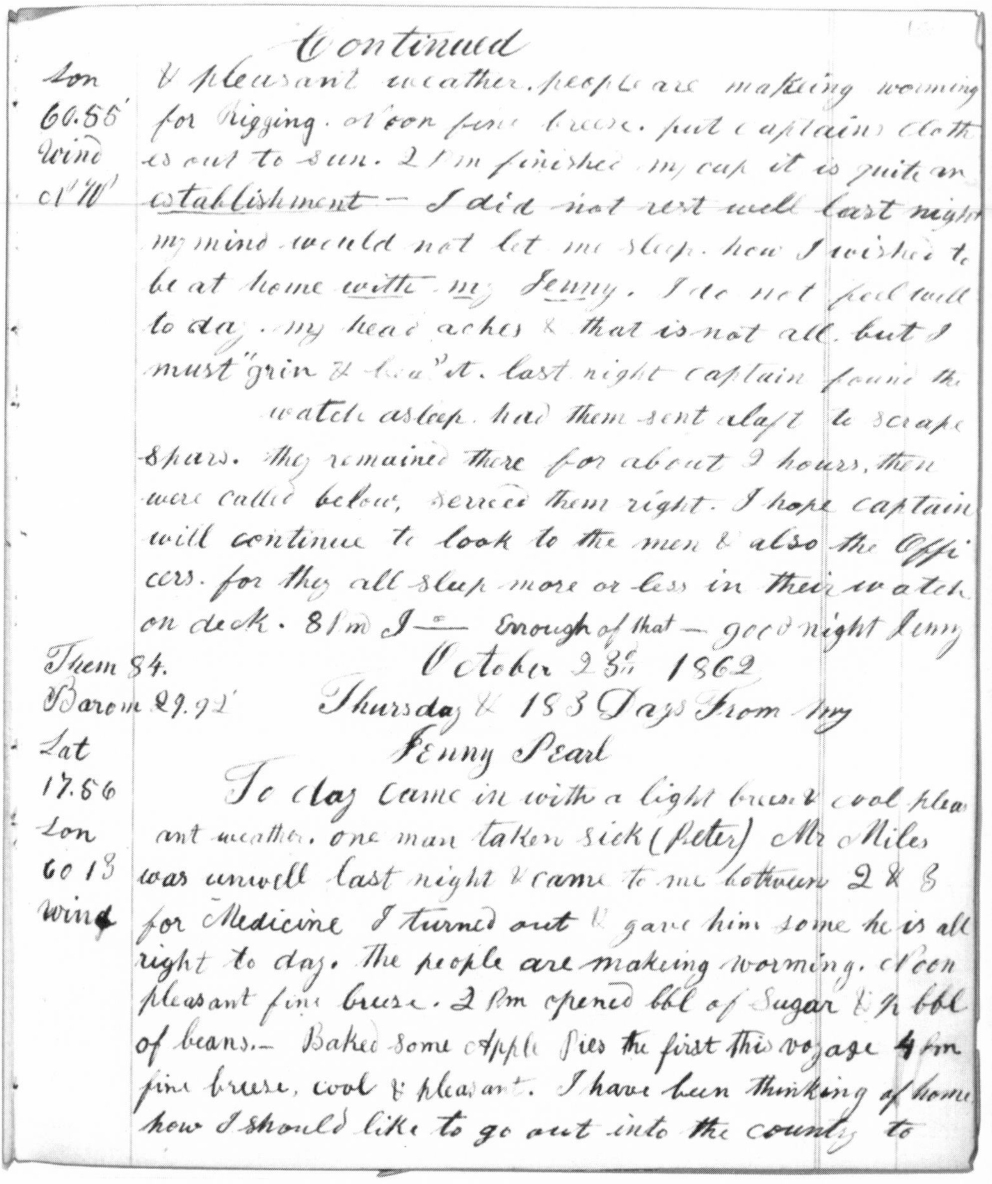

Continued

Son
60.55'
Wind
ɴ'ᴡ'

& pleasant weather. people are making worming
for Rigging. at noon fine breeze. put captains cloth
es out to sun. 2 Pm finished my cap it is quite an
establishment — I did not rest well last night
my mind would not let me sleep. how I wished to
be at home with my Jenny. I do not feel well
to day. my head aches & that is not all. but I
must "grin & bear"it. last night captain found the
watch asleep. had them sent aloft to scrape
Spars. they remained there for about 2 hours. then
were called below, served them right. I hope captain
will continue to look to the men & also the Officers. for they all sleep more or less in their watch
on deck. 8 Pm I — Enough of that — good night Jenny

Them 84.
Barom 29.92'

October 23ᵈ 1862
Thursday & 183 Days From my
Jenny Pearl

Lat
17.56
Lon
60 13
wind

To day came in with a light breeze & cool pleasant weather. one man taken sick (Peter) Mr Miles
was unwell last night & came to me between 2 & 3
for Medicine I turned out & gave him some he is all
right to day. The people are making worming. at noon
pleasant fine breeze. 2 Pm opened bbl of Sugar & ½ bbl
of beans.— Baked some Apple Pies the first this voyage 4 Pm
fine breeze, cool & pleasant. I have been thinking of home
how I should like to go out into the country to

FIGURE 8. Charles Benson's journal entry for October 22–23, 1862. Benson's direct allusions
to sexuality are unique among maritime journals.

nineteenth-century morality and marital fidelity prevented him from patronizing local prostitutes or entering bigamous marriages in the ports he visited.[31] As for sexual intimacy with other men, Benson gave no sign that his interests lay in that direction; moreover, even if he did desire sexual intimacy with any man aboard the *Glide*, his professional, social, and racial alienation from others on board the vessel precluded the easy formation of such a liaison.[32] His sole remaining sexual outlet was masturbation, a practice often prompted by his thoughts, both conscious and subconscious, of his wife.

Benson's guilt and distress over his behavior are easy to understand. As early as the eighteenth century, European and American culture came to view masturbation, especially by males, as a serious threat to the practitioner's physiological and psychological well-being. By the nineteenth century, masturbation was characterized as a form of "self-pollution" that reflected sexual inadequacy and a lack of true manliness. Victorian men were warned that indulgence in "the solitary vice" would have dire mental and physical consequences and could lead to insanity, visual myopia, impotency, genital shrinkage, tuberculosis, and even death. In the context of the nineteenth-century culture of manly self-denial and controlled behavior, masturbation signified a lack of willpower; this in turn led to a breakdown in the individual's mental and physical strength and health. The evils of masturbation were linked to larger social consequences, as well. Men who masturbated not only exhibited female personality traits such as weakness and hysteria but also removed themselves from the energetic world of the self-made man. Thus their behavior would result in their social and emotional isolation from others.[33] Under such circumstances it was only natural for Charles Benson to experience extreme guilt over his thoughts and deeds, even to the point that he applied "caustic" (perhaps saltpeter) to his penis to prevent further misbehavior.

It is remarkable that his journal contains any sexual content at all. Some of the thousands of unexamined sea journals in existence very likely contain some sexually explicit writings. Yet maritime scholars have unearthed only a handful of journals that discuss sex. Seafaring diarists generally shied away even from discreet or coded references to sex; while they often complained of missing their wives or sweethearts, sailors were unlikely to describe explicit fantasies or sexual yearnings in their journals. Although the practice must have been widespread among lonely sailors, few ever discussed masturbation in their diaries. Besides Charles Benson's journal, only two of the diaries I have encountered even

mention masturbation at all: one was kept by marine Philip C. Van Buskirk and the other by a mate on a whaler, Marshall Keith. Like Benson,
both of these men expressed guilt over their behavior. And like Benson,
neither was a foremast hand: Van Buskirk was a marine (whose responsibilities and status were different from sailors) and Keith an officer.[34]

When the men of the fo'c'sle wrote about sex they generally referred
to the women they met on their travels. It was not uncommon for single
or even married sailors to have intercourse with women they encountered in port cities, often prostitutes who frequented the docks for that
very reason. Nevertheless, though most sailors were familiar with the
port "'sailortown[s]' of brothels, cribs, and grogshops," few of them commented openly about their activities there in their journals or correspondence. A ship's boy named Harry B. Mitchell demonstrated sailors'
discretion about such matters when he described his encounters with
Shanghai prostitutes in 1862. Mitchell wrote of "Nacking Shanties" where
he, along with the ship's carpenter and steward, passed some liberty time
in the company of hired women. On one occasion the teenaged diarist
proudly reported that he had "spent the night with two fine Chinese girls"
before returning to his vessel at five o'clock in the morning. In every one
of these instances, Mitchell was extremely circumspect: all of his references to prostitutes were written in a special code, which he reserved for
descriptions of illicit activities such as drinking, gambling, and stealing
(usually alcohol, which he pilfered from the ship's stores).[35]

Briton Cooper Busch argues that the paucity of sexual references in
sea journals is correlated to the relative shortage of writings by "common" sailors. Most existing journals were written by officers born into
New England's middle class. Their sensibilities, formed and shaped by
mainstream Victorian culture, affected their attitudes toward and writing about sex. Of course, ship's boy Harry B. Mitchell is a prime example
of a common sailor who was equally unwilling to openly discuss such
sensitive subject matter. Yet Busch makes a valid point when he distin-
guishes between foremast hands and officers. Among crewmen, he writes,
"courtship, love, purity, and other aspects of dominant Victorian culture
had little place . . . respectability among the poor did not necessarily mir-
ror middle-class respectability." Officers, in contrast, exhibited the values
and attitudes that distinguished middle-class New Englanders, which
most of them were.[36]

Once again, Charles Benson stood apart from virtually the entire seafaring community. He was certainly not an officer, as his race and rank at-

tested, yet his worldview was similar to theirs, as his journals clearly show. His adoption of middle-class codes of romantic love and sexuality, along with his definitions of manhood and fatherhood, his identification with illustrations of middle-class subjects, and the middle-class forms he used in his personal diary, indicate that he subscribed to the values and imperatives of the dominant culture. Although Benson's economic and social status could have aligned him with the culture of sailors, in his private writings he chose otherwise. The steward's greater contact with officers and his voracious appetite for reading exposed him to the dominant culture's outlook. At the same time, his critical and meticulous temperament were suited to the rigid, controlled value system of mid-nineteenth-century America.

In essence, Charles Benson shared the perspectives of privileged middle-class whites. At sea he felt that he followed the precepts of this group to the letter. He thought of himself as a breadwinner, a caring father and husband, and as a seeker of self-improvement, in both intellectual and behavioral terms. The solitude of his shipboard life allowed him to keep this self-image inviolate, immune to the slighting attitudes of the other sailors aboard with whom the steward had little sustained contact. Yet at all times and in all ways, Charles Benson remained a black man aboard a white ship. The same things that allowed him to create and maintain his personal self image—his unique rank and responsibilities on the *Glide*, his solitude, his close relationship with the cook, his free time to read and think—only reinforced his essential difference from those around him who were not of his race. Although he chose not to confront issues of race in the pages of his journal in any direct way, his race and race-related attitudes played a very important subconscious role as he composed his journal entries by lamplight in his cabin, alone.

CHAPTER SIX

"It seams odd to be confined on ship board"

AT SEA, 1862–1864

"WHAT A MISERABLE life a sea fareing life is," Charles Benson wrote in 1862. "I will stop it if I live & that soon (that is if I get any thing to do on shore)."[1] But Benson knew that would not be easy. Discrimination and economic fluctuations had spoiled his chances at steady shoemaking work in Middlesex County a decade earlier, leaving him in the uncertain position of a day laborer. Prospects were equally poor for black men seeking employment in larger cities like Salem or even urban centers like Boston, New Haven, or New York. Limited by racist hiring practices to short-term unskilled work, black men and their families were forced to live on the margins of urban society, destitute and destined to remain so. After years of trying to make a living in Framingham, Natick, and eventually in Salem, Benson was well aware of his meager prospects ashore.[2]

At sea, however, he was sought after. As a capable, experienced hand Benson was one of the last of a vanishing breed of career mariner. He was also one of a dwindling number of black men able and willing to fill the berth of ship's steward on yearlong trading voyages around the globe. His employment record of thirteen consecutive voyages between 1854 and 1864 are one indication of his value. His worth could also be measured by his position on the pay scale. According to the *Glide's* papers, "Charles A. Benson, steward" was paid $20 a month for his 1862 voyage. His salary was exceeded only by the first mate's $35 a month and the second mate's $25 a month. The cook, John L. Jones, earned only $18, while the remainder of the crew took home far less each month, their wages ranging from $6 for ship's boys to $14 for the best-paid able seamen.[3]

Despite his ranking in the vessel's salary structure, Benson's annual pay of $240 for a year at sea was still insufficient to support his family.

One contemporary estimate by the Massachusetts Bureau of Statistics of Labor fixed yearly expenses for a family of four in Essex County, Massachusetts, at $590 in 1860. That figure rose to over $700 by 1863 and peaked above $800 the following year, mostly because of the severe inflation that plagued Northern cities throughout the Civil War. According to the same study, seamen like Benson averaged far less than the cost of living. So too did Salem's black day laborers, who faced the additional obstacle of seasonal unemployment for between three and six months out of every year. As a result Essex County's black women were forced to supplement their family incomes through live-in domestic work, which paid nearly as much per day as men's jobs. Those who did not turn to live-in work, like Jenny Benson, tried to subsist by taking in washing or sewing for more affluent neighbors. Such work was hard to find and paid only pennies an hour. The circumstances facing Salem's impoverished blacks would only worsen in years to come; after the war ended, the cost of living remained high while wages receded slightly.[4]

Unable to "get any thing to do on shore" besides even less remunerative day labor, Benson appreciated his secure position as steward aboard John Bertram's trading vessels. And it was his race, the very characteristic that barred him from finding a good job ashore, that allowed him to achieve job security at sea. Salem's black community had long depended on the preference of local merchant captains for black cooks and stewards as a source of employment. Even now, in the waning days of Salem seafaring, a small but distinct group of black men continued to find regular maritime work, Benson among them. In an unusual twist these black men found that the distinction of their race could work in their favor. Excluded from the fo'c'sles of Salem's merchant barks, brigs, and brigantines because of their race, black mariners of the mid- to late nineteenth century willingly accepted billets that paid them better than the foremast hands who might disdain them and their berths.

Despite the wage disparity and Benson's own misgivings about common sailors, there was apparently very little interracial tension aboard the *Glide*. In his journal Benson reported no incidents of discrimination or racial insult at sea. He also admitted that he liked the bark's officers "well enough," and they seemed to bear no ill-feelings toward him in return. Captain McMullan's ship's log made no reference to the steward at all, indicating that he fulfilled his duties without incident or problem. Additionally, although First Mate William Churchill had a series of clashes with other personnel, including a number of spats with the captain and a "tumbling on the deck" with the second mate, he and Benson got on well. In fact, both the *Glide*'s officers and their trading partners in East Africa and the Middle East held Benson in such esteem that they trusted him with large amounts of cash and presented him with gifts.[5]

Moreover, the distance between the black steward and his white shipmates shrank as the voyage progressed. At the start of their journey, Benson had seen little good in the "pack of fault-finding, ignorant men" with whom he sailed. Consequently his journal entries referred to the sailors only in the aggregate, describing how "the people" went about their business, performing "ordinary work" or "common ship duty." But three months after the vessel left Salem, Benson began identifying several of "the people" by name. The first individuals distinguished in this manner were a pair of sick crewmembers whom he was nursing back to health in his capacity as de facto medical practitioner aboard the *Glide*. "The boy George on the sick list," he wrote in July 1862. "Gave him a dose. I gess he will be 'round' by night. Boy John quite unwell."

This was the first time that Benson had referred to the ship's boys, John O. Donnell and George Plander, by their forenames. This pattern continued over the ensuing weeks as Benson began to mention the names of several of his white shipmates, including "one man (Jo)," "one man (Peter)," "one man (Bill)," and "the man Harry."[6]

With the passage of time and several thousand miles, Benson began to contradict his earlier assertion that he had "little to do with a sailor." One day in Aden when he was on shore and short of cash, he reported "I borrowed three dollars of one of our men (Peter)."[7] Clearly, the distance between Benson and his white shipmates had shrunk. A sort of reciprocity, if not outright camaraderie, between black steward and white crewmen could be discerned in Benson's attitude and behavior toward the *Glide*'s white complement. Once in 1864 Benson and one of the ship's mates perpetrated a series of pranks against each other, tossing items of clothing overboard with no apparent hard feelings on either side. Later that same voyage, on Thanksgiving Day, Benson "gave the people Dates in their Duff, & gave one large mince pie to each watch." He added, "I done it on my own hook for fun; Captain did not know it."

This entry came on the heels of another passing remark. "'Sail ho'!" he wrote, "Frank 'made a sail' on our weather bow stearing about West," omitting the prefix "the boy" when he identified ship's boy Frank Mellus.[8] The growth of ties between the steward and the rest of the men reflected the congeniality that suffused the vessel. The voyage was going well, encountering salubrious weather and trading conditions. With a skilled captain at the helm and officers and men who knew their jobs and performed them with a minimum of disruption, the *Glide* was a relatively happy ship in 1862. The fifteen men aboard more or less became a family that included even the black steward and cook, despite the racial barriers that set them apart from the others.

The bonds between the men of the *Glide* precluded the formation of ties with outsiders, as Benson's off-hand references to two black men taken on the *Glide* temporarily in late 1862 suggest. The first was an American seaman, like Benson the steward of a merchant bark outbound from Salem. The *Glide* crossed his path at Mozambique in July 1862, when he lay gravely ill and in need of immediate medical care that was unavailable on the island. Benson wrote:

> (in port of Mozambique) 5 Pm the people all came on board in good order. there came with them a man who was steward of the Storm King that Captain Pond left here sick. he has had a hard time of it, half starved, been sleeping out of doors for 6 weeks, has got the fever & ague, is as poor as "jobs Cat"—we will keep him for a while.

Although Benson recorded the names of the man's vessel and commanding officer immediately, he waited nearly two weeks before identifying the steward himself. Only when they reached their next scheduled stop at Zanzibar did he elaborate, and then only in passing.

> 9 am the sick steward & a man Harry went on shore to the hospitol to see the doctor. 10 am they returned the steward (Robert Hill) taking his things—for he has a good little fitout given him—& went on shore for good to the hospitol. . . . 2 pm one man (Peter) taken sick gave him some medicine he went below.[9]

Robert Hill was on his first deepwater voyage out of Salem. Born in "King and Queen County, Virginia" and newly come to the city at age thirty, he had probably paused there just long enough to meet Captain Pond and accept his offer of employment before departing on the vessel that would soon abandon him at Mozambique. Benson's interest in the man was limited to sympathy and professional notice of the 'good little fitout' that Hill kept with him. Hill would eventually find his way home aboard another Salem-bound vessel and recover sufficiently to ship out once again aboard the bark *William H. Shailer* in October. Charles Benson would never spare another thought for the transient figure of the "sick steward" he had met on his travels.[10]

A few days after Robert Hill was taken in, another stranger boarded the *Glide*. As the vessel prepared to leave Mozambique, Benson wrote, "Captain came on board & brought a collored man, to work his passage to Zanzibar." This man was an African, one of many Benson met during his sojourns in the waters of the Indian Ocean. Most of the "collored" men he encountered were slave laborers set to work loading and unloading cargo at Muscat, Aden, Mozambique, and Zanzibar by their Arab and Indian masters. Americans commonly described these menial workers as "coolies," a term employed often by the *Glide*'s master John McMullan in the ship's log. Benson preferred to call them "natives" in the pages of his journal, occasionally referring to them as "collored." Long accustomed to the presence of Africans, Benson found nothing extraordinary about sharing his vessel with yet another black man and did not mention him again (fig. 9).[11]

For many leading black Americans of the nineteenth century, Africa played an important symbolic role in the formation and meanings of their black cultural identity. As the drama of slavery's end played itself out through the American Civil War, issues of black nationalism and personhood came to the fore, at times linked to a reexamination of the importance of black America's African roots. The settlement of Sierra Leone and Liberia by American emigrés added new layers to the relationship between blacks on the two continents, especially when the Northern press and voluntary associations, such as the American Colonization Society, mounted a highly publicized campaign to spur black colonization after midcentury. For years after the Civil War, black religious leaders would build on this prewar rhetoric as they expanded their own missionary activities in Africa.[12]

Charles Benson of Salem, Massachusetts, was in no sense a black nationalist or missionary, and he had little use for rhetoric in his personal writings. As his observations on Africa and Africans confirm, Benson, like most of his shipmates, considered himself an American first and foremost, and his experiences in faraway lands prompted a good deal of gawking at the exotic but no contemplation of his own African heritage. Although thousands of East African slaves populated Zanzibar at the time the *Glide* anchored there in August 1862, Benson recorded no comments about them or their lives. Instead he played tourist, like innumerable other American sailors visiting ports around the world.

FIGURE 9. Slaves carrying merchandise. Although slave laborers were commonly called "coolies," Benson referred to them by the less derogatory term "Natives."

"The natives are haveing a gay time on shore," he wrote to his wife Jenny. "The 'tum tums' are Beeting & men & women are shouting & singing. I should like to have you here to night to see & hear what is going on in a Arab port." He elaborated further when he reached the Omani port of Muscat later in the voyage. On the night he inscribed the following journal entry, a troupe of performers came aboard the *Glide* to stage a "Notch," or native dance.

> we are to have a 'Notch to night. 7 Pm Muser came with chairs & Rugs. 10 P Notch Girls, Fiddler, & Boy with Tum Tum came. 10½ Ludder, Bimigee, & other Banaan's came & then an Arab Dhow captain & mate, we had the after part of the maindeck divided from the fore part at the main mast with the American Ensign & then the sides were hung with flags of different discriptions festooned in a very pretty stile, & then the deck was covered with Rich Rugs from Pershia & Turkey, lanterns were hung around which spread a mellow light togather with the full moon (almost) throu the curtains. about 11 Pm the grand preformance Began. it consisted of singing danceing & music in the perfect native style & lasted until about

> ½ past 3 in the morning, the preformers collected about 30 dollars from
> the ordiance during the night, some of the Banaans went to sleep, so did
> Muser, Mahommed & Easer. They staid all night but the others went on
> shore at the breaking up of the preformance. ¼ to 4 I will now turn in for
> I am tiered. I wish you were here to have seen it. good night Jenny.

Like his captain and officers, who enjoyed "Notches" ashore whenever
they had the time to attend them, Benson appreciated the entertainments
of foreign lands. Dazzled by the colorful sights and sounds, he remained
mute regarding the slave entourages that accompanied the Arab "natives" and strained to load and unload the *Glide*'s cargo.[13]

At Muscat Benson caught a glimpse of the royal family of Oman's
Sayyid Thuwaini, son of the empire-builder Sayyid Said. Benson was especially taken with the young prince of Oman, who went sailing several
times with Captain McMullan.

> captain came on board with the prince. I gave him a glass of water. he is a
> fine looking Boy light complection black hair, & large black eyes. his arms
> & ancles were adorned with gold rings his dress which was pure Arab was
> made of gold silver & silk threads.

On one memorable October day Benson witnessed the arrival of the
Sayyid's most impressive sailing vessels, bearing some most unusual passengers.

> 2 of the Kings man of Wars came to anchor in the harbor Each fireing a
> salute of 21 guns, which was returned by the forts on shore. one man of
> war brought some of the Kings concubines, which he has had with him in
> the country for 5 monts they are Georgians & are said to be very white &
> handsome & cost $7,000 for the two & then $7,000 to dress them. what do
> you think of that Jenny. his Wife is here in Muscat & was looking out of
> the window to see them come. they are to live with the rest of his concu-
> bines in a house clost to his own. he has about ———— in all.

The pennywise steward, so careful to account for every dollar he spent in
port, was intrigued by the ostentatious displays of ruling-class wealth.
But his interest was also captured by the prince's 'light complection'
and the whiteness of the Sayyid's Georgian concubines. Most Americans
would have found it jarring to see someone who was "very white" being
bought and sold as a commodity, particularly in the context of the on-
going American Civil War and its implications regarding slavery. Nevertheless, Benson seemed most interested in the more titillating aspects of
his story, such as the dollar amounts being spent or the sexualized aspects

of the ruler's multiple-concubine-plus-wife household. At heart he was an American sailor abroad, seeing sights no landlubber could. He remained detached from the larger concerns of black America, even at a time when the collective consciousness of black communities was at its height.

In Benson's homeland, Northern blacks were gripped by the upheavals of the growing conflict, which Frederick Douglass termed the "Second American Revolution." For them the Civil War was the culmination of decades of abolitionist agitation—a cause Charles Benson had never served nor mentioned in his journal—and the chance to finally do something themselves to advance toward the goal of achieving full "manhood rights" for all black Americans. On the home front, blacks initiated their participation in the war by organizing efforts to assist former slaves as they began to make their way North, providing them with work and basic necessities. As the war progressed and black enlistment in the Union Army became a reality in 1862 and 1863, more than 175,000 black men volunteered to become "champions for liberty," fighting not only to bring an end to slavery but also to prove themselves as full-fledged citizens of their nation. Soldiers and orators affirmed black masculinity through military service and support for the war, dedicating themselves to achieving full manhood for all black men through the eradication of slavery.[14] Black newspapers debated the meaning and implications of the war, as the fight for emancipation began to broaden into a larger struggle for full citizenship and civil rights. The war experience politicized the black communities, spurring them to consider their place in American society.[15]

Charles Benson expressed his own concerns about the national conflict in his journals, but with a different focus than that of the black leadership cadre of the North. At the time, the Civil War was at its height. Although Benson was far away at sea on the Atlantic Ocean and out of touch with current events, his few comments regarding the Civil War reflected his keen interest in its progression. On May 30, 1862, for example, he wrote:

> I have been reading some last years papers about the war. How I should like to hear from home now to hear how the war rages. But above all how my Jenny Pearl gets on.

About two weeks later, a bored Benson reported:

> I have been overhauling my newspaper to find Dec. ones. Could find only 3. It is to bad for there is that Trent Affair I did not read or hear all when at home.

He spent the following day reading the papers he found, adding the terse comment, "I have been reading about the war." After landfall at Muscat Island in September 1862 the crew of the *Glide* could obtain slightly fresher information about the Civil War, and Benson scribbled a worried note: "we hear bad news from home. I hope it is not true, but we fear the worse." That same year, Benson pasted a newspaper illustration into his notebook showing two women, one labeled "North" and the other "South," gripping a flagpole from which a thirty-four-star American flag proudly flies. Benson's final mention of the Civil War was dated October 6, 1862, shortly after the Union victory at Antietam and President Lincoln's issuing of the Emancipation Proclamation.

> We got very discouraging accounts from home. How true they may be we do not know, but it is evident that the war is far from being ended. It makes me feel rather down to hear such news from home, but I must hope for the best.[16]

Despite his apparent interest in the war, Benson did not discuss American slavery at all. His only reference to slavery in general was a passing remark that the *Glide* encountered an "English man of war steamer . . . on the look out for [Arab] slavers" at the port of Mozambique.[17] Otherwise Benson expressed no opinions about the institution that had enslaved his great-grandparents and great-great-grandparents and continued to hold millions of his own contemporaries in bondage. This was atypical of black diarists, who usually indicated a heightened interest in the war with regard to its potential to end slavery. Charles Benson, far from the black communities of home and isolated from the concerns of most black Americans, merely demurred.[18]

Meanwhile in Salem, where organized black communal activity had always been minimal before, there was a sudden surging of patriotic commitment to the Union cause. Salem's first black soldier was George Johnson, who enlisted in the First Massachusetts Volunteer Infantry in October 1861; the light-skinned mulatto shoemaker probably passed as white to dodge the military's proscription against black enlistment.[19] Around the same time, while Charles Benson was busily scrubbing floors far away in the Indian Ocean aboard the bark *Dorchester*, as many as twenty-five of Johnson's fellow black townsmen joined the U.S. Navy, the only legal way for them to join the Union forces.[20] When "colored regiments" were finally created for black volunteers in 1863 and 1864, eighteen more black Salemites enlisted in the Fifty-fourth Massachusetts Infantry. By the time they did so there were so many black men enlisting that all but two of the Salem volunteers had to be transferred to the Fifty-fifth, which accommodated the overflow from the Fifty-fourth. Two of Salem's black men were instrumental in the successful black recruitment drive that filled these units: the abolitionist Charles Lenox Remond, who turned his orating skills to help the Union cause, and Francis H. Fletcher, then twenty-two and a recent migrant to Salem. Fletcher, who served as secretary at a major recruitment meeting at Boston's black Joy Street Church in February 1863, was one of the first to enlist in the Fifty-fourth Massachusetts and would eventually attain the rank of sergeant.[21]

After living in Salem for more than a decade, Benson knew many of the city's forty-three black enlistees and was well-acquainted with at least a dozen. He knew William Stearns, the *Glide*'s cook on her 1861 maiden voyage and a sea cook for decades before joining the U.S. Navy at age fifty-four. York Lee, another Navy man, was the younger brother of Benson's black shipmate aboard the 1857 voyage of the *Elizabeth Hall* to Zanzibar, George Lee. Other enlistees included career seafarer Jacob C. Chase and Daniel J. Cooper and Abraham Williams, the sons of seamen who sailed in Benson's era. Simeon J. Wheatland, another Navy volunteer and the son of the Salem porter John Wheatland, was familiar to Benson from his days working in the Derby Square marketplace a decade earlier alongside the elder Wheatland.

Marching in the ranks of the Massachusetts Infantry were several of the men Benson knew best in Salem. John Cassell, a barber, had been a Cedar Street housemate of Benson's for several years. Cassell's brother-in-law George W. Morris, who would ship out with Benson on the *Glide* in the late 1870s, was another army volunteer; he and his mother, Mercy Morris, were the Bensons' neighbors on Creek Street, where they moved a short time before the end of the Civil War. In addition to his closest neighbors, one of Charles Benson's oldest Salem contacts also joined the army. James L. Sherman, the middle-aged restaurateur who had provided Benson with his first steady job in Salem more than ten years earlier, enlisted in Company E of the Third United States Colored Cavalry. Along with his son William Sherman, who began in the Fifty-fifth Massachusetts Infantry before transferring over to the navy, the oyster-dealer joined the ranks of black Salemites who heeded the call of their country and their consciences.[22]

It is inconceivable that Charles Benson was entirely unaware of the dangers facing his many friends and acquaintances in uniform. Yet he mentioned none of them by name and evinced no interest in how they were getting on in the military. Instead, the only specific wartime incident he referred to in his journal was the *Trent* Affair of November–December 1861, a diplomatic crisis between the United States and Great Britain triggered by an incident involving a U.S. warship and a British mail packet in international waters. While most black Americans were more interested in the proliferation of early battles, or the vital issues of slavery and emancipation, Benson focused only on a story whose political ramifications had little impact on blacks or the overall war effort.

Benson's dissociation from the larger black world and his own compatriots at home hint at the ambivalence he continued to experience in matters of race. Since childhood Charles Benson had spent most of his time alienated from the company of other blacks, in terms of both his physical and emotional geography. His isolated upbringing and inexperience in black communal affairs left him without the instincts of a dedicated "race man." As a result, he was less sensitized to issues of race than he might have been in the midst of a thriving black community. Writing in his journals as an adult, he remained disengaged from a broader black culture that he had never fully experienced. Alone at sea in a world of his own making, Benson was not entirely conscious of his disengagement. But it bled through into his journals, the place where Benson expressed his innermost self.

BENSON'S AMBIVALENCE about race was deepened by the values he absorbed from his reading. He read constantly, countering the solitude he experienced at sea. With only a limited supply of material available, Benson read and reread his "Books & papers." In his cabin were "a goodly number" of newspapers, including local papers such as the *Salem Gazette* and *Salem Register* and some national periodicals published in the North, such as *Harper's Weekly*. He had a Bible, which he made a special effort to read each Sunday. "Thanks to kind friends" at home, his collection included a few popular novels. Crowding Benson's sea chest aboard the *Glide* was a cross-section of publications that graced middle-class parlors throughout New England (fig. 10).[23]

In the pages of his reading, Charles Benson found affirmation of the ideology that guided his life. The publishers of these selections advocated the rewards of hard work and self-discipline and emphasized popular concepts of religious Christian duty and romantic love. Illustrations accompanied the prose portraying confident middle-class men and de-mure middle-class women; black steward Charles Benson cut out and pasted these images into his journal, labeling them "Charles" and "Jenny." Once he clipped a long love story titled, "A Chapter of Married Life" that followed a "young and handsome" romantic couple from estrangement to reconciliation. At the end of the piece he wrote, "Jenny read this and tell me what you think. was there not one other Margaret that was cold & in-different & almost drove her husband to despare[?]" Charles Benson saw his idealized self in his reading material.

Because he identified himself so closely with the texts he devoured, he used them as authorities to shape his own opinions. He was predisposed by his religious leanings to consider the Bible that "blessed book that god has given to show our souls the way to heaven." But he was equally

FIGURE 10. Sea chest and contents. Benson's "donkey" would have contained his journal, readings, and pictures from home.

influenced by the secular writings he brought along with him. If the *Trent* Affair was important enough to command significant attention in the Salem papers, it merited Benson's special attention as well. Conversely, popular apathy toward some issues important to black Americans matched Benson's tendency to remove himself from black communal concerns.

Not once during the war, for example, did Salem's newspapers, like Benson in his journals, acknowledge the military contributions of the city's black residents. The papers did, however, address the issue of black military participation in the Civil War. White Salem was generally favorable toward the unusual step of allowing blacks to fight, but the city's periodicals expressed some uncertainty. The *Salem Gazette* took the position that former black slaves might make good Union soldiers, primarily because they would be easier to satisfy with lower wages and poorer quality food than their white counterparts. Blacks' physical strength and natural deference would compensate for their limited intellectual capacity, wrote the *Gazette*, since black enlistees boasted "a willing hand without the meddling head."[24] But this mild editorial support for black military participation was tempered by a strong note of caution. The *Gazette* article concluded that harsh disciplinary measures would be required to keep primitive black warriors in line, such as "instant death" as a punishment for any "indulgence of private license or vindictiveness." A month later, the *Gazette* retreated even further when it noted that "we are not among those who have anticipated much benefit in our present contest from emancipation and the arming of the blacks."[25]

Despite his ambivalence regarding race, or perhaps because of it, Benson was drawn to readings on racial subjects. One such book was the popular novel *Cudjo's Cave*, which occupied his attention for an extended time in 1864. Written the year before by John Townsend Trowbridge, a Bostonian whose friends included Henry Wadsworth Longfellow and Oliver Wendell Holmes, the book was set against the backdrop of early Civil War Tennessee. According to its author, the book was intended to convey the message that "the war of secession was a war of emancipation from the start." *Cudjo's Cave* was written and published in the wake of the Emancipation Proclamation and the July 1863 New York City draft riots that victimized hundreds of blacks and portrayed an array of white and black characters fighting side by side against slaveowning rebels. Aided by a massive publicity campaign by its publisher, the book soon became a bestselling specimen of wartime propaganda, and a copy eventually wound its way into Charles Benson's sea chest.[26]

While the hero of *Cudjo's Cave* is Penn, a white schoolmaster transplanted from the North, two of the main characters are black slaves. The titular character, Cudjo, is "a native African . . . brought to this country a young barbarian." He is deformed and ugly with the "countenance of an ape," and his defects are linked explicitly to the brutal treatment he receives as a slave. Speaking in exaggerated dialect and alternating between childlike and bestial personae, Cudjo embodies nearly every popular black stereotype of his era. Notably, the character refers to himself in the text as a "nigger."[27]

Cudjo's closest companion and antithesis is Pomp, also an ex-slave but otherwise unlike him in every way.

> There was something truly grand and majestic, not only in his person, but in his character also. He was a superb man . . . the most perfect specimen of a gentleman . . . always cheerful, always courteous, always comporting himself with the ease of an equal in the presence of his guest. . . . He was, in short, a lion of a man.[28]

Described as a "negro" rather than a "nigger," Pomp is meant to represent the peak of black advancement. He is portrayed as educated and articulate, and he delivers several monologues arguing for emancipation as well as an end to racism in both the North and the South. Charles Benson, who faced the occupational and social restrictions that afflicted all Northern black men, may have felt the resonance of Pomp's statements. If he did, he gave no sign in his journal.[29]

Notwithstanding Cudjo's tragic heroism and Pomp's nobility, the unquestioned hero of *Cudjo's Cave* is Penn, who emerges at the end of the book as "a bronzed and bearded young man, robust and rough, with an eye like an eagle's." At its core this work, produced by a scion of Bostonian respectability, was meant to illustrate the same journey to manhood once traveled by Richard Henry Dana in *Two Years Before the Mast.* The qualities of bravery and grit exhibited by the protagonist are couched in the familiar terms of middle-class principles of manliness, hard work, and self-mastery. This was a moral that Charles Benson understood very well, since it affirmed the principles he held most dear. Whether or not Benson responded to the racialized aspects of the book was a question he steadfastly refused to address in his daily writings.[30]

While he was working his way through *Cudjo's Cave,* Benson also read a three-part article that had appeared in 1863 issues of *Harper's New Monthly Magazine,* titled "The Religious Life of the Negro Slave." "The life of the negro slave is a peculiar one," it begins, "and hence Christianity in him must manifest itself in many respects in a peculiar manner." One of the article's central vignettes is a description of a Southern black preacher addressing his flock. According to the author, "it was the exhibition of what is one peculiar element of the Negro character—his simple receptive nature, and his earnest emotional faith. 'He believeth with the heart,' and 'receiveth the truth as a little child.'"[31] The innate simplicity of blacks constitutes the central thesis of the *Harper's* article, which reproduces long snatches of stereotypical dialect as testimony to their lack of sophistication. Charles Benson did not respond in his journals to the contents of the article, which he referred to as "Harper, on Nigger Religion."[32]

Benson's choice of words is especially interesting in the context of the article's own use of the word "Nigger" as a backhanded compliment for one of its subjects, the black preacher.

> There was nothing repulsive about him; none of those indefinable, repellant characteristics which so many Negroes possess, and which is best described by the epithet *Nigger.* There was nothing of this, but, on the contrary, a wholesome, genial, winning presence, and an air of such manly self-respect and genuine humility that you felt attracted rather than repelled by his society.[33]

It was common for nineteenth-century Americans, even blacks, to associate the word "Nigger" with slaves like the ones described in "The Religious Life of the Negro Slave;" Houston Baker points out that even Frederick Douglass did so. But black speakers and writers addressing a public audience used the word for the express purpose of "uplifting the race," to bring about educational advancement and civil rights for a black population denied them under slavery. Black public figures encoded their own meanings into a word that whites used to condemn blacks by classifying them as subhuman menial laborers.[34]

Charles Benson decidedly was not writing his diary for public consumption. But his casual use of the phrase "Nigger Religion" likewise signifies his appropriation of the term for his own use. Like slang-slinging black men born a century later, Benson did not necessarily intend to convey any pejorative meaning. Clarence Major argues that blacks who use the word informally between themselves convey "undertones of warmth and good will—reflecting, aside from the irony, a tragi-comic sensibility that is aware, on some level, of the emotional history of the race." The black newspaper *Chicago Defender* affirmed this point in the early twentieth century when it reported that "Nigger is a common expression among the ordinary Negroes and is used frequently in conversation between them. It carries no . . . sting when used by themselves, but they object keenly to whites using it because it conveys the spirit of hate." Charles Benson, informally jotting down his thoughts for a private audience of himself and his wife, was less concerned with propriety than were black leaders who used the term with more circumspection.[35]

But consider the following: *Cudjo's Cave* and "The Religious Life of the Negro Slave" differentiated between "Niggers" and "Negroes." Both were written by white authors and intended for predominantly white audiences. But Charles Benson was a mixed-race individual who was defined by society as "black" and whose relationship with race was complex and conflicted. The fact that he read these sources indicates that Benson was interested in understanding race and how it was portrayed, but his decision to mute his reaction to his reading reveals his desire to bury these issues without consciously addressing them. Always anxious to avoid discord, he was particularly unwilling to force himself to face his own feelings about his racial place in the world around him.

Benson's discomfort about the impact of race on his life was brought to the fore on a very few occasions. One of these occurred early in his 1862 voyage to East Africa when Benson and the cook John L. Jones engaged in one of their customary "long talk[s] about Salem people." Although he would not elaborate on the cause, Benson reported that the conversation ended abruptly when "——s [Jones] got mad—as usual." A month later the two were at it again, this time when they "had a long arguement about northern & southern people."

Certainly the differences in temperament between the two men helped spark their "arguements." The evidence of his personality and habits suggests that Benson found it easy to obey authority and follow prescribed roles. His entire working life was defined by a strict hierarchy of status and task that Benson found familiar and comforting. In contrast, Jones's tendency to "get mad" identifies him as a man less willing to submerge himself in the passive acceptance Benson often demonstrated. But as they fought about their views on "people" the two black men likely touched on their individual views on race as well. Originally from the town of Alexandria on the outskirts of Washington, D.C., Jones was one of fewer than two dozen Southern-born blacks in Salem.[36] Unlike Benson, who had no firsthand knowledge of the American South, Jones was familiar with the "southern people" they were discussing and had grounds for comparison with the Northerners Benson had known for his whole life. In their divergent opinions about black or white "people" from the South, the North, and their home town of Salem, Jones and Benson indicated how each contextualized his experience of being a black man within a larger society. Benson, reticent and cautious and largely disconnected from black America, consistently took positions that angered and frustrated his companion. Uncomfortable with the confrontational direction taken by their discussions, Benson apparently avoided them as the voyage went on.[37]

Although Benson limited his conversations thereafter, he still thought of home constantly. "I love to talk of home sometimes," he wrote, "but to think of it always." Along the way, his meditations often brought forth memories of friends and acquaintances at home and some of the places they frequented together. Sundays aboard ship were especially lonesome as Benson recalled the social aspects of church attendance in Salem, "went to the galley & sat & read the bible," he inscribed on one dreary November Sunday in 1864. "How I should like to be home to night. I suppose they begin to have meetings in the Nigger Meeting House now."[38]

The "Meeting House" to which Benson referred was Salem's black church, long the only communal institution maintained by the city's black community. In an unpublished monograph written in the 1960s, the Salem historian Eleanor Broadhead summarizes virtually all that is known about this short-lived institution.

> [In 1827] an advertisement in the local paper asked that anyone interested in digging the cellar for a Church to be erected in South Salem for the Colored People, apply to John Remond, William Williams or Prince Farmer, Building Committee. A chapel was built on South Street, later known as Mill Street. . . . First called the "United Bethel Church," this had six names in all by 1854 when it became the "First Free-Will Baptist Society." Its closing seems to have been about 1861.

The closure of the church building did not mean the end of the meeting, for Benson referred to the meeting in his journals as late as 1864 and a Salem newspaper did so in 1866. The likelihood is that regular meetings continued in a small brick structure on Warren Street.[39]

Benson had mentioned the meeting in the previous volume of his journal, when he expressed his weekly hope that his wife had attended it in his absence. At the time, however, he never once referred to the services

as anything other than "meeting" or "church," omitting any racial desig-
nation that identified it as a black house of worship.[40] His choice to des-
ignate the church as "the Nigger meeting house" was certainly unusual,
at least by the written standards of his time. The establishment and
maintenance of separate religious services provided a sense of communal unity, accomplishment, and pride to nineteenth-century black New
Englanders. Consequently, black writers and community leaders were always careful to maintain a scrupulous reverence when writing about
their houses of worship.[41] By choosing an epithet (at the very least a common vernacular term) instead of a more traditionally respectful descriptive for his church, Benson continued to eschew communal conventions.

CHARLES BENSON's idealism, which was so pronounced in the areas of
romantic love and the code of manly behavior, did not extend into the
realm of black nationalism and racial pride. Such idealism was not consistent with the conditions of his upbringing and past experiences. Regardless, any expression of such sentiments would have been out of place
aboard ship. Benson's world was his vessel, a floating wooden cocoon
where he would spend most of the foreseeable future in close quarters
with thirteen whites and but one other black man. In this limited environment, race-based rhetoric was unwelcome for the strife and conflict it
could cause. As a black steward on a predominantly white ship, Benson
was always careful not to jeopardize himself or his position.

As he knew after spending a decade at sea on seven different merchant
vessels under the command of six different captains, sea life could be
especially cruel to black men. By the time he joined the complement of
the *Glide* in 1862, Benson was well-acquainted with the racist notions
that circulated among the white sailors of the fo'c'sle. Most working-class
whites of Benson's era subscribed to the pervasive racism of American
culture, indulging in the stereotypes, mockery, and devaluation of nonwhites that was embedded in the Victorian worldview. Sailors were no
different, their conversations and personal writings sprinkled with racial
invective aimed toward their black shipmates.

Benson knew too that when those black shipmates were cooks or stewards, sailors' racist attitudes often turned to antipathy. Aside from the issues of seafaring skill or manhood, both of which were considered lacking in the galley personnel, there was the matter of shipboard food, which
was roundly detested by nearly every merchant sailor who went before

the mast. One contemporary of Benson's who sailed out of Salem aboard the merchant vessel *Sooloo* in 1861 provided a detailed indictment of the miserable fare served up to seamen. The hard ship's biscuit provided at mealtime was nearly inedible, he reported, so much so that it had to be broken up "with an axe or perhaps a hammer if you have patience enough," then soaked and sweetened and "christened 'Dandy Funk' . . . and served with stinking beef and muddy coffee." With a sarcastic flourish he added, "this is called breakfast." Dinners were worse, consisting of "Rotten Salt Fish . . . Rotten Potatoes . . . [and] Stinking Water 1 Yard." The men of the *Sooloo* blamed their unpalatable fare and growling bellies on two men: the cook, responsible for their food that was so "poorly cooked," and his compatriot in the galley, "the miserable apoligy for a man we have for a steward."[42]

Black stewards and cooks faced not only the anger of a hungry and dissatisfied crew but also their preconceived racial views. As W. Jeffrey Bolster writes, "all cooks and stewards were accused of being 'dishonest, filthy, and neglectful of . . . duty'—but African-American men even more so." Whites assumed that blacks were innately slothful and unintelligent, dirty and careless. Although few white sailors reared in small-town New England had met many blacks during their upbringing, their opinions had already been shaped by a racist culture that introduced blacks as figures of stereotype. In the Salem newspapers that seafarers like the men of the *Sooloo* and Charles Benson scoured for news of home and loved ones, they encountered blacks who worked as menial laborers, displayed simple-minded childishness, and acted as the butt of "darkey" and "nigger" jokes. Sailors, already angry at their black shipmates for rationing their vessel's food supplies, saw little reason to deny racial hatreds inculcated in them since childhood. Black stewards like Charles Benson, uncomfortably aware of the hostility of the crew, could best avoid confrontation by keeping to themselves. They also took to characterizing the bulk of common sailors in unflattering terms, as Benson did when he referred to them as "a pack of fault-finding, ignorant men" in 1862.[43]

In the peaceful, stable world of the *Glide*, where interracial tensions were absent or at least muted, Benson was never the target of any significant malice or violence. As his feelings of kinship and affection toward his shipmates grew, he had little cause to alter lifelong patterns and rush to join in racial solidarity with other blacks. Although he lived in a defining historical moment for black Americans everywhere, at sea Charles Benson was as far from the epicenter of change as it was possible to be in both a psychological and an actual sense. Ashore, he had never found a clearly defined place that properly suited him, not in terms of his occupation or his race or his self-image. But aboard the *Glide* he knew exactly who he was: Charles Augustus Benson, ship's steward, with all of the rights and responsibilities that position entailed.

During his three voyages on the vessel, the longest tenure he had yet spent anywhere at sea, Benson had grown more ensconced in "his" pantry, familiar with the habits of his captain and attached to the bark that was his home. As the days flowed into months and eventually years, his memories of his home ashore took on the quality of dreams. Reality was the *Glide*, not the phantom community he had left behind. In danger of losing that sense of himself within his daily routine on the *Glide*, Charles Benson clung to his relationship with his beloved Jenny Pearl as a means of anchoring himself to his home ashore. But after a decade at sea, he was losing that sense of connection to his family in Salem.

Over the ten years since he first went to sea in 1854, Benson had made more than a dozen consecutive sea voyages with only intermittent periods at home in Salem. Since 1857 every one of those voyages was a lengthy one to Zanzibar and the Indian Ocean, separating Benson from his family for about a year at a time. Afflicted with homesickness, loneliness, and guilt over his extended absences from home, Benson passed much of his time at sea in misery. Though he was no stranger to feelings of isolation, the cumulative effects of spending long years alone weighed heavily upon him. He had been married for nearly twelve years to a woman he loved to distraction but enjoyed her companionship for only a fraction of that time. He considered the city of Salem to be his home, yet he was rarely there. By 1864 Benson's emotional suffering was further exacerbated by a decline in his physical health, another consequence of ten years at sea.

Charles Benson was burning out at age thirty-four, his body and soul exhausted by the harsh life of a mariner. As the *Glide* neared the end of her voyage in late November 1864, Benson returned to the familiar cabin that had been his home for nearly three years. "I began to stow & pack away books & other nicknacks," he wrote. Bone-tired and weakened by illness, the steward was exhausted. "If I was at home, I should not be out of my bed long," he confessed on one of his bad days. He was nearly

desperate for a respite, his dearest wish to be home where he might recover. Toward the end of the voyage, late in the evening, he concluded his
day with the weary observation that he "sank to rest in the dark blue
wave."[44] Whether he knew it or not, this would be one of the last nights
he would spend at sea for more than a decade. After the end of this, his
thirteenth sea voyage, Charles A. Benson would go home to remain
ashore in the arms of his Jenny Pearl.

CHAPTER SEVEN

"I feel more than half sick"

AT SEA, 1864

CHARLES BENSON'S thirteenth sea voyage, his third aboard the bark *Glide*, was unusual even before it began. The vessel's prior voyage to Mozambique, Zanzibar, and Aden had been the most profitable in its three-year history, yielding more than three times the value in hides, senna, spices, and ivory than its previous trip. The *Glide* had made her way home fully laden with lucrative cargo and reached Salem on January 11, 1864. The spectacular success of this voyage was underscored by its duration of only nine months and four days, bringing the vessel home months ahead of a schedule that would ordinarily end only in February or March. But despite the *Glide*'s early return, wind and weather conditions dictated that another trip back to Zanzibar could not begin until early spring. The delay may have been further augmented by the necessity to secure outward-bound trade goods, financing, and a suitable crew, all of which were difficult to assemble under the wartime conditions that prevailed that year. Thus, the *Glide* remained at anchor in Salem Harbor for just over three months, the longest layover Charles Benson had enjoyed in his ten-year seafaring career.[1]

Once the *Glide* was finally ready to set sail on April 13, 1864, it embarked from Boston rather than Salem, its typical point of departure. As a result, for the first time Benson found himself taking a train down to Boston amid piles of his gear, then ascending the familiar gangplank off an unfamiliar pier. Aboard the *Glide* he found more changes in the area of personnel. William Churchill, the young first mate on both of Benson's prior voyages on the vessel, was gone, replaced by C. W. Emery, a large man nearly six feet tall and with a quick temper and quick fists. At age thirty-nine Emery was a career mate without a command of his own despite being five years older than the bark's master, Captain John McMullan. Neither proficient nor likeable as an officer, Emery would soon alienate many aboard, including the steward, who came to consider him "a mean man, in most every thing." Emery was one of many men new to the *Glide*, several of whom were in their forties, a consequence of the paucity of available young men at the height of the Civil War. Benson, now thirty-four, was in the novel position of being among the younger crewmen, one of whom, James Adams of Maine, was close to fifty.[2]

The biggest change for Benson was the absence of John L. Jones, the black cook who had accompanied him on his journeys around the world for the past five years. Unwilling or unable to wait around until the *Glide* was ready to leave, Jones apparently left Salem for good in early 1864, perhaps in search of better opportunities in Boston or elsewhere. His replacement was Aaron Moses, a black mariner and lobsterman who had come to Salem from his native Nova Scotia around the same time as Benson in the early 1850s. The two men may not have known each other well; Moses lived on the other side of town from the Bensons, maintaining a home in northerly Salem Neck on Webb Street. But Benson had probably heard of the cook before, if only because he was one of the rare black Salemites to appear in the local newspaper. Moses' brush with notoriety came in 1859, when a boarder of his named Edward Owens twice attempted to shoot him over an unrecorded dispute. The irate Owens, a black barber, was thwarted by the quick action of Mrs. Moses, who snatched away his weapons and tossed them into Salem Harbor. The story of the shooting and Owens's subsequent arrest and trial was a source of gossip in black Salem for years, particularly because he was acquitted in Superior Court despite persuasive evidence against him. After the incident had faded into memory Moses went back to sea, eventually winding up aboard the *Glide* five years later. Owens stayed in Salem, presumably in new lodgings, but fell back into trouble in 1866, when it was reported that the "insane colored man (the one who shot another named Moses a few years ago)" was arrested by the police, who determined that "his insanity was of a dangerous character." Aaron Moses, who was back home in Salem by then, was likely relieved to hear the news.[3]

His contretemps with Edward Owens notwithstanding, Aaron Moses seemed to have little trouble getting along with his new shipmate. Benson enjoyed Moses' cooking, perhaps a welcome change after five years of eating the fare prepared by his predecessor, John L. Jones. Benson liked Moses' fried fish and his baked goods, including gingerbread and his specialty, "Sugar Cakes." When Benson felt poorly he could go "to the galley & lay down on the Cooks 'Donkey'" (sea chest) for a quick snooze, a measure of the two men's easy relationship. Together they chuckled over an "Irish story" Benson dug up to share with his comrade. Benson recorded no disagreements with Moses that approached the ferocity of his "arguements" with Jones, and at the end of the voyage Benson would make sure to find a way to express his personal affection and regard for his friend. About a week before they reached Salem, he "gave the cook a bottle of currie, Pickle Limes, Mutton tallow & a bottle of chutney for his wife & a bottle of Dates for his little ones." They passed the remainder of the evening "in the galley spinning yarns . . . about Salem." They would remain close friends for years afterward.[4]

The 1864 voyage the two men made together turned out to be brief, lasting only seven months and twenty-four days. Although this quick passage could be attributed in part to favorable winds and currents, it had more to do with the vessel's contracting trade markets. The cornerstone of Salem's commerce in the region had always been inexpensive textiles, the cotton cloths, calicos, and "domestics" produced in massive quantities by New England mills. Because of the Civil War, cotton was now in short supply and the mills in shambles. As cotton prices soared, American traders could no longer fill their vessels' holds with yards of sheeting, and local traders in the Indian Ocean could no longer afford to trade in the little cotton they could find. In a corollary development, the war also diminished American demand for former trade staples such as ivory and gum copal that had once filled the hold of the *Glide*. The impact on the economy of Zanzibar, which funneled goods in and out of the East African interior, was devastating. The dropoff in American trade, which had accounted for over one-quarter of the island's foreign commerce before the Civil War, caused Zanzibar's overall trade to drop by more than one-third within only a few years. By the time the war ended, the special relationship that had once existed between Salem's mercantile interests and the Zanzibar trade region had ended.[5]

The consequences for the *Glide* were enormous. In 1863, the bark's most profitable year to date and forever after, the inbound cargo contained more than 650 pieces of ivory along with more than 5,000 animal hides and nearly 2,000 bags and packets of various spices accumulated at Zanzibar, Aden, and Mozambique. A year later, under diminished circumstances, brief trading stops at virtually closed markets yielded only 22 bags of gum arabic, fewer than 1,000 bales of animal skins, a miserable 9 pieces of ivory, some coffee, 2 barrels of limes, 4 bundles of reed mats, and 4 bags of candy. Although the voyage still made respectable profits, the total came to less than one-third of the previous year's. In 1865 the merchandise brought home by the *Glide* would fall off in value by another two-thirds. That figure plummeted further in 1866 and again in 1867. Just as they had in Brazil a decade earlier, Salem's mercantile fortunes were fading fast in the Zanzibar trade.[6]

Nevertheless, Charles Benson seems to have enjoyed the short-lived 1864 voyage of the bark *Glide*. Virtually every hardship he had experienced in 1862 was minimized this time around. With fewer stops and trade partners, he had less work to do when the *Glide* was in port. And, at sea, he spent less time on his hands and knees scrubbing the cabin floors. Best of all, the excruciating homesickness that had plagued him in earlier years was eased by the short duration of this voyage and the long stay at home that preceded it.

The tone of the journal Benson kept on this voyage is less despondent and suggests that his discomfiture at being far from his home had ebbed. This time he indulged in a sly humor that was new for him, at least in his personal writings. The changes in his attitude may have stemmed from the quickness of the voyage or, since this particular notebook was composed on the homeward-bound leg of his journey, may have been the result of his anticipation of homecoming. Still, there is definite evidence that the stylistic differences in Benson's writing reflect changes in him. Although his values and inner conflicts had not changed, he no longer retreated into the idealized sphere that once sustained him. Older and more experienced, Benson was now comfortable with the realities that faced him.

On Friday, October 28, 1864, Benson wrote, "205 days from home," in his first journal entry in a new notebook. This opening differed from the formula he had used two years earlier when he began keeping his journal. Back then he had always begun each day by noting the number of "days from my Jenny Pearl." Benson ended his daily entries differently as well, changing "good night Jenny" to "good night, Dear Pearl." These alterations, subtle though they were, held great meaning for Benson. On his previous voyage his wife, Jenny, had centered his existence. He mentioned her name at least once a day in his journal, and thought about her constantly. The "dear, dear Jenny" that he carried within him was his most constant companion at sea, the only other inhabitant of the intimate world he constructed in his mind and writings. In an extreme reading of Victorian ideals of romantic love, Charles Benson filtered everything in his experience through his image of Jenny. Whether he was taking in the sights at sea or in foreign ports, "reading in the Bible," or reminiscing about people and places he knew in Salem, he always interpreted things in terms of what Jenny would say or how she would feel. The homesickness that afflicted him throughout 1862 was little more than a yearning to be with his absent wife. Since its continued grip on his emotions served as a testimony of his great love for his "dear little wife," Benson displayed his lonesomeness as a badge of honor. It may be a bit strong to say that Benson reveled in his misery, but to the extent that he linked it to his feelings for Jenny, he did.

By late 1864 Benson no longer needed to prove his love for Jenny this way. He certainly continued to love her and desire her company. But at some point during his two visits home, for one month in 1863 and three months in early 1864, his idealized vision of his relationship with Jenny was dispelled by the daily realities of married life. For the first time in a decade, and perhaps the first time since they had met, Charles came to know his wife as an independently functioning adult. The fifteen-year-old girl with whom he had fallen in love was now a hard-working woman determined to secure the continued survival of her family. Back at sea several months later, he tacitly acknowledged his new understanding of Jenny. He dispensed with flowery avowals of love and misty-eyed gazing at her photograph and contented himself with a single statement of his devotion: "I think Jenny is ———— how fare."[7]

In his journals Benson began to address his wife with a wry affection he had rarely demonstrated before. One afternoon in late November he was in the galley preparing dinner when this mood struck him:

> 4 Pm killed a duck. we have 2 more left. I suppose the Salem Market is full of ducks & poultry for Thanksgiving I hope you will have a Turkey, Goose or something, & will save me some old rusty Chickens legs, that is if you happen to have any laying around loose.

Just a few days earlier, another galley experience jogged thoughts of his wife, making him smile. "Cook makeing 'Sugar Cakes,'" he wrote. "ha ha. how are you Sugar Cakes." He was still chuckling the next time the cook baked up another batch of "Sugar Cakes" some weeks later.[8]

Benson's new frame of mind also extended to the subjects of sex and

sexuality. In the past his physical needs had driven him to either sentimentalism or guilt, depending upon whether or not he had acted on his
desires and turned to masturbation. But this time around the stirring of
his libido only made him droll.

> I feel <u>funny</u>. did you ever feel <u>funny</u>? well if you ever did you know just how
> I feel. I wish I was at home I would try to get rid of this <u>funny feeling</u> but
> I suppose I must grin & bear it until I get home.

He had had "funny dreams" before, of course. Once in 1862 he had even
showed a rare flash of humor about his sexual need to be "with Jenny,"
stating "my head aches & that is not all. but I must 'grin & bear' it." But
for the most part he had regretted his "<u>trouble</u>" and the "bad deed[s]"
that followed, acting appropriately mortified at the intrusion of his
fleshly lusts into the spiritual realm of romance he had concocted for
himself. But a newly realistic Benson was more comfortable with this
side of himself and less prone to feeling guilty.

He was not entirely free of insecurity, however. One October morning,
after a night of unfulfilled desire, Benson confessed, "one time I dreamed
that I should have trouble in <u>seeing</u> you when I get home." Always wary
of unharnessing his sexuality, Benson feared that impotence might be his
just punishment for his deviant behavior while alone at sea. "I wonder if
it will be so," he added, "I hope not." He reiterated his concern several
weeks later on the day he felt "<u>funny</u>." He wrote, "the days seem very long
& I am getting as nervous as can be. I hope when I do get home I shall
find <u>every</u> <u>thing</u> <u>all</u> <u>right</u>." Nevertheless, it was not merely impotence he
feared but also his reception from a less-than-willing wife. "if I dont," he
warned, "I shall ———." If he remained true to form, the dash that ended
his sentence referred to masturbation, which might be his only sexual
outlet if his amorous intentions were rebuffed upon his return home.
Once again it would appear that practical experiences during his last visit
home were shaping Benson's expectations for the future.[9]

He had certainly learned where authority lay in the Benson home,
even when he was around. Although he was the nominal head of his family, Benson no longer attempted to cast himself in the role of patriarch
and provider. Nor did he ask useless questions about why Jenny found
trips to Salem Market unromantic. Long months at home had taught him
how capable his Jenny was at handling finances, organizing her workday,
and dealing with the myriad of details that went with running a household on her own. More aware than he had ever been in eleven years of

marriage, Benson ceded full authority over the family's domestic affairs to his wife.

> if we have any kind of good luck we shall be home before Christmas, & I hope we may for I want to eat my Christmas dinner with my family this year. it is a long while since I did so, & if we do get home & every thing is well, I shall have a dinner party Christmas day. what say you Jenny. can we aford it. good night dear Pearl.[10]

As with his sexuality, Benson was not entirely comfortable putting aside the middle-class ideology of masculinity that had guided him for so long. Deprived of his rightful role in the family by the circumstances of his occupation and his wife's aptitude, he worried about his place in his own home. "how I want to get home," he wrote two weeks before his arrival in Salem, "& yet I some times dread the thoughts of going home, for it seems to me at times as though I was not wanted there. is it so? am I not in the way some times?" Benson was finding it increasingly difficult to reconcile the realities of his home life with the gender rules he had followed throughout his adult life. When he signed off that night he made a minute change to his usual farewell and wrote, "good night & happy dreams dear Pearl." This was shorthand for a sentiment he had expressed one day in 1862 when he was especially fretful: "I must put more faith in you, for I well know you will do what is right." At his most stressed, Benson relied on romantic sentiment to make everything all right, even when he was less than sure of himself. Wishing his wife "happy dreams" affirmed the love he hoped would continue to see them through the difficulties of living together.[11]

Even at his most "nervous," Benson did his best to maintain his good cheer in late 1864. He enjoyed his growing closeness to the rest of the crew and began to display a volubility about others aboard, especially first mate Emery, in his journal. "[O]ur mate makes funny work fitting ship," Benson remarked after more than six months at sea; "he don't seem to understand his business. he seems more like an old rough farmer than he does a sailor." A few days before they got home, Benson observed, "Mr. Emery is giving his room a cleaning out. it needs it." Whether he was being whimsical or pointed, humorous or slightly edgy, Charles Benson was easier in mind and spirit than he had ever been as steward of the bark *Glide*.

It was remarkable that he could maintain his composure at all, let alone a cheerful attitude. Benson was sick throughout the entire voyage, sicker than he had ever been before. He had been ill at sea in the past; in

1862 he had suffered a lingering "severe cold" that left him with a "verry sore throat" and a "bad head ache," signs of the "Neuralgia" that had him in its grip. But those pains and "troubles" paled in comparison to the intestinal malady that afflicted him for most of 1864.[12]

Nearly every day his suffering grew worse, as he described in his journal.

[October 28] I have had a severe pain in my bowels most all day. took Peppermint Laudanum. it stoped the pain but made me feel bad otherwise.

[October 30] I have severe pain in my bowels. the pills that I took last night did not operate good.

[October 31] All the morning I suffered greatly with violent pain in my bowels & lateral parts. . . . I have had several painfull discharges of Blood & slime.

[November 1] I feel miserable to day. . . . I yet pass blood most every time I have a stool . . . feverish & bad.

[November 2] I feel miserable to day. I feel as though I should vomit all the time. 2 Pm went to the galley & lay down upon the Cooks "Donkey" & fell asleep. 4 Pm I turned out & felt some better for a while, but soon the sickness returned.

[November 3] I feel some better than I did yestoday, but am far from feeling well. I continue to pass blood at most every discharge. 3 Pm went to the galley to sit & read, but soon fell asleep. 4 Pm awoke with a severe pain in my bowels, had several discharges of blood & other foul matter, black as ink, when shall I get well.

[November 4] I feel rather slim to day. have pain in my bowels.

[November 5] I had violent pain in my bowels all the fornoon. took various things to stop it but they seemed to do no good. at last it seemed to wear itself out. I feel much better this afternoon. have not had much pain & have not been in the head since dinner.

[November 6] I washed me & changed my clothes. I was surprised to see how much I have fell away. I am very poor I don't believe I weigh more than a hundred pounds. I feel much better to day.

[November 7] my Disentary started with renewed vigor this morning. I keep up a continual running in the head & blood runs free from me almost as water.

[November 11] I have felt pretty well to day, but at times I have had severe pains in my bowels, & have had several bloody stools.

[November 13] have severe bearing down pain in my lower extremitys.

[November 17] my Diarrhea does not trouble much to day, but the pills are horrid.

[November 20] I turned out at half past three to go into the head. my bowels pained me nearly all night. I feel more than half sick am quite feverish. I continued to have frequent, painfull, bloody, discharges until about 10 am. then I took some Laudanum & Peppermint & that seemed to relieve it.

[November 23]I have another trouble the Catarrh in my head troubles me much. no peace for the wicked.

[December 2] I washed cabin windows outside & in. I had a very severe pain in my bowels all the while took some Laudanum it did not seem to do any good.

As he knew (for all the good it did him), Benson was the victim of a case of diarrhea, or dysentery. The symptoms were as Benson described them: excessive peristalsis, or muscular contractions in the body's alimentary tract, accompanied and aggravated by a flux, the inordinate discharge of liquid matter from the body through "frequent stools." Medical texts of the time differed on the specifics of dysentery and diarrhea, associating the former with "marked tenesmus [straining]" during bowel movements and the latter with a lack of straining. They also distinguished chronic forms of the disorder, which could last months and cause serious long-term damage to bodily organs and blood vessels, from short-term acute cases, which frequently wound up being chronic in the end anyway. Benson, who reported "violent pain in my bowels & lateral parts" accompanied by "frequent, painfull, bloody, discharges," would likely have been diagnosed with chronic dysentery. However, most ordinary people such as Benson used the terms "dysentery" and "diarrhea" interchangeably. So did many physicians, who also used the catchall phrase "looseness of the bowels" to describe the condition.[13]

Benson's malady was the subject of much discussion and debate at precisely the time he was suffering the most. Hundreds of thousands of Civil War soldiers on both sides of the conflict were afflicted with the flux. Contemporary studies asserted that 54 percent of all Union troops and nearly 99 percent of Confederates had the disease at one time or another, and estimates of the resultant death toll range from sixty thousand to one hundred thousand. The widespread incidence of diarrhea and dysentery was attributed to several causes. Army camps were squalid with stinking and befouled latrine trenches, poor drainage arrangements, and

unwashed, slovenly soldiers. The spread of bacillary and amoebic dysentery, infections spawned amid the unsanitary crowding of military bases,
was furthered by the dearth of healthy water supplies. Another cause was
the soldier's diet, which was appallingly low on fresh fruits and vegetables but provided plentiful quantities of salt pork and beef. "Death from
the frying pan" was one Union medic's description of recruits' cooking,
which consisted of flour-and-water cakes, rice, beans, or meat fried in
whatever greasy fat was available.[14]

Charles Benson faced many of the same hazards as these soldiers on
his voyage aboard the *Glide*. Fresh water was always in short supply on a
seafaring vessel, and sailors became accustomed to water turned stale
and brackish in wooden casks. Stocks of vegetables ran out, and dishes
made from "home potatoes" were eventually replaced on the table with
"bread hash" or other flour concoctions. Sailors' rations were much the
same as those allotted to soldiers, as Benson recorded in his descriptions
of his stewarding duties. Barrels of hams, beef, pork, and "salt junk" were
hauled up each day from the pantry to the galley to be fried for dinner.
Supplementing the meals were large quantities of beans, so renowned in
the army for their diarrhea-causing properties that one Civil War surgeon proclaimed they had "killed more [men] than bullets." And while
the cabins that Benson so diligently scrubbed were clean and free of dirt,
the port cities he visited during the course of his journey were not. Zanzibar Town, the island's capital and trading center, was "the dirtiest place
in the world," according to one contemporary British observer. Poor san-
itary arrangements and crowded conditions combined with the equato-
rial heat and humidity, forming a lethal environment where disease was
endemic.[15]

The causes of Benson's ill health were relatively clear, but treatment
would prove complicated. He contracted his illness at a transitional time
in American medical practice, when leading authorities were divided over
the fundamentals of causality and cure. The predominant philosophy of
the early-nineteenth-century orthodox establishment held that diseases
were essentially *sthenic*, or stimulatory, in nature. The physiology of the
sick individual was overexcited or "morbidly animated," as evidenced by
high pulse rates and quickened heartbeats. Prescribed curatives were intended to drain the body of excess excitement and restore its natural balance. These curatives often took the form of purgatives that would both
cleanse and deplete the system by expelling bodily fluids, either cathartics that did so through the bowels or emetics that induced vomiting. Use

of the lancet for bleeding patients was another popular solution of this kind, especially in the middle Atlantic and southern regions of the country, where the ideals popularized by the eighteenth-century physician Benjamin Rush held sway. Opiates, which calmed patients and aided their ability to sleep, were also considered effective therapies, particularly after a violent purging.[16]

Beginning in the 1850s, the medical community began to move away from older ideas toward a new understanding of illnesses as *asthenic*, or enfeebling. During the 1860s and 1870s many physicians came to question the value of weakening agents such as purgatives, which they saw as exacerbating patients' conditions rather than healing them. The new theory advocated stimulants instead, in the form of judicious quantities of alcohol, iron compounds, and supportive diets that would lend new strength and life to systems weakened by disease. Thus, Charles Benson was one of more than a million victims of dysentery at a time of change and uncertainty about the basic character and goals of therapeutics.[17]

To complicate matters further, there were also disagreements over appropriate dosage. The early nineteenth century was known as the era of "heroic medicine," when the medical establishment believed very aggressive therapeutic intervention was warranted. Doctors plied their patients with "heroic" or massive quantities of medication in the belief that such huge dosages would cleanse the system and restore natural balance that much faster. One of the foremost practitioners of the heroic school was John Esten Cooke of Kentucky, who prescribed hundreds of grains and even pounds of purgatives as therapy for his bile-centered theory of sthenic disease. Even after many physicians began rejecting Cooke's approach to pathology in the 1850s, his philosophy of heroic treatment was retained. Through the late 1860s, a significant number of medical professionals continued to administer their remedies in huge portions, often to the detriment of their patients.[18]

The response of the public to the dictates of the allopathic authorities was primarily one of cautious acceptance. Most Americans agreed with the principles of maintaining the body's systemic balance through the prudent use of drugs to treat illnesses. They were less comfortable with the extremes of heroic medicine, feared by many patients for their side-effects and other attendant dangers. Popular resistance to the heroic school, which hastened its demise in the second half of the nineteenth century, often took the form of skepticism or outright refusal to cooperate with doctors' orders. In an ancillary development, many people turned to homeopathy, which rejected the medical orthodoxy. Originating in eighteenth-century Germany, homeopathy stressed the role of nature in effecting recovery and advocated minimizing pharmaceutical doses or even eliminating them altogether. Brought to the United States from Europe in the 1820s, homeopathy gained adherents by the thousands in the ensuing decades. Despite rancorous opposition from the medical establishment, or perhaps because of it, the system spread so widely that homeopathic organizations and treatment facilities were created and maintained independently of mainstream institutions.[19]

With a bewildering array of medical philosophies and courses of treatment at his disposal, Charles Benson took an eclectic approach to curing his dysentery and tried them all, purgatives, opiates, homeopathic remedies, and folk medicine. In the end, every one of the pills, powders, and liquids had the same curative effect, which is to say none at all. Instead, many of them only made things worse (fig. 11).

The first curative Benson reported taking was "Peppermint Laudanum," which he ingested to relieve "a severe pain in my bowels" on the October 28. He again combined the two substances two days later, and did so one last time in late November. Benson took unadulterated laudanum on two other occasions, the largest quantity an "injection of . . . 40 drops." He may also have meant a laudanum-based concoction when he wrote "took some pain killer" on December 2, the last time he reported medicine use on the voyage.

One of the most popular nostrums of the nineteenth century, laudanum was a tincture of opium, mixing opium with alcohol. Entirely legal and readily available in the United States, the drug was so inexpensive that it was affordable even for the lowest-paid workers. It became a medicinal staple, prescribed by physicians as a painkiller and applied to the same use by a host of individuals who self-medicated their own bodily complaints. Laudanum and other opium compounds were thought to cure a wide variety of conditions, ranging from head and muscle aches to respiratory problems, infant colic, gynecological and obstetric disorders, and neuralgia. It was also applied quite effectively to cases of diarrhea, since one of the chief side-effects of opium is constipation.

The peppermint that Benson used in conjunction with the laudanum was *mentha piperita*, a plant cultivated in the American midwest beginning in the 1850s. He may have used powdered or dried leaves, or possibly peppermint oil mixed with his laudanum solution. Peppermint was a well-known herbal remedy that could be used for fevers or aches and

FIGURE 11. Medicine case. With free access to the ship's medicine case,
Benson tried many curatives for his dysentery.

was also thought to be helpful for digestive disorders affecting the bowels or colon.

Of all the remedies he tried, laudanum was most likely to have allevi-
ated Benson's condition, but, as Benson wrote after his last attempt in
December, "took some Laudanum it did not seem to do any good." There
may have been several reasons it did not. The limited doses he took, only
five over the course of six weeks, may have been insufficient to ease his
peristaltic distress. Furthermore, the diluted solution he was drinking
likely contained too little opium to be effective, especially given the small
size of his dosage, which he measured out in liquid drops. Most important, the benefits gained from the laudanum were counteracted by the
cathartics he was taking at the same time. Contrary to his intentions,
Benson's drugs were working at cross-purposes, extending his suffering
rather than ending it.[20]

Another opium compound was Dover's powder, which was a mild
combination of opium and ipecacuanha. Principally prescribed as a pain

reliever, it was to a lesser extent used as a remedy for diarrhea, like its liquid counterpart laudanum. Little-known in the early part of the century, Dover's powder became one of the most prominent drugs in America in the 1840s and 1850s, surpassing laudanum as the chief source of opium use in the country.[21]

Benson reported using "Dovers Powders" only once, on November 1, the latest opium compound he employed after three incidents of laudanum use earlier in the week. The tiny amount he took, "5 grains," contained only one-half grain of opium. This was probably not enough to accomplish his purpose.

On five different occasions he also reported the use of different types of pills: two of them, "Blue Pills" and Lees Pills," he identified by name, while the other three he did not (although he did say of them that they were "horrid"). Pharmacies and dispensaries of the time did a thriving trade in pills of all kinds, alleging cures for a wide variety of ills. While "Lee's Pills" were likely a specific brand, the phrase "Blue Pills" sometimes referred to a spectrum of quackeries peddled by any number of unqualified medicos with little or no training. By the time Benson took his Blue Pills in late 1864 they were in common use among soldiers in the Union Army; at least one recruit's diary mentions taking "Pills for Diarrhea [and] Blue Pills for Jaundice" during military campaigns in South Carolina.

Any or all of the pills Benson took may have contained opium, which was often administered in pill form and was probably a main ingredient in "Pills for Diarrhea" soldiers reported taking.[22]

The corrective Benson used most often after laudanum was calomel, or mercurous chloride. Grains of the metal were counted out and dissolved in a bitter liquid to be taken orally. A powerful cathartic, calomel was a keystone of heroic medicine's dedication to eliminating harmful secretions from the body. Uncertainty about how the drug worked or how much remained in the body after purging did little to dissuade physicians from applying it liberally to their patients. In small quantities calomel was thought to be a stimulant, in large ones a depletant, and always salubrious for the system. Following the example of Dr. Cooke of Kentucky's Transylvania University, medical practitioners all over the South and West administered huge dosages as a cure for nearly everything, to adults and children alike. The general public shared the perception of calomel as a wonder-drug and took to guzzling it down at the first sign of ill health. During the Civil War, military medical personnel dispensed huge quantities of calomel to soldiers in both the Union and Confederate armies, most notably to the thousands of men with diarrhea and dysentery.

The worst potential effect of calomel was mercury poisoning. Ingestion of calomel led to salivation, causing the mouth to turn brown from the effects of mercury. This discoloration was often followed by a rotting of the gums and soft tissue of the mouth. When gangrene set in, the mouth would ulcerate, teeth and gums would slough off and fall out, and significant amounts of bone would be lost from the jaw. So frightful were the consequences of calomel abuse that in 1863 the surgeon general of the United States, William Alexander Hammond, issued a Medical Department circular banning it (and tartar emetic, another solution of mercury) from the Union Army's supplies. Calomel use was so deeply entrenched in the national consciousness that the circular not only was ignored but was even partially responsible for Hammond's eventual ouster from his position by physicians antagonized by his attitude toward their miracle cure.[23]

Charles Benson was lucky to escape the worst effects of taking calomel. He took only low dosages of the metal, a caution inbred in him by the tendency among New Englanders to take medicine only in moderation. Although he limited his intake to between 3 and 10 grains once a day, he still suffered for doing so. On November 1, the morning after he took his largest 10-grain dose, Benson reported "I feel miserable to day. the calomel that I took last night gave me a terible working, but made me feel no better." That night, after mixing "5 grains of Dovers Powders with 3 grains of calomel," he felt even worse, "feverish & bad." Benson lasted less than a week on the calomel regimen, having the good sense to stop once he noticed that his mouth had become "very sore takeing so much calomel." He stayed away from mercurous chloride for the remaining five weeks of the voyage, a providential decision considering that the cathartic substance had probably been making things worse all along.[24]

"I HAVE TAKEN so much medicine," Benson wrote in November 1864, "that now I am at my wits end to know what to take." The failure of calomel to mitigate his distress prompted Benson to try organic remedies, complementing the allopathic strategy he had already attempted with the more holistic course known as homeopathy. "I am taking some Homopathic Medicine," he reported in mid-November, not specifying the precise nature of the potion, which he may not have known anyway (it might have contained sulphur, the universal panacea of homeopathics). Benson was tired of the pain and frustration that attended each failed attempt to get well through conventional ingredients from the medicine case. But after trying the new method for nearly a week, from November 5 through November 11 Benson conceded defeat. "I am taking Homopathic Medicine," he repeated, "but don't see as it does me much good."[25]

At this point Benson added two more natural remedies to his long list of pharmaceuticals. The first, tincture of Peruvian bark, had the distinction of being the original theraputant that sparked the creation of homeopathy a century earlier. *Cinchona succirubra*, as the bark was properly known, was the source for the alkaloid quinine, which was considered even more efficacious than calomel by many Civil War–era authorities. Quinine itself would have been almost impossible for Benson to obtain; at the height of the war, black-market stashes of quinine reputedly commanded prices up to $188 an ounce. But unprocessed cinchona bark could be procured in the faraway marketplaces of Zanzibar and Mozambique, giving the sick steward a chance to sample the medicinal touted as the *ne plus ultra* of diarrheal remedies. He supplemented one of these samplings with "a dose of Rhubarb," another root imbued with cathartic properties, which of course only aggravated the problem. By December 2, four days before he finally returned home, Benson was out of ideas. "I have taken so much medicine that nothing seems to have much afect on me," he sighed.[26]

DESPITE HIS near despair over his physical problems, Benson maintained his strong sense of humor throughout the voyage. In addition to his good-natured jibes at his wife, companionship with the cook, and prankishness with the mate, he even managed to poke fun at his own frailties. In the middle of November, after running his disastrous course of medicinals, Benson chuckled at his own discomfort.

> the Piles trouble much. I now know how to pity you. if you have them any thing like me you must suffer dreadfully. it seems to me as if I was agoing to have a child all the time such bearing down pain. I don't know when I could have got in the family way, good night dear Pearl.

Even so, Benson yearned for a respite: "if I was at home, I should not be out of my bed long," he confessed on one 'miserable' day. "[T]his is some of the pleasures of sea life. work as long as you can stand."[27]

His health in ruins, Benson no longer felt nurtured by the world of work in which he lived. One prominent casualty of his transformation from idealist to realist was his working identity, which had so dominated his sense of self years before. The transformative events of this year, beginning with his illuminating period at home in Salem and continuing into his singular voyage on the *Glide* and the collapse of his once-healthy constitution, changed him irrevocably. Although he did not indulge himself in the rhetoric of homesickness that once filled the pages of his journal, Benson wanted nothing more than to be beside his wife in Salem.

"[W]here will this end, I continualy ask my self. I think not while I am at sea, but if I live to get home I think I may get well."[28] These words, written six weeks before the bark *Glide* dropped anchor in Salem Harbor, were prophetic. Charles Benson did "live to get home," to his great relief and that of his wife and family. And though it took some time, Benson did indeed get well. But by then the *Glide* had headed back to Zanzibar without him. For the first time in more than ten years, Benson was no longer a ship's steward. Instead he had been granted his fondest wish, the one he had expressed innumerable times in the sea-journal he kept when he was a mariner. He was home in Salem, where he had always said he wanted to be.

CHAPTER EIGHT

"How I wish that I could live on shore"

SALEM AND AT SEA, 1865–1878

WHEN CHARLES BENSON took his last step off the gangplank of the *Glide* on a chilly December day in 1864, he had little intention of ascending it ever again. For the first time since he began his seafaring career in 1854, Benson was determined to avoid shipping out on any voyage for at least a decade. He had been sick for months and was in precarious health, his weight down to less than one hundred pounds and his alimentary tract wracked with clenching tremors. He missed his wife and family and was plagued with uncertainty about his place in their home and in their lives. He was also curious about the people he knew and the momentous events that had passed him by in his absence, and he was eager to learn for the first time in his life what it meant to be part of a larger community. Consequently, when the *Glide* began her fifth voyage out of Salem on March 23, 1865, Charles A. Benson, steward, was not aboard. He was not alone in this decision. Only three of the vessel's crew returned for another voyage: Captain John McMullan, seaman Daniel Riley, and the former cook Aaron Moses, who now replaced Benson in his higher-paying position as ship's steward.[1]

Benson may have suffered mixed feelings at the *Glide's* fleeting departure from Salem Harbor, but he likely felt vindicated by the time the bark limped home eleven months later. A spectacularly unsuccessful trading voyage, one of the poorest in the vessel's history, was marred further by the specter of death at sea. For the first time in his career the captain had brought along his wife, Kate, to accompany him on his long journey, the prerogative of shipmasters with some seniority. A little more than halfway through the voyage, Kate McMullan took ill in the steamy tropical waters off East Africa; perhaps she fell victim to a disease similar to the one that laid Benson low a year before. In early August she died en route from Aden to Muscat, leaving her bereaved husband to carry on with his responsibilities as commander and lead trader. Because the ship's log for the voyage no longer exists there is no way to determine his health or state of mind at the time. They could not have been good, for within two months the captain, then only thirty-five years old, was dead as well. The *Glide* was brought in by the first mate, William Hathorne, who was promptly promoted to command and sent back to Zanzibar shortly thereafter. Charles Benson, doubtlessly shocked by this sudden and tragic turn of events, could only count himself lucky for surviving his own ill health.[2]

By then Benson was comfortably settled back in his favorite haunts in "Old Salem," his reentry into the community aided by its resemblance to the one he had left to go to sea ten years earlier. The majority of Salem's blacks continued to live in the two major neighborhoods they had occupied in the 1850s, the Mill Pond and Salem Neck areas. The two predominant occupations among the city's black men were still those of seafarer and day laborer. Many of Salem's black women, including Jenny Benson, continued to take in washing and perform domestic service, and the women of the Remond family still maintained their hairdressing establishments along Essex Street (Charlotte Forten had finished her schooling and departed in the late 1850s). As in the 1850s, the largely working-class black community consisted mostly of small living units, which frequently expanded to provide an extended-kin network for black youths (fig. 12).[3]

On the streets of Salem Benson could see many of the faces he knew from years past. Susan Seymour and her daughter Mary still lived with the Bensons, as they had for a decade. Benson's former boss, James Sherman, came back to Salem shortly after Benson, fresh from a wartime stint in the U.S. Navy. Many of Benson's former shipmates and housemates still lived in Salem with their families, including the mariners William Capela and Aaron Moses. Even Jenny Benson's old Porter Street neighbors, the Colmans, Drews, Fullers, and Williamses, all remained in Salem; so did Robert and Hannah Dailey, who had helped raise her.

Benson arrived home just in time to celebrate the end of the Civil War. Although he had shown little regard for military participation in the past, perhaps he felt some of the black pride and sense of accomplishment that grew out of black military successes in the Civil War and the end of slavery in America. Benson may have stood on the sidelines among some of his fellow townsfolk in September 1865 when the fighting black men

FIGURE 12. Creek Street, Salem. Benson returned to the family home on
Creek Street in 1865. Along with most of the Mill Pond area, the street was later
destroyed in the Great Salem Fire of 1914.

of the Massachusetts Infantry, several of them from Salem, marched
through Boston streets crowded with people cheering their victory. Less
than forty years earlier, Charles Benson's parents had stood beside their
Belknap Street neighbors and watched as blacks marching through
Boston were pelted and heckled by whites deriding "Bobalition" parades.
As late as 1857 the members of the Liberty Guard, an informal military
company of black men, were harassed by rowdies when they attempted
to march down Charles Street. Now, a procession of black soldiers in full-
dress uniform paraded to the acclaim of large crowds of black and white

Bostonians. This great transformation was recognized by the black veterans on display, including some from nearby Salem.[4]

During the months and years following the war Benson may have come to recognize the racial pride of the war veterans, who returned home with a pronounced dedication to improving the welfare and position of people of color. In July 1867, Sergeant Francis Fletcher of the Massachusetts Fifty-fourth and three other Salem black veterans enlisted fifty black men to the cause of creating a colored company in the state militia. Three years later, "a meeting of colored people of Salem" that Benson could have attended, had he the inclination, chose Fletcher to represent the community at a black national labor convention held in the nation's capital. During the ensuing months, Fletcher circulated pamphlet copies of the meeting's proceedings and gave a speech about the convention at Salem's Goodell Hall.[5] He also contributed several columns and letters to the *New National Era*, a black newspaper published in Washington, D.C. In his pieces, "Frank H. Fletcher" discussed national political developments of interest to blacks and extolled the accomplishments of Charles Sumner Wilson, the first black cadet appointed to West Point and the son of one of Salem's black soldiers.[6] Years of fighting bloody battles at Fort Wagner, Olustee, and Honey Hill had shaped Fletcher into a passionate and outspoken proponent of racial uplift and brought him to a position of leadership in black Salem. Charles Benson, discussing these events with his cronies and reading about them in the newspapers, was being exposed to these ideas for what may have been the first time in his life.

At the same time, Benson was receiving decidedly mixed messages from the culture around him. Along with the other Salem residents observing or reading about the Boston parade in 1865, Benson may have wondered at the contrast between the stateliness of the city's black warriors and the more humble posture blacks had assumed in a Salem procession several months earlier. On the Fourth of July in 1865, the city had celebrated the nation's birth and the recent end to the war with a grand parade. Among the 130 displays and floats presented by the city's schools and churches were two with black themes. The first, "Waiting for the Hour," was described by the *Salem Gazette* as

[A] group of negroes, watching for the hour of twelve, Dec. 30th, 1862, carrying the following banner: — "Proclamation: Whereas **** Persons held as slaves on the first of January, 1863, shall be forever free. — A. LINCOLN, Dec. 31 st, 1862, and Jan. 1 st, 1863."

South Church presented the other race-related float in the parade, which
followed "Home Again," a tableau of a white "widow with her family welcoming the return of her soldier boy." Titled "The Negro Question," the
float offered

> a design in three parts, illustrating the motto, "Past, Present and Future."
> The first, a slave wearing manacles, under the protection of the govern-
> ment, which was represented by a young lady wearing the American Flag;
> —the second, a young lady teaching a negro to read; —the third, a negro
> depositing his ballot at the polls.

"The Negro Question" to which the float referred was one of the major concerns of the white politicians and intellectuals planning the coming Reconstruction of the South. In speeches and newspaper editorials,
the issue of black citizenship and voting rights played out in arguments
about the pros and cons of improving the social, cultural, and economic
status of former slaves.[7] In the 1865 procession, the representations of
blacks as Southern slaves overshadowed their representation as freemen.
Moreover, the role of Northern black soldiers who helped fight and win
the Civil War was disregarded in the parade, including those from Salem.
On July 4, 1865, Salem's blacks watched the floats roll by; perhaps some
of them even stood atop them in the posture of slaves. But despite all the
spectacle, blacks' real lives remained obscured, hidden from public attention and discourse. When Salem's whites discussed blacks seriously,
mean, they were not referring to those who lived among them in Salem.

The contrast between the dedication of the black community to racial
uplift and the very real white barriers to black advancement was the same
in Salem as it was in cities throughout the urban North in the late nineteenth century. After the Civil War, as before, blacks were excluded from
employment in the growing sectors of the economy. Discriminatory hiring practices restricted black workers to menial, pre-industrial jobs, and
unemployment was rampant among blacks, who could not attain those
positions. Even the most secure jobs paid only low wages and offered
no opportunity for occupational mobility. Entrepreneurial efforts were
equally handicapped by blacks' lack of access to financial resources, and
so black-owned businesses suffered dismal failure rates as well. Mired in
poverty and trapped in the poorest neighborhoods that presaged the
coming of residentially segregated ghettoization at the turn of the century, urban black communities were well on their way to an era that historians would identify as the nadir of race and race relations in America.[8]

In large black urban communities, the response to racism and discrimination was a surge in institutional development and political activism. The black church, so vital in spearheading the antebellum abolitionist movement, played a central role in defining the community by providing much-needed social and economic services for established families and new migrants, particularly those from the former slave South. Denied advancement at work or in the white political arena, blacks concentrated on achieving success within their own sphere. They formed voluntary and charitable organizations to sustain themselves and their growing settlements and established newspapers that helped shape a growing racial consciousness among urban blacks. A leadership cadre developed, dedicated to bringing about black advancement and equality in the wider world. Although long decades would pass before their efforts would bear fruit, black urban communities across the country continued to sow their seeds with care and deliberation throughout the last third of the nineteenth century.[9]

In Salem, where the black population had historically proven diffuse and ineffective, the intracommunal efforts of the post–Civil War era would be limited and short-lived. Despite the dedication of the would-be community leader Francis Fletcher, black Salem lacked cohesiveness. Deep divisions appeared within Salem's black church, the population's only formal voluntary association. The source of the split was a unilateral decision by the congregation's landlord John Remond, who had been instrumental in founding the church in 1828, to sell the building, despite the protests of the congregation. The controversy grew so heated that it attracted the attention of the local newspaper, which reported, "the 'Mill Street Chapel' seems getting to be a sort of 'bone of contention' among our colored brethren." Long the only black institution in Salem, the weekly meeting faced extinction if it were evicted. Although the resolution of this particular contretemps was never recorded, Salem's black church disappeared from written records and soon ceased to function entirely. Not a single communal organization took its place to serve the needs of the town's black population.[10]

Salem's blacks were so busy trying to eke out an existence that they may have been unable to find the time or resources to build or maintain communal institutions. But blacks in other cities faced the same challenges and met them head-on.[11] James Horton and Lois Horton point out that in Boston "poverty and discrimination did not force disorganization, but often actually encouraged organization." The blacks of Worcester,

Massachusetts, whose circumstances were similar to those in Salem and who numbered only about five hundred individuals, maintained two thriving churches and a colored branch of the Odd Fellows and even made inroads into an overwhelmingly white military veterans' organization, the Grand Army of the Republic. Worcester's blacks also staged several public exhibitions in the post–Civil War 1860s to celebrate the anniversaries of the Emancipation Proclamation and the abolition of slavery in the British West Indies. The crowning difference between black Worcester and black Salem was demonstrated by Worcester's version of a gala Independence Day parade in 1865. As in Salem, several black participants marched in the parade. But whereas Salem's blacks appeared as slaves, the Worcester marchers distinguished themselves as entrepreneurs. Three of the city's black citizens entered their own horse-drawn cars in the procession to advertise their trades.[12]

The moribund state of black Salem's public image was an indicator of the community's inner weakness. By the time Charles Benson returned there in the mid-1860s a marked decline had begun, particularly in terms of population. Only 270 blacks remained in Salem in 1865, almost 35 percent fewer than the 412 who lived there fifteen years earlier.[13] The disparity in the ratio of black women to black men had grown since 1850, as the proportion of women rose from 48 percent to 62 percent of the total number of blacks. Those who remained were also older, as the average age of black residents was now thirty-two as opposed to the 1850 average of twenty-seven. There were fewer children as well: the number of blacks under age fourteen dropped from 104 to 62.[14]

This pattern grew more pronounced in the ensuing years. In 1870 there were 262 blacks living in Salem, but many of them were recent migrants from Canada or the South who would leave the city shortly thereafter for a new life elsewhere.[15] By 1880 only 203 blacks remained in Salem. Over the course of only three decades, Salem's black population had diminished by more than half. The steep population decline of black Salem was even more glaring in comparison to the general trend in the city, which was in a period of rapid growth and expansion; Salem's overall population had risen to 27,500 by 1880, a growth rate of more than 25 percent over thirty years.[16]

Salem was not unique in terms of black residential instability. Stephan Thernstrom and Peter Knights have noted that "the black population of Northern cities in this period was exceptionally volatile."[17] Elizabeth H. Pleck's work on post–Civil War Boston also reveals that blacks of the

North were exceptionally transient at this time, more so than whites.[18] Nevertheless, by 1880 only 42 people remained out of more than 400 blacks who had lived in Salem in 1850. Furthermore, 86 of Salem's 203 black inhabitants—nearly half of the black community—had been in the city for less than a decade (in many cases for less than five years) and would soon move on.[19] The much larger black enclave in Boston, nearly 6,000 in 1880, could withstand this transience. Salem's smaller black community, in contrast, had few resources to attract or hold migrants.[20]

One underlying cause for the instability of black Salem was the near-total collapse of the city's maritime fortunes. Cursed with "a mediocre harbor and a barren hinterland," in the words of Robert G. Albion, Salem was no longer the bustling seaport it had been at the dawn of the century, when the town's ships traded around the globe. Unable to accommodate the larger American merchant ships being built at midcentury, Salem Harbor was forsaken even by small barks and brigs. By the 1860s and 1870s most vessels shipped out of ports better equipped with ancillary commercial facilities and services than Salem, mainly Boston and New York. Furthermore, Salem had based its maritime success on commercial ventures in South American and Indian Ocean ports, especially Brazil and Zanzibar. During the 1850s and 1860s those trades disintegrated, hastening the demise of Salem shipping. Even local tourist guides were forced to acknowledge the end of Salem's mercantile dominance, noting that "the days of Salem's commercial prosperity have passed into history."[21]

These changes had particularly severe consequences for Salem's black community. At midcentury, just before the onset of decline, seafaring was the favored occupation of Salem's black men. In 1850, crew lists for Salem vessels reported that 56 black mariners lived in Salem; five years later that figure was 53.[22] By 1865, however, only 18 black men were still "mariners" or "seamen." As of 1880 only 3 black mariners remained in Salem, and all were career mariners over fifty years old (one, of course, was Charles Benson). Clearly, black seafarers were a dying breed, and Salem's black community was fading with them.[23]

The depression in the maritime trade and the population attenuation in the black community led to other losses. As black Salem declined, so did the opportunities generated by black communal networks and entrepreneurs. The most prominent black victims of the disruption of Salem's trade were the wealthy business owners of the Remond family. Their fortunes depended on the income generated by the oyster- and wine-selling ventures of John Remond and his son-in-law James Sherman, and both were devastated by the economic downturn. By 1870 Sherman was out of business, and in 1874 old John Remond died at the age of eighty-eight, the remains of his commercial empire dying with him. With their business ventures destroyed in the wake of disruptions in Salem's maritime trade, the remaining members of the Remond family had no way to keep the family business empire solvent. With the sole exception of Cecelia Remond Babcock's establishment, all of the black barbershops of Salem also went out of business by the mid-1870s. In the wake of these calamities, the Remond family dispersed. The Putnam clan moved to Worcester, and several of the Remond women left Salem to live in Europe. Black Salem, now dwindling and bereft of its uppermost class, would never recover.[24]

To counter its seafaring losses, Salem underwent a large-scale transition to manufacturing during the 1860s and 1870s. The city's commercial interests now focused on the coal and lumber trades and the tanning industry, which made use of the imported hides arriving aboard the few Salem-owned merchant vessels still engaged in the African and South American trades.[25] This commercial expansion did not translate into greater opportunities for blacks, however. The new manufactories opened up many new jobs in Salem, but most went to white immigrants. The federal census returns for 1880 emphasize blacks' woeful absence from Salem's industrial workforce. Out of a population of 203 people of color, only 7 were employed in industrial settings: one man worked in a tannery, one woman at "machine stitching," and the remaining five in the shoe industry. As in other industrial cities of the late nineteenth century, employers excluded blacks from the expanding industrial sectors of the economy. Thus the city's growth did not provide jobs for blacks, and even fewer black in-migrants came to Salem.[26]

With financial disaster looming, the apathy that was the hallmark of black Salem took permanent hold in the community and was aggravated by the lack of success that plagued even the most dedicated of Salem's blacks, Francis Fletcher. Proud though he was of his military service, public lobbying, and newspaper writing, Fletcher was dogged by failure in the causes that mattered to him most. His pleas for the formation of a black militia company were ignored by the governor and state representatives. Fletcher's support of the first black West Point cadet, Salem-born Charles Sumner Wilson, came to naught when the young man's appointment was foiled by political opponents of integration at the military academy. Fletcher's misfortunes extended into his working life. Although

he had attained a respectable clerking position during the years following the end of the war, his job was short-lived. By 1869 he was forced to
seek employment as a house painter, a position far more typical of the
low-paying manual labor generally available to black people in Salem.
Shortly thereafter, defeated and bereft of opportunity, Fletcher slipped
into the stream of black emigrants and left Salem.[27]

WHEN CHARLES BENSON returned to Salem in early 1865 he was less
concerned with the big picture than he was with his two uppermost pri-
orities: getting well and finding work. The emaciated condition that
necessitated the former also precluded the latter, and so he spent most
of the next several months to a year recuperating. Scribbled notes in the
back pages of an old sea journal indicate that he spent some time assist-
ing in his wife's home-based laundering, keeping the books as "Mrs.
Jenny M. Benson commenced work for Mrs. Marg. Chandler . . . at two
dollars per week" and performed "washing & ironing for Mrs. Harden at
one dolar a dosen." The rows of painstaking figures and lists of shirts,
sundries, and "Garabaldies" were dated January through August 1865;
interspersed with them were newspaper clippings regarding "costive"
bowels and advertisements for "rupture trusses." Perhaps Benson bought
a truss or followed newspaper guidelines for "how to eat grapes," for his
health steadily improved. By the end of 1865, he was working again.

For the first time since his days as a cordwainer in Natick in the 1840s,
Benson found shore work in semi-skilled positions. From 1866 through
1869, the former steward put his literacy to good use by working as a
clerk in two different establishments. He began at a restaurant in Derby
Square, working for Joseph Morris, an oyster-dealer and "restorator"
since 1850, and brother of a mariner, William Morris. After some time he
moved on to a "dining-room" on Front Street, owned and operated by
Aaron Moses, his former shipmate and close friend. He was still there in
1869, when he referred to the establishment in his listing in Salem's annual *City Directory.*[28]

The black community of two Benson had lived in at sea now benefited
him ashore. His job with Joseph Morris, for example, may have been related to the interpersonal connections he made as a black sailor; he surely
owed his position in Aaron Moses' establishment to the friendship the
two men developed during several voyages together. A decade and a half
earlier the new emigrant had secured work in another black-owned

restaurant, Sherman's oyster-house. Black business owners such as Sherman, Morris, Moses, and the female hairdressing entrepreneurs of the extended Remond-Putnam-Babcock circle provided jobs for many black Salemites, including higher-status positions like Benson's clerking job that were otherwise unavailable to working-class blacks.[29]

Benson was fortunate to find steady work, for his decision to remain with his family in Salem had some direct and immediate consequences. When Benson settled down in Salem in late 1864, it had been over ten years since he and his wife had shared their marital bed for an extended time. As Benson finally brought his "funny dreams" and sexual longings to fruition, their family life changed drastically. When he first returned home, his family consisted only of his wife, Jenny, and their eleven-year-old daughter, Fransisca. Now that the years of infrequent contact between the Bensons had ended, their family started to grow at a more rapid rate. In 1868 Charles W. was born. In 1869 Ida Lois was born but died in infancy before her second birthday. In 1871 the Bensons' fourth child, Hannah J., was born, and in 1875 the last child, William Henry D. was born. For the first time in his life, Charles was present to help raise his children and fill the unfamiliar role of father.

Just as his growing family needed his income the most, the deterioration of black Salem began to have adverse effects on his occupational prospects. By 1875, both of the black-owned restaurants where Benson had recently found work were out of business. Joseph Morris's restaurant, which had been open for well over a decade, had apparently ceased to exist by 1869; by 1874 the same was true of Aaron Moses' dining-rooms, which operated for less than five years altogether. Benson's position did not last even that long, for by 1870 he was let go by Moses, whose meager earnings may have been insufficient to pay his salary. Benson went on to secure a job at another Salem restaurant, around the corner from Moses' Front Street "dining-rooms," in Derby Square, where he had found his first Salem job in 1853. In line with the changes in Salem, though, Benson found himself laboring under altered circumstances. No longer did he work for a black proprietor, like James Sherman, Joseph Morris, or Aaron Moses. Instead, his employer was a white man named Davenport. At Davenport's he was also hired as a cook, not a clerk, at a wage lower than even what he had received as a seafarer five years prior. Nevertheless, Benson held onto his position as "cook, eating house" for five years. As his contemporaries died or left Salem, as more Benson children were born, as he celebrated the marriage of one daughter and mourned the death of another, Benson stayed home. After spending ten

years away at sea, Benson had kept the promises he had made to himself
on the *Glide* and passed the next decade at home with his wife and family in Salem.[30]

Some of the most important personal events of his life took place during these years, including the births of most of his children, the death of
his daughter Ida, and the marriage of his daughter Fransisca to William
Wentworth, a young waiter from New York living in Salem. He was also,
finally, sharing the struggles and pleasures of black Salem life that his
wife had experienced alone in his absence during the first decade of their
marriage. Side by side the Bensons struggled for their daily bread, as
Charles worked in the best jobs he could find and Jenny took in washing
from Salem's white families. For the first time in his adult life, Benson
committed himself to remaining with his wife and family full-time. By
doing so, he doubtlessly hoped to trade in homesickness and isolation for
family and companionship, the pantry and steward's cabin for home and
hearth. Yet the complexities of real life did not match the idealized version Benson constructed in many of his earlier journal entries, and he encountered unforseen difficulties and challenges ashore. Because Benson
did not keep a journal when he was at home, he did not reveal his innermost feelings in writing. Only after 1875, when he returned to the sea
once more, did he hint at the inner dynamics of his family life in Salem
and what it was that drove him away.

BENSON LEFT home in summer 1875. At forty-five he was old for a seaman, but he had been offered the berth of steward aboard the merchant
bark *Taria Topan* and chose to accept it (fig. 13). The *Taria Topan* was
newly built, completed, and launched in Salem Harbor in 1870 in front of
a large crowd gathered at Derby Wharf, which Benson may have joined.
Named for an Indian merchant who was the longtime customs master at
Zanzibar, the bark joined the *Glide* along the easterly trade routes to and
from Zanzibar, Aden, and Muscat. Now, ready to begin a sixth voyage as
part of Salem's dwindling mercantile fleet, the *Taria Topan* was in need
of a replacement steward, preferably one with experience in the deepwater Zanzibar trade. When the offer was made, Benson obliged, returning to a life he had forsaken nearly eleven years before. After a thirteen-
month stint aboard the *Taria Topan*, Benson along with the captain,
William Beadle, switched to a different vessel, one as familiar to Benson
as his own home in Salem, the bark *Glide*. He remained on the *Glide* as an
active mariner for the rest of his days.

FIGURE 18. *Taria Topan* at anchor. Benson went back to sea on the bark *Taria Topan* in 1875.

No Benson journal exists from his first two voyages in 1875 or 1876; either Benson did not keep a diary, or these particular volumes were somehow separated from his personal papers and lost. For whatever reason, there is no documentation of the bittersweet initial reactions he had upon his return to the sea and seafaring. However, a journal does exist from his 1878 return voyage aboard the *Glide* from Zanzibar, his third in three years since resuming his maritime career. In this journal he does not often reminisce. When he does, he writes of some of the pleasures of home: long walks, market days, and romantic Saturday nights spent in the company of his wife, the same warm scenes that he had envisioned in his journal entries in 1862. But even then his narratives had a new bite to them. During the intervening years he spent in Salem Benson had been stripped of his tendency to idealize his home life. His previous journal volume, composed after a three-month stay at home in 1864, had exhibited the rudiments of a more realistic approach toward marriage. His later narratives, written after he spent ten years in his family's rented house, brought his realism to its full fruition. Where he had once quavered at the vague feeling of being "not wanted" in his own home, Benson now understood with certainty that his proper place might very well be at sea.

In one of his first journal entries after leaving home in 1878 Benson confessed "some of the Blues have worne off & I can begin to feel that I am realy upon the Ocean once more." Although he was still "home sick," Benson admitted, "I know it is for the best that I am away. for there are too many temptations at home, & again how can I ern my bread without it on the mighty deep." His earlier journals expressed despair and despondence at the outset of voyages, especially when he allowed himself to wallow in homesickness. By the 1870s the journal entries he wrote less than a week after he left home balanced his loneliness with his recognition of the necessity of his choice. After a decade at home Benson now knew that he could not "ern his bread" in Salem, for he had tried that and failed. Although he knew he would miss his family over the course of his voyage, he was also aware that life at home was fraught with difficulty. His reference to the "temptations" of home, perhaps referring to sexual intimacy with his wife and her resultant pregnancies, reflected his awareness that his being home meant more children, adding to the burdens of the Benson family.[31]

There were others difficulties at home. In April 1878, en route home from Zanzibar, Benson hinted at these when he wrote:

I feel lonesome to day, my mind is much on home, trying to penetrate the
future, to see what I shall find when I arrive home. it is well I cant, for
troubles come fast enough as time passes away.[32]

Eight months later, on his next voyage, Benson was more clear.

I am real homesick, my mind is continualy at home. How I wish that I
could live on shore, But there are many things that stand in my way on
shore, it is better for me to be at sea. But it is hard. I suppose I must stand
it as long as I can work. & when I can't work I want to "step out."[33]

The journals Benson composed a decade earlier rarely mentioned
"troubles" at home. He had certainly never argued that he was better off
at sea, fixated as he was on the various miseries he experienced on his long
voyages away from home. In the past, when Benson discussed his reasons
for going to sea he did so with regret and sometimes defensiveness, focusing on the economic necessities that had impelled him to leave Salem
and his family. Writing in 1878, well after the end of his decade at home,
Benson now recognized that "many things" prevented him from remaining in Salem. Certainly the tensions of daily family life played a major
part in his discomfort in his own home, something he had first alluded to
in 1864 when he reported feeling "not wanted there." But his reluctance
to identify the "things" that obstructed him ashore suggests that he also
felt some guilt for his decision to leave once again. But now he knew he
could no longer lay all the blame for his wanderings on monetary need,
for he had come to acknowledge his own inner drive to go to sea.

Unwilling as always to be too explicit, Benson expressed the attractions of the sea indirectly. Most often he did so by displaying a new san-
guinity toward the conditions of a seafarer's life, a subject that once suffused his journal. He still mentioned the discomforts and loneliness of
seafaring, but now he restricted such comments to moments of particular shipboard tension. In 1878 and 1879, for example, Benson complained
about his lot only during an encounter with rough seas and stormy
weather, and again during the last days of the voyage when he anticipated
getting home.

The Bark Rolls heavily. There is not much comfort any where. Comfort
was there any comfort any time, or anywhere at sea? I cannot really say I
ever did. it is the excitement, danger, and money that a sea life Brings, that
keeps me at sea. nothing else.[34]

Clearly Benson was proud of the "excitement" and "danger" of his manly occupation, just as he had always linked his job with his sense of manhood.

Despite an occasional note of weariness with life on board ship, Benson seems to have been more content on this voyage than ever before. There was even a spark of humor in his complaint that "this is not liveing it is only Glideing out an existance." And within a few days he resolved, "I will not complain we have been very lucky to get so far, so well. Thank God for it."[35] In general, he was troubled far less by homesickness, which no longer incapacitated him. Now when he thought of home he was more reflective than agonized. "I wish I could stop this fretting about home," he once wrote, "but I cannot it always was so when away."[36] His broadened perspective on his relationship with the sea came not only from years of experience—he had now been a seaman for nearly a quarter-century—but also from the total commitment he had made to seafaring. For the first time ever in his journal entries Benson looked past his arrival home and openly made plans for his "next voyage." He was willing to state, "when I can't work I want to 'step out.'" This from a man who, nearly two decades before, had written, "what a miserable life a sea fareing life is. I will stop it if I live & that soon." With no trace of his former fatalism or melodrama, Benson openly acknowledged that he was a seagoing steward, that he would remain one for the rest of his working life.[37]

Benson now saw little cause for pessimism. He was comfortable with his choice to return to the sea, with his surroundings, and with his role aboard the *Glide*, enough to allow his sense of humor to come to the fore. In late December 1878, for example, shortly after the bark began the last leg of a long voyage, Benson recorded the following story:

> I forgot to state last Monday that we had quite an addition to our famiely, in the shape of 150 Birds. (Paroquets) They were sent on board by Mr. Rider (Joshua) "Gummy" As the sailors on board the Bark Nubia used to call him about 20 years ago. They are part for Mr. Webb & part for Rider I believe. A fine job I have got to take care of them. I don't like them they are noisy & smell sour all the time. I like birds, But nothing of the Parrot kind. My little Canaries are doing well so far. I hope to get them home.

Within two days, Benson noted that he had "Changed the Paroquets from the After to the forward house" because "they have already spoiled more than 500 gallons of water." Later that afternoon he remarked, "looks like rain. I hope it may for we want *Good* water." He concluded, "of Bad we have enough."[38]

Over the next several weeks, it became increasingly obvious that a sailing vessel made a poor aviary. One by one, "Gummy" Rider's 'paroquets' met their untimely end. Two of the birds flew off almost immediately, and soon after Benson reported "No. 3 Paroquet departed." Almost every day Benson noted the death or disappearance of one or two more. Sometimes he would merely note "1 Paroquet gone." On other occasions he would grow more lyrical. "2 Paroquets gone where the 'Woodbine Twineth,'" he wrote on the thirteenth of January, and on the twenty-eighth, "1 paroquet flew out of the cage & lit upon the rigging. he is a 'gorner.'" Benson never recorded how many birds remained by the end of the voyage, but it is unlikely that a significant number of the 'Paroquets' survived the trip home.[39]

At times the *Glide* seemed a lot like a floating menagerie to the steward, who was also charged with the care of other animals aboard the vessel. On a voyage where many of the humans had trouble getting along with each other, including the captain, mate, several of the men, and even Benson and the ship's cook George Morris, Benson took greater pleasure in the company of his own pet birds and the ship's cat. His "little Canaries," who had been his companions on more than one voyage, gave him pleasure: "I have had these Birds a long time," he wrote, "and got quite attached to them." As for the cat, Benson was willing to tolerate misbehavior. "Put lounge cushings & covers out to air," he announced one late December day. "The cat ——— on them last night." Even so, Benson was understanding. "He is apt to do such things," he added, without further comment.[40]

Even such mild scatology would have been out of character for Benson in earlier years, when he confined his observations on bodily functions to clinical descriptions or guilty confessionals. Now he was freer with his pen, more willing to dip into the salty sailor's world. His 1878 journal notebook was adorned with newspaper illustrations of beautiful, curvaceous women, none of them labeled "Jenny" as in days past. They appeared to be there solely for Benson's viewing pleasure, not as representations of middle-class marriage. One picture was especially revealing. It depicted a woman sitting slouched in a chair, her legs slightly apart, with striped stockings visible between the hem of a calf-length skirt and the top of her boots. In a special code that he used for many of his most sensitive statements, Benson captioned the picture, "let me see your cunt," a vulgarism that was atypical of his prior circumspection in his journals (fig. 14).

This particular notebook also contained several other lurid illustrations of melodramatic figures accompanied by Benson's descriptive captions, some coded and some not. A threatening female figure with raised knife is marked "die" in Benson's hand, while another young woman cowering in the arms of her male lover pleads, "save me." In the picture-pages of his journal, cads abound, clutching pretty girls as they demand, "is that so?" or chatting up attractive misses before the eyes of their outraged wives. A proper Victorian gentleman, poised beside his lady as if

FIGURE 14. Image of a woman at a table from Benson's 1878–79 journal. In contrast with earlier years (see figure 7), Benson favored more lurid images by the 1870s.

the two were preparing for a footrace, is urged in code to "catch her, sam!" In middle age, Benson reveled in plebeian tastes he had never before demonstrated. It was as if he had decided to abandon the *Salem Gazette* in favor of the *Police Gazette*. He was acting less like a middle-class officer in his journal and more like a sailor, for all his affectations and protestations to the contrary. Instead of trying to replicate the respectable world of the shore at sea, as he had in the early 1860s, Benson now took on some of the rough-and-tumble characteristics of the working-class fo'c'sle. He was privileging the sea over the shore, choosing to fit his image of the former where he had once yearned for the latter.

At various times in these later years Benson felt more at home at sea than he was ashore. Early in 1878 the relief in his writing was palpable after his "Blues" passed and he felt he was "realy upon the Ocean once more." As he remarked several days after leaving home, "things begin to feal natural again."[41] Benson also expressed greater pleasure in other aspects of his life on the "mighty deep." At sea he witnessed sights unseen by shore dwellers in Salem;

> at sundown saw the sun just on the Western horizon & the Moon just on the Eastern. it was a Glorious sight. Oh! if I only had language to describe the scene. I will say it Looked first rate.[42]

In the 1860s Benson usually concluded his descriptions of the wonder and beauty of the sea by wishing that his wife were there with him. Not so on this occasion, when he merely expressed his reactions without further comment. On another "lovely night," with the moon "about full & there is not a cloud to be seen in the heavens," Benson did "wish Jennie was here"—but only "for a while" (fig. 15). When Benson saw "an Eclips of the moon" in 1880 he again enjoyed the "glorious sight" without expressing his wish to share it with Jenny. He even gloated, adding, "they could not see it at home."[43]

Of course Benson still missed his wife and family, and he continued to express his desire to remain ashore with them. "May God help me," he wrote at the outset of his 1878–79 voyage, "for I want to stop with my famiely." Benson knew from long experience that months of loneliness, discomfort, boredom, and homesickness awaited him on his journey, and he acknowledged this when he wrote:

> I felt very sad. . . . it was time to turn in, Oh! dear How lonely I felt, no Jennie, no Willie, no Charlie. don't blame me if a few tears droped on my pillow. no man loves his family better than I.

FIGURE 15. The *Taria Topan* under sail.

Yet he ended philosophically: "I must take things as they come, I suppose."[44] Benson had a new outlook, a more realistic one. He was and would remain torn between the competing attractions of the sea and the shore. But he now accepted the likelihood that he would spend most of the rest of his life at sea.

Benson reserved his strongest appreciation of sea life for his vessel, his familiar and beloved bark *Glide*. As he wrote once when leaving Zanzibar,

> Thank god we are free from the land once more. I love the wide Ocean to sail on. I don't like this being pokeing around the land. I never feel right until all land is out of sight.[45]

In fact, Benson's home was not the sea itself but the *Glide*, his vessel. In several journal entries his sense of connection to and pride in the vessel that sheltered him is palpable. In the aftermath of a dangerous encounter with a waterspout, Benson thanked "the Bark" for saving all aboard from "the Whirlwind." After one "perfect Hurrycane," when the bark "tossed & pitched about like mad," he observed, "our good Bark rode it out nobely, she is a fine sea boat." And when the *Glide* had the opportunity to outdistance a French vessel on the open sea, he described how "Mistress Glide tossed up her head, and off she sped leaveing the poor french man behind." After a similar incident he wrote, "Hurah, Hurah! for the Bonie Glide. She is, and always was my Joy and Pride." Benson felt he belonged at sea, and he belonged aboard the *Glide*.[46]

By the end of the 1870s Charles Benson was back at sea for good aboard the *Glide*, and he had made his peace with that life. His attempt to fit into shore life in Salem had lasted a decade but was ultimately doomed. Three years after that period of his life ended Benson could admit this with some equanimity. But when he first returned to sea in 1875, Benson may have experienced some severe misgivings about going back to seafaring. As he would discover on his first voyage aboard the *Taria Topan*, he faced many new circumstances in the maritime world he had once known. Like Benson himself, seafaring had changed while he was ashore in Salem.

CHAPTER NINE

"I am realy upon the Ocean once more"

AT SEA, 1875–1880

WHEN CHARLES BENSON lugged the sea chest that held all of his important belongings up the gangplank of the merchant bark *Taria Topan* in July 1875, he was boarding a vessel that had not even been built the last time he had been to sea. But he surely felt right at home within moments. Commissioned by the owner, John Bertram, the *Taria Topan* was evocative of Bertram's *Glide*, although its 630-ton capacity dwarfed that of its smaller 490-ton predecessor. The two vessels were also commanded by many of the same officers during this era. Among others, captains William Hathorne, Nathan Bachelder, Edward Trumbull, and William Beadle all transferred back and forth between the barks, in some cases after serving first as mates and later as masters on either or both vessels. When Benson returned to sea in 1875, he made the same transition from *Glide* to *Taria Topan* as the officers he served and settled himself in the *Taria Topan's* pantry and galley. He would switch back the following year.[1]

Once aboard, Benson discovered that little had changed since his last voyage eleven years earlier. The physical layout of the vessel and the mechanics and conditions of seafaring were all familiar, and the tasks of a steward were second nature to a man with his extensive experience in that position. Benson had made numerous lengthy journeys before his retirement from seafaring, so the 382-day voyage he now took aboard the *Taria Topan* represented nothing new for him. The vessel's trading routes to and from ports in the Indian Ocean and Red Sea were also well-known to Benson, who had made at least eight consecutive trips to the same destinations between 1857 and 1864.[2]

Yet changes had occurred in the years that he had been ashore, and these altered the rituals of Benson's departure. In prior years, Benson's voyages began at the wharves of Salem, and most ended there as well.

However, by the time Benson shipped out in 1875 practically no foreign-bound vessels sailed from Salem any longer. The *Taria Topan* had departed from Salem but once, on her maiden voyage to Zanzibar in 1870; after that the vessel was never seen in Salem again, from her return to Boston Harbor in 1871 until her loss off the South American coast in 1894. The last vessel that came to Salem after rounding the Cape of Good Hope at Africa's southern tip had been the *Glide*, which arrived there in 1870 shortly after the *Taria Topan*'s launch. After her subsequent departure from Salem five weeks later, the *Glide* too returned to Boston Harbor, the vessel's U.S. port of call for the remainder of its existence. So when Benson left home in 1875 for the first time after a ten-year layoff, he did not head toward the familiar Salem docks but to the city's Eastern Railroad station. There he caught the train that would henceforth transport him to his place aboard vessels docked in Boston.[3]

Benson's new routine reflected the differences in the maritime commercial world he was rejoining. Over the prior decade Salem's maritime fortunes had continued to dip, and by 1875 fewer Salem-owned vessels traversed the globe than at any prior time in the nineteenth century. Also, the number of men, particularly black men, employed in the maritime trades had decreased dramatically. Benson's return to deepwater sailing coincided with demise of maritime Salem, as he was surely aware. Benson no longer traversed Salem streets crowded with sailors from around the world. Even during his years ashore Benson must have noticed the disappearance of his company of black cooks and stewards. In the 1850s Benson had more than fifty fellow black townsmen who made their living at sea; by 1880 he was one of only three active black mariners in Salem.

Drastic changes had also taken place around the world during Benson's retirement from seafaring, especially in Zanzibar, where he had spent so much time in earlier years. In April 1872 the island of Zanzibar was blasted by a powerful hurricane. The winds that buffeted the small island were powerful, destructive, and unexpected. The yearly monsoon, or "Great Masika," did not usually begin until mid-May, but the 1872 monsoon was not only early but explosive in its force. Virtually all of the island's trees were felled or uprooted, and the clove trees that were the island's staple suffered grievously. Cloves were Zanzibar's major crop and export good and were virtually the only home-grown product of Zanzibar's plantation-based agricultural system. After the hurricane, the clove groves and stored supplies were almost entirely wiped out. Although clove supplies were still sufficient to meet worldwide demand thanks to

operations on the nearby island of Pemba, which had better weathered
the hurricane, the island's planters were unable to recover from this disaster. As a result, clove prices rose sharply when Zanzibar's wealthiest
traders imposed high export taxes in an effort to cut their losses as much
as possible.[4]

The hurricane struck Zanzibar at a moment when the commercial center was already reeling from the forces of political, economic, and social
change. The most recent scion of the Al Bu Said dynasty, Sayyid Majid,
had been ruler of the island and its commercial empire for over a decade;
Benson had glimpsed Majid's "very white" Georgian concubines at a distance in 1862 and served lemonade to his son the "young prince." When
Majid died in 1870, his death came as a sudden and unexpected shock. His
successor, his brother and former rival for the throne, Sayyid Barghash,
proved to be far less capable. Within only months of ascending the throne
Barghash became embroiled in a conflict with local representatives of
the British government over his empire's longstanding, large, and lucrative trade in African slaves. Zanzibar also faced a major economic crisis
related to both the hurricane damage and its political power structure.
Most of the landed Arab aristocracy of Zanzibar, including the dynastic
rulers, were deeply indebted to Indian moneylenders and traders. Zanzibar's overproduction of cloves had led to economic stagnation and planter
indebtedness over the previous quarter-century, leaving most of the
island's Arab-owned plantations mortgaged to the Indian contingent.
Attempts to raise revenues through higher duties or heavy borrowing
from foreign governments ended in failure, and during the early years of
Barghash's rule the Indians, especially the customs master Tharia Topan,
came to dominate Zanzibar's economy.

The completion of the Suez Canal in 1869 and the establishment of
regular steamship travel to Europe in 1872 led to further upheaval in
Zanzibar. The island was now at the center of a flurry of new trading and
political activities by European nations eager to exploit their access to
the Indian Ocean region. These changes were accompanied by a rapid
rise in urbanization as migrants converged on Zanzibar Town, which became crowded with people and refuse. In 1869 and 1870 this influx led to
a massive cholera epidemic that killed nearly half of the town's eighty
thousand residents. Between the transformations caused by disease,
population movement, and changes in the island's rulership and leading
traders, Zanzibar was already in severe upheaval when the hurricane hit
it in 1872.[5]

These profound changes coincided with the marked deterioration in America's trading position in Zanzibar, which had eroded steadily since the onset of the Civil War. As Benson remembered from his last voyage to that part of the world in 1864, the markets for U.S. trade goods were drying up and the number of U.S. vessels active in trading was dwindling. In the absence of any significant U.S. commercial presence, gum copal and ivory prices fell, hurting Zanzibar's traders throughout the 1860s. As European nations took more of an interest in Indian Ocean commerce in the 1860s and 1870s, the American presence and importance in Zanzibar corroded further.[6]

The decline of the U.S. trade in Zanzibar was neither complete nor irreparable. Benson's return there aboard the *Taria Topan* in 1875 came at a time of revitalization, when the poor trade in cotton was replaced by the growing East African demand for inexpensive American kerosene. Vessels like the *Taria Topan* sailed for East Africa loaded with lighting fluid, and some small quantities of cotton cloth. As one contemporary Salem ship master noted, they also bore "notions of all kinds, which the captains took out for ventures" for their own personal profit, ranging from silks and linens to alarm clocks. U.S. trading vessels returned home carrying Omani dates and coffee, dried and salted animal hides from Zanzibar and Aden, and generous quantities of ivory, a market in which American traders had a large share. This was thanks in no small part to their close ties to powerful Indian merchants like Tharia Topan, perhaps the most powerful segment of Zanzibar's economic community. At the forefront of this effort was Captain John Bertram of Salem, baron of the most successful of the three American mercantile houses remaining on the island by the 1870s, and the same man who had first opened the island up to American commerce four decades earlier.[7]

So in 1875 Charles A. Benson, steward, returned to seafaring under similar but altered circumstances. His employer, destination, and vessel were all familiar but not quite the same as they once were. John Bertram was aging and less involved with his business, which now operated free of the Salem mercantile competitors with whom he had struggled in prior years. Although Benson's experiences in foreign ports were basically the same in terms of the people, places, living conditions, and responsibilities he had in the trading centers he visited, the commercial, political, and social environments in Zanzibar and its tributary ports of Aden and Muscat had changed a great deal in his absence. The existing volumes of Benson's journals give no indication that he had any difficulty adapting to these subtle alterations, just as he had adapted to the conditions he had already encountered over his first decade of seafaring. But Benson's journal entries do identify one major change that disrupted his own shipboard life as well as the equilibrium of everyone aboard: new commanding officers.

By 1875 few if any of Charles Benson's former captains still served as active shipmasters. Over the years most had retired from seafaring, and many had already been middle-aged or older by the time they rose through crowded ranks of seamen to become captains. Some of Benson's captains had died during his self-imposed retirement, including Captain John McMullan. McMullan's replacement, William Hathorne, formerly a first mate, became one of a new breed of ship captains when he took charge of the *Glide*, his first command, on that 1865 voyage. Hathorne had some seafaring experience from his U.S. Navy service during the Civil War. Yet he had spent the latter part of the war ashore as a Washington bureaucrat and had not been to sea for some time when he signed on as mate of the *Glide* after the end of the war. He was also extraordinarily young when he assumed command; the crew list for the *Glide's* 1865 voyage listed his age as twenty-two.[8]

Bertram's decision to overlook Hathorne's youth and inexperience and keep him on as captain of the *Glide* and later the *Taria Topan* reflects the circumstances he faced in the postwar era. Hathorne was a capable mariner, but more important, he was a skilled negotiator and a shrewd trader. These qualities garnered him a role as U.S. consul (and, not coincidentally, as Bertram's business agent) at Zanzibar when he gave up his command of the *Taria Topan* in 1875. John Bertram had need of such men in the volatile East African trade of the 1860s and 1870s, especially at a time of maritime decline, for the attrition of Salem's maritime fortunes was accompanied by a contraction in the pool of suitable officers. Relatively young men, like Hathorne and contemporaries such as the thirty-one-year-old Edward Trumbull, who rose to the captaincy in 1884, were given the opportunity to prove their mettle on Bertram's behalf. Both Hathorne and Trumbull ably carried out their responsibilities and even prospered. Others were less successful, including one in particular: Captain William Beadle, Benson's commander on all of the voyages he made during the latter part of his career, between 1875 and 1881.

William Beadle was thirty-four years old when he became master of the *Taria Topan* in 1875, on the voyage that also marked Benson's return to the sea after his decade ashore (fig. 16). Beadle had been a seafarer since he was fifteen, when he served as a ship's boy aboard the Salem bark *Iosco* on a voyage to and from Mozambique and Zanzibar. Over the ensuing years he rose to the level of officer, serving as mate aboard at least six vessels before gaining command of the schooner *Julia Parsons*, which was wrecked on his first voyage as captain. Beadle then returned to service as a first mate, finding a berth aboard the *Glide* under the command of the novice captain James S. Williams, a longtime mate aboard the vessel. Williams, too, was recovering from the wrecking of his first command, the maiden voyage of the new Bertram-owned bark *Jersey*. Like Williams, Beadle would also receive a second chance at command from Bertram, whose desperation for captains with East African experience may have influenced his choice of Beadle as master of the *Taria Topan* in 1875.[9]

While Benson's observations about his voyage with Beadle aboard the *Taria Topan* are unavailable, he did write at length about the man's personal habits and professional skills in the journals he kept aboard the *Glide* in 1878–79 and 1880–81. The picture that emerges is one of insecurity and inability in a man who may have been the least capable officer Benson ever met in a long seafaring career. Beadle's weakness as a commanding officer were obvious and frequently grating to Benson and many of the other men of the *Glide*, causing tension aboard the vessel that sometimes spilled over into violent outbreaks between the men and even the officers. When Benson returned to sea in 1875 he sought peace—relief from the tensions of his home life and all the other difficulties of life on shore, a sense of occupational and financial stability, and even the serenity of quiet moonlit nights at sea. Instead he encountered the "Everlasting Quarreling" between the captain and his officers, among the mates, and between the officers and the men. To his consternation Benson became embroiled in all this "growling," and he too found himself at odds with the captain, the mates, the cooks of the *Glide*, and even with his beloved Jenny. Of all the changes Benson faced this was the most drastic and difficult, and it contributed to the unhappiness that overtook Benson with greater frequency in the last years of his life.

Benson's 1878–79 journal volume began in Zanzibar, the last stop of a voyage "from Boston to Tamatave Madagascar. Madagascar to Aden, Arabia. Arabia to Zanzibar & from Zanzibar . . . to Boston Mass." The continuation of a previous volume (Benson wrote "my first book was too small. I had to bye this one in Aden"), this journal was composed on Benson's fourth voyage since his return to active seafaring, and his fourth with Captain Beadle. It differed from the journals of the 1860s in several important ways. Benson was more free with his personal opinions and more garrulous and generally less self-absorbed than in earlier writings. For the first time, he regularly allowed his experience and familiarity with the ways of sailing vessels and the sea to rise to the fore. He also revealed other changes in his perspective on marriage, family, work, and life in general. Like all journal-keeping sailors, he continued to devote much attention to doings aboard ship, reporting anything interesting that occurred on board the *Glide*. As a result of Benson's new concerns and writing style, his journal entries are usually lucid, expressive, and at times extremely frank. This new candor is particularly true of his direct and detailed assessment of Captain Beadle.

In March 1878 the *Glide* began the homeward-bound leg of an eight-

FIGURE 16. William Beadle, a poor seaman and commander, was Benson's captain for the last six years of his life.

month voyage, a passage that would take only sixty-six days, breaking speed records for the Zanzibar-Boston Atlantic crossing. Most aboard, however, were preoccupied with a rash of sickness that affected many of the men of the *Glide*, including both mates, the cook, five crewmen, and Benson. After several days most of the sick men felt better, but when the *Glide* began to encounter rough seas Benson reported:

> the mate was quite unwell, & is not much better to day. Captain is rather off the hooks, he always is in rough weather. I gave Captain a dose of Senna this afternoon he wanted it.[10]

Over the next several days Benson described the conduct of an obstreperous sailor on the sick list named "Peaterson," whose condition prompted Benson to write "his name ought to be Job for he is filled with boils." Peaterson's work-shirking and back talk to the mates and the captain resulted in his disratement as a seaman, a procedure that included Benson's participation and signature as an official witness in the captain's private log. Shortly thereafter Benson recorded the following exchange between himself and the captain:

> Captain not feeling very well . . . 8 Pm strong breese, & the weather feels to me like a change, a storm, of wind or rain or both. I mentioned it to captain, he laughed at me & said there would be no change until the barometer fell. I said I think there will in less than 24 hours.

Benson's entry for the following day read:

> This day came in with a gail of wind & heavy sea. Last night it blew very hard, in squalls, & rained in torrents at times . . . *the change came.*[11]

Shortly thereafterward the captain was confronted with more insubordination. The ship's parrot had the temerity to nip the captain on the finger. His response was to "beat the bird" so violently that it flew (or more accurately, fell) overboard, "swallowed salt water," and expired. "Moral,' wrote Benson, 'never beat loose Parrots at sea.'"[12]

These early 1878 journal entries introduced many themes that would recur in Benson's descriptions of Captain Beadle's command of the *Glide*, beginning with the captain's intestinal indispositions. On several occasions Benson noted that Captain Beadle was "not very well," once mentioning the "pain in his bowels" and once that the shipmaster was "very bilious." Benson did not mince words when explaining the causes of the captain's difficulties. In May 1878 Benson wrote,

Captain . . . has had a bad look for full a week, there has been a cold working in his system for some time. He does not wear <u>appropriate</u> <u>clothing</u> for
all the different changes we have to undergo.[13]

On more than one occasion, Benson linked the captain's poor health to
his eating habits. In early 1878 he wrote,

Captain & Mate not feeling very well. They have been eating lots of Hot
pastry of late. I have told them that it would hurt them, but they said no.
They find I was right, but will not give in. Oh! how some people love their
belleys.[14]

On his next voyage Benson reported that the first mate of the *Glide*,
Charles Welch, was "not very well last night nor to day." Welch's discomfort was due to overeating, as Benson described: "Captain and mate both
eat very hearty of Buckweat Cakes every morning and both are takeing
medicine for Dispepsia."[15] After Captain Beadle's biliousness recurred
Benson observed that Beadle "may have a fever. He don't seem to want to
stop eating long enough to take medicine." The captain's capricious behavior regarding medicine compounded his condition, as demonstrated
by his choice to follow the medical advice and prescriptions advocated by
a quack homeopath named Doctor Cate. The Cate plan cost the captain
fourteen dollars; "Captain thought it real cheap," Benson commented,
adding "I did not think so." After prolonging his agony with steady doses
of this "Homeopathy" for a week, Captain Beadle finally stopped taking
Cate's medicine and improved rapidly. Benson did not hide his sense of
vindication from his journals. "I do not believe in Doctor Cate," he wrote.
"Captain has taken his Madicine & followed all the rules strictly & is
worse to day than he was the day he left. How is that for Cate?"[16]

Benson's criticism of immoderate behavior was not limited to Captain
Beadle. In the pages of his journal Benson also scolded the *Glide*'s cook,
second mate, and several of the men for smoking, drinking, or whoring
to excess. In 1880, he reluctantly set out to cure Bill, a ship's boy, of "the
Ladies Fever." "I am sorry for him," Benson remarked, "But them that will
dance must pay."[17] He showed the same mixture of sympathy and exas-
peration toward the master of the *Glide*, whose standards fell far short of
Benson's personal and professional ideals.

Captain Beadle was not merely an idiosyncratic commander. Benson's
journals testify that at times Beadle's seamanship approached a level of
ineptitude that was dangerous enough to imperil the welfare of all aboard

the *Glide.* His deficiencies also extended to interpersonal relationships with those under his command. Captain Beadle's technical and personal missteps sowed tension and discord on several of the *Glide*'s voyages. His crew suffered the consequences, to their chagrin and his.

Beadle's poor skills as a shipmaster were apparent from the outset of his career as a commander. After the wreck of his first vessel, the schooner *Julia Parsons*, and his subsequent demotion to mate, he did not regain command until some years later, when he captained the *Taria Topan* on an 1875–76 voyage from Boston to Zanzibar, Aden, and Muscat. The voyage took over a year to complete, and it is probable that the trip was lengthened by Beadle's lack of seafaring aptitude. This ineptitude was demonstrated by the vessel's performance on the last leg of the voyage. Whereas the *Taria Topan* took over four months to complete the passage from Zanzibar to Boston, the *Glide*, under the command of the senior captain Nathan Bachelder, left Zanzibar over a month later but arrived in Boston on the very same day as the *Taria Topan* in May 1876. Beadle's poor performance as captain of the *Taria Topan* resulted in his transfer off the larger vessel after only one voyage; his replacement was Captain Bachelder, who would remain in command of the *Taria Topan* for nine voyages before his retirement from seafaring in 1884, at the age of sixty-three. Beadle exchanged posts with Bachelder, moving to the smaller and older *Glide* after his removal from the *Taria Topan*. With Beadle as captain, his brother Charles Beadle as first mate, and Charles Benson as steward, the *Glide* left Boston for Zanzibar in September 1876. Shortly after her arrival there in December, the *Glide* ran aground on the northern tip of the island.[18]

With the exception of Benson's weather-related disagreement with Captain Beadle, his journal entries from the *Glide*'s following voyage from August 1877 until June 1878 do not mention any severe mistakes on Beadle's part. Of course, this volume of the journal covered only the last three months of the voyage, which consisted of relatively smooth sailing on the homebound passage. Benson's account of the next voyage, from 1878 to 1879, tells a different story. All seemed uneventful on the first leg of the journey, which took the vessel to a preliminary stop at Zanzibar. Once there, however, things began to deteriorate. As Benson later reported,

> November 1st . . . The mates accounts don't agree, with accounts on shore. I do not know who is right. *They* are haveing lots of trouble about Ac-

counts this voyage, in Zanzibar it was confusion all the time. Captain & mate had sharp words in the hold about stowing Cargo.

The vessel's next scheduled stop was a mainland port in the Red Sea, Abdul Kori. When the bark sighted the destination, more chaos ensued when the captain misidentified it as an unknown island. Unmoved by the remonstrances of both the mate and Charles Benson, his most experienced sailor, Captain Beadle refused to change his opinion until several men aboard proved conclusively that he was mistaken. Beadle thereupon admitted that he had been not only wrong but stubborn, adding that he really did not know Indian Ocean navigation.[19]

Despite the captain's admission, this scenario recurred a month later, when the *Glide* was on her way south to Tamatave, Madagascar, the last stop before the passage home to Boston. On November 29 Benson wrote that Charles Welch, the first mate, "said twice he saw Plumb Island from aloft . . . the captain says no." The following day the mate insisted that he was right, noting that if that was indeed Plumb Island then the *Glide* had missed Madagascar entirely and was now far off course. "Captain says no & stands down south," Benson wrote that morning, but a noon observation confirmed the mate's suspicions: "by observation we find our selves nearly 50 miles to the southard of Tamatave." After two days of northerly backtracking the captain was certain that they had reached Tamatave, and so set the studdinsails to move the vessel toward a stretch of coastline visible off the bow. Benson suspected otherwise, and so, he reported:

> I watched the land sharp & was soon satisfied that we were a long way to southard of Tamatave. I made a noise which awoke Captain (He haveing turned in & was fast asleep) and told him that I had been looking at the land (He had asked me three times during the forenoon if I had looked & I had told him no I was too busy) and should say we were full 25 or 30 miles south of Tamatave. He immediately got up, took his Mariene Glasses & went aloft. Soon came down & ordered studdinsails in & the Bark braced sharp on the wind . . . I wish I was at Salem.[20]

Benson probably wished he was at Salem again on the following day when the bark, still sailing northward, sighted another island. A nettled Captain Beadle declared that this was in fact Plumb Island, implying that the mate's identification of Plumb Island to the south a week earlier was wrong. Benson, unconvinced, peered through the thick rain and fog enclosing the vessel and noticed a "Bunch" (of trees, probably) on the island. He concluded that they were at Fong Island, which lay between Plumb

Island and Tamatave. With some difficulty Benson persuaded the mate that he was right, but the captain was another matter.

> At the Dinner Table the Mate remarked "That is Fong Island" Captain asked "How do you make that out? "That is Plumb Island[.]" the Mate said No sir "Fong Island." Then they had a hot argument, both left the table & went on deck. Captain took his book to prove his words, & the Mate pointed out the different points on shore to prove his statement. The mate was right He soon proved to Captains satisfaction that he was right & Captain wrong
>
> it was well Mr. Welch convinced him he was wrong, for we soon could all see, if we had gone a few miles farther in shore, we would never have come out again, for the water was breaking over the reefs all around & about these Islands, (for there are several Fong Islands) & the wind was blowing in shore, & also a very heavy ground swell sitting us in shore. . . .
>
> The truth is The Mate saved the Bark. At the dinner table Captain Beadle made these remarks. Said he, "To tell the truth I do not know any thing about this damned land, I can only tell Tamatave when I get near enough to see the Goveners Flag Staff, & see both reefs & get hold of certain points Then I know where Tamatave is and not a damned mite be fore.["] These are his very words.[21]

William Beadle had first traveled to the Indian Ocean as a boy of fifteen and had spent as much time in East African waters as he had at home in Salem over the course of the next twenty-two years. Now a mature ship captain, Beadle was forced to admit that his knowledge of his craft came only from books and that he had developed little in the way of seafaring skill as he rose through the ranks. Beadle proved that his reluctant confession rankled a bit three days later, when the first mate sent word through Benson that he was unwell (a sickly man, Welch often suffered painful spells and headaches). Welch requested relief from his duties. As Benson reported afterward, "I told Captain. Mate did not get relief."[22]

Relations between Beadle and Welch had never been good, except, perhaps, when the two men sat at a table together eating too much. On numerous occasions Benson noted "Captain & Mate <u>XXX</u>," "Captain & Mate had sharp words," and "Captain & Mate cannot agree about hardly anything these days."[23] After the Fong Island episode the tension between the two men became almost unbearable, causing Benson to remark:

> 6 Pm light wind, but heavy weather between Captain and mate. They are haveing another of their Growls They are ever at it one way or the other,

They have no comfort themselves & don't seem to want any body else to have any. it has been thus nearly the whole of the Voyage, & I shall be glad when it is at an end, for it is very uncomfortable to be where there are two forever a growling & fault finding. Well! there it is, & here we are![24]

The constant difficulties between the two officers affected every aspect of shipboard life. "Each one seems to try to anoy the other," Benson wrote in obvious frustration, "& let every thing else have a miner consideration."

> one will not give in & the other will not give in so there it is many things are destroyed, many things are not done, The vessel is not cared for, the cargo is not stowed, & in fact every thing about us is at heads & points just because Captain & Mate are ever at varience.[25]

Conflict spread throughout the vessel. Crewmen shirked their tasks, defied orders, and administered "poundings" to one another. Their behavior prompted beatings at the hands of officers or got them clapped in irons by the captain, who would brook no insolence from the men after his own difficulties with the mate.[26] As the ship's parrot discovered to its detriment in May 1878, Captain Beadle's temper grew increasingly violent. He would explode at the least provocation, and in the absence of animal targets—Beadle was fond of shooting at whales, hawks, and other wild creatures the *Glide* encountered at sea—he directed his fury at people.[27] When a ship's boy angered the captain on one such occasion, he was put in irons, beaten severely, and knocked repeatedly against the heavy ship's wheel on deck. The captain, wrote Benson, "beat him until the 2d mate asked him to stop. . . . the Boy cried & screached both times he was Beaten by Captain Beadle." This all took place before the horrified crewmen, who were forcibly prevented by the mate from leaving the fo'c'sle to interfere with the captain's justice. "The cause of this I don't Pretend to know or say," Benson concluded. "All I know it was done."[28] Although Captain Beadle never raised his hand against his officers, they were also not immune to punishment. After exchanging "hot words" with the captain in 1878, the second mate, Charles White, was put in irons and demoted just one day before the *Glide* docked in Boston after 291 days at sea.[29]

Benson often found himself trapped in the middle of the conflict on board the *Glide*, as both Beadle and Welch attempted to draw him into their feud, constantly talking "about . . . one the other" to the steward. At times the captain purposely sent Benson on errands that would draw the mate's ire, dispatching him to bother Welch for course changes or to "change the kerosene in the Mates lamp & put in Whale oil." The resentful mate responded by flying "into a great pashion" of rage. After the lamp episode Benson remarked that the mate "was very angry, he cursed and swore at me in a very disagreeable manner." More than once the mate expressed his anger at the captain by verbally abusing his steward.

Benson's response in almost all of these cases was to avoid joining the conflict as best he could. When the mate took umbrage at Benson's offering navigational advice to the captain, Benson "made no reply." Nor did he tell the captain afterward exactly what the mate had said to him about the matter, although Beadle asked him about it "several times." Once, when Benson heard "angry voices" in the Aft cabins of the officers, he wrote that he "stoped" on his way there to stay out of the quarrel. And when Beadle administered his brutal beating to "the Boy Antone," Benson wrote, "When I saw Captain Beadle Beating the Boy upon the deck, I went into the galley out of sight, so as not to witness it." But although Benson remained aloof from the many quarrels of the *Glide*'s officers and men, he still became embroiled in contretemps of his own that were more painful and affecting than the "growls" between the officers, making Benson's last years at sea especially difficult.[30]

By 1880 Charles Benson was old for a seafarer and a northern black man. He was fifty years old, around the same age his father probably was when he died. He had outlived most of his relatives and one or more of his children. Though he was in fairly good health for a career seaman, the stress of his sea life was getting to him. More than ever, Benson had to look to his own inner values and strength to complete his own sense of self. Cut off from nearly everyone around him by both the requirements of his occupation and ever-present interpersonal conflicts, Benson's psyche was taking a beating. His body fared no better, battered by the same shipboard conditions that had nearly taken his life long before. "this going to sea it will kill me," Benson once wrote. He was right.

CHAPTER TEN

"This going to sea, it will kill me"

AT SEA, 1880–1881

"I SHALL BE glad when we get home, so to get free from this everlasting quarreling," Charles Benson wrote in February 1879.[1] He referred to the quarrels of others aboard the *Glide*—the men, the officers, and especially the captain and the mate. But Benson's life would never again be free of conflict. Being at home in Salem freed him from the quarrels of the *Glide*, but he faced his own domestic disputes when he remained there for any extended time, as well as the alienation and isolation he had come to feel among the black community there. His disagreements at sea, with the cook or the captain, also disrupted the peace that Benson wished to cultivate for himself. Even in the privacy of his own thoughts, Benson faced conflicts about his race, his values, his role within his family, and the choices he made in his life. During the last decade of his life Benson really did face "everlasting" conflict, for he was never without it very long.

Benson's isolation at sea had come to extend even to his relationships with his black shipmates. The values he espoused in his journal, such as pride in his work, love of family, and moderation in personal habits, were those of the respectable middle class. These values brought him into conflict with other working-class blacks who did not necessarily share his views. They, like Benson, were black men in low-status jobs; but unlike Benson, they did not always attempt to propagate middle-class values and apply them to their own experiences. Moreover, when these men went to sea they did so only for the short term; they spent the remainder of their days ashore as members of working-class black communities. Charles Benson had always remained aloof from communal life, an attitude that put him even further out of step with the younger black men with whom he shared the *Glide*'s galley. As Benson appeared to reject his closest peers in his quest for respectability, they in turn rejected him and his philosophies. Benson never let go of the personal code that had guided

169

him for most of his adult life, but he grew increasingly alone in his dedication to these values.[2]

Benson often found himself at odds with the various cooks of the *Glide*.
The first cook who clashed with Benson was George Morris, a black
Salemite in his forties and a contemporary of Benson's. In 1878, as in earlier years, Benson's judgments of the cook took the form of small sniping
jabs at his personal habits: "Cook has a pain in his 'Donkey,'" Benson
wrote when Morris complained of chest pains. "I think he uses altogether
too much Tobacco."[3] At the same time, Benson was often far more critical of Morris than he had been of his cooks in the 1860s. On July 21, 1878,
Benson remarked, "the cook is not much company this voyage." He then
elaborated further:

> He has finished all his small talk & he is not booked up either on Politicks,
> History, Poetry, or Religion. I was surprised when I found George so defi-
> cient about the things of the world. He has never read much, & has
> thought less. He has a great many old, crude ideas.

Perhaps Benson, a voracious reader himself, put some effort into fur-
thering his shipmate's education; he later noted that "[Morris] has taken
to reading & I see that there is a great improvement in his manner of
thinking of many things." It would appear that these changes were not
permanent, however, for several months later Benson wrote, "Cook out
of sorts, he often is. He has some odd, oldfashion, funny ways that makes
it hard to get along with [him]." In the end, Benson's attempts to provide
guidance may have caused additional friction between the two men. "It is
getting very disagreeable to have one jealous & suspicious of every move
they don't seem to understand," Benson wrote in reference to Morris.
"Well, such is life."[4]

After Morris left the *Glide* in 1879, the atmosphere in the galley took
a turn for the worse. The man who signed on as cook for the *Glide*'s 1880
voyage was a drunkard, and his frequent imbibing interfered with his
work and his relationship with Benson, the ship's steward.[5] While in port
at Majunga in June 1880, Benson reported that "Cook drank so much rum
that he got on a sick Tight, had a vomiting spell, insulted me, & turned
in." Over the next few days the cook remained out of sorts. Benson wrote,
"Cook not perfectly in order ... underweigh again, but makeing bad
weather." Less than two weeks later, with the bark still anchored in port,
Benson noted tersely, "Cook Tight."[6] No doubt Benson feared the worst,

and indeed the cook's condition deteriorated even further. On July 9, 1880, Benson described his latest run-in with the cook in his journal.

> Cook has been drinking early this morning. I smell the Confounding Rum. He is full of talk & seems to think he is deceiving every one, yet all hands are takeing notice of it. The Cook and I had some sharp words. He got so tight that he turned in. I with great difficulty awoke him, telling him that Captain was comeing and we were to go to sea. He arose with great confusion at first & then broke out in great rage, calling me names not belonging to me. I tried to reason with him, there was no such thing as reason in him. He is a bad man to get tight—he will listen to no one. 4 Pm Cook to tight to work, turned in. I went into the gally & got supper, & cleared away. 7 Pm. Cook awoke and was very insulting in his language. He ever is when in rum.[7]

Three days later, the cook was drunk again, "half knocked up," as Benson put it. The drunken cook, who remained unnamed throughout Benson's diary of the voyage, did not return for the *Glide*'s next voyage. However, his replacement caused similar problems; on the day of departure Benson reported, "I went on board every thing was in confusion the cook was not there . . . in about half an hour My cook came drunk."[8] Benson disapproved of this behavior, and expressed his feelings mildly by writing "it is all his own fault," and "Smart <u>man</u>, I do not think."[9]

And so his isolation was exacerbated by his rifts with the cooks of the *Glide*, his only black companions on his long journeys. In 1880, during his difficulties with his drunken cook at Majunga Harbor, Benson wrote, "I am real lonesome, more so since the Cook gives me trouble."[10] In the 1860s Benson and the cooks John L. Jones and Aaron Moses had spent a great deal of time together, talking about the familiar people and places of black Salem. But on these later voyages Benson lacked this camaraderie that made seafaring bearable. In the absence of any close personal relationship, Benson had to live without the sense of community that had sustained him on his voyages two decades earlier. This was even true in 1878, when the *Glide*'s cook was George Morris, an apparently responsible man who did not drink or neglect his duties, and an acquaintance of Benson's before the two men even shipped out together. Back in the late 1860s Benson had clerked for Joseph Morris, George's brother, in his oyster-house; the two men were also neighbors on Creek Street, where the Bensons, at number 6, lived adjacent to George and his mother, Mercy

Morris, who dwelled at number 5 Creek Street. Yet despite their prior connections, Benson and Morris did not forge a tight personal bond with each other.

Benson's journal suggests that their individual temperaments and attitudes had a great deal to do with that: according to Benson, Morris's old-fashioned ways and suspicious nature made any close relationship impossible. Yet Benson's own idiosyncracies must have been equally off-putting for Morris, who apparently did not share Benson's more esoteric interests or enthusiasm for reading. Benson's journal entries show a penchant for criticizing others who somehow did not live up to his personal standards of proper behavior, cleanliness, or efficient work habits. It is very likely that when Benson expressed these sentiments in conversation he alienated other people. In the 1860s Benson reported that the cook John L. Jones frequently became angry in the course of their discussions about Salem; perhaps George Morris felt the same way after being cooped up on the *Glide* in Benson's company for several months. Two years later, the insults a drunken cook hurled at Benson in Majunga Harbor could conceivably have stemmed from the hostility and anger the cook felt after months of the steward's fussy chiding and scolding over his "Confounding Rum." Benson took pride in his work and expected others to do the same, but these expectations could have driven a wedge between Benson and the only other black men on the *Glide* who were in constant contact with him.

In addition to the onboard conflicts that consumed Benson in this period, his journal entries also hint that he was experiencing some difficulties in his relationship with his wife. His written references to Jenny Benson differed from those he expressed in earlier journal volumes. Benson no longer ended his entries "good night Jenny" or "Good Night Dear Pearl," and when he marked off time on his voyage he counted "days from home," not "days from my Jennie Pearl," as he had in 1862. In his later writings Benson rarely followed his older custom of writing as if he were speaking directly to his wife. Clearly he did not expect her to read his journals any longer, and he seemed to have lost the sense of her presence accompanying him on his journeys.

While Benson did not make any direct mention of marital quarrels, he did hint at them. He may have had marital difficulties in mind when he wrote, "there are many things that stand in my way on shore, it is better for me to be at sea." In December 1878 he was slightly more revealing when he wrote, "I wonder if Jennie thinks of me to day, we have been Married now almost 26 years and Jennie in all this time never told me she loved me." In 1862 Benson rhapsodized about the love letters he received at sea from his wife. Less than twenty years later he complained (inaccurately) that she had never expressed her love for him. This complaint was quite unusual, since, for the most part, Benson still wrote of his "dear Jennie" without any added insinuations about a lack of love or affection. Still, Benson's insecurities about his marriage had deepened by the 1870s, even after a quarter-century of marriage.[11]

As in the old days, separation played a large role in his marital fears. Even after spending ten years at home with his wife, Benson continued to worry about his place in her heart and in her home. He continued to fret, "I wonder if they think of me at home," as he always did at sea. But his years in Salem left him even less secure about his status in the family, particularly because of his wife's aptitude at running the Benson household with or without his presence or help. In 1878–79 Benson pasted a rather telling newspaper clipping into the back of his journal, attributed to a writer identified only as "S.W.": "Although a married woman can possess property in her own right, she cannot sell, convey or mortgage the same without her husband. He must join her in the conveyance." Anxious about the depth of his wife's need for him, Benson at times felt alone and unloved. Although he could keep his anxieties at bay by adopting a positive outlook and concentrating on his tasks as ship's steward, it was less easy for him to overcome his loneliness aboard a vessel where he felt close to no one. As the years passed, his loneliness only intensified.

Benson's unhappy voyages with Captain Beadle were marked by an isolation that resembled his experiences of earlier years but often surpassed them in this regard. He remained apart from the ordinary sailors, whom he still regarded with disdain. He wrote less than ever about "the People" in his journals, and once went so far as to complain "I am tiered & sick at the sight of sailors."[12] Furthermore, by the 1880s many of the sailors on New England merchant ships were immigrants who were the only men willing to put up with the poor living conditions and relatively low wages of seafaring; Benson mentioned two of these men aboard the *Glide*, a "Du[t]chman" and "a Jew," who remained otherwise unidentified by name in his journal. This further alienated Benson from the other men on the bark who did not share his New England background.[13] Moreover, as ship's steward Benson was considered to be in the camp of the unpopular and underqualified Captain Beadle, and this association resulted in unpleasant exchanges with others on board who were hostile to the captain. Finally, Benson's age set him apart from the rest of his shipmates. When Benson turned fifty in 1880, he was the oldest man on the *Glide*, older even than Captain Beadle, who was not yet forty. Surrounded by quarrelsome, inexperienced, immigrant sailors, Benson was especially alone on these voyages to Zanzibar.[14]

Lonesome and conflicted, Benson was plagued further by issues of racial uncertainty akin to his inner conflicts of the 1860s. His notebooks were again adorned with clipped newspaper illustrations of whites in respectable middle-class garb, with only one image of a nonwhite. This was a published sketch of a black man in a desert scene, perhaps one of the "Natives" Benson saw in Zanzibar or Aden, leading a camel with a monkey on its back. The racial message reflected by this image is unclear: did Benson select it because it showed a black man? Was it a reminder of the exotic places and people he saw in his travels? Was it interesting to Benson because of the incongruity of its subjects?

Whatever his reasons, Benson's inclusion of this sketch as the sole illustration of a nonwhite in his journals is notable. Benson remained an American black who did not manifest great solidarity with nonwhites from other parts of the world. He made not a single reference in his journal to prominent black Americans or issues of interest to them. In an era when many blacks were outraged over the myriad failures of Reconstruction, when Frederick Douglass maintained a high level of racial activism and visibility, and when a large number of ordinary blacks migrated west to Kansas as Exodusters, receiving attention and charitable aid from a number of sources in Benson's home town of Salem, Benson was conspicuously silent. As ever, he chose not to identify himself with the mainstream of black America, exacerbating his alienation from virtually every group.[15] On these final voyages Benson was alone, isolated from his wife and children, other blacks, and even from his fellow mariners aboard the *Glide*.

Given his insularity, it is unsurprising that Benson continued to experience bouts of homesickness. "I for one wished myself at No. 9 Rice St. Salem, more than once," Benson wrote in a typical entry in 1878.[16] "No.9 Rice Street," the home that Benson now missed, was the family's new house in the northeast corner of Salem. They had left their ten-year home on Creek Street sometime between 1875 and 1878, after Benson returned to seafaring. For the first time since their marriage, Charles and

Jenny Benson moved away from the Mill Pond area, once the center of black Salem. The decision to move may have been eased by the fact that few blacks still lived in the Creek Street neighborhood on the west side of the Mill Pond by the late 1870s. But instead of crossing to the other side of the pond, where many blacks still dwelled on Porter, Pond, and Cedar Streets, or to the Salem Neck neighborhood where blacks still inhabited English and Webb Streets, the Bensons headed in a new and different direction. Accompanied by their daughter and son-in-law, Fransisca and William Wentworth, who rented a house next door, the Bensons moved to Rice Street.[17]

The living conditions on Rice Street were similar in many ways to those that Salem's blacks had always endured in their Salem Neck and Mill Pond homes. Rice Street was only one block south of the tracks of the Eastern Railroad. As on Creek Street, the Bensons' residence was located near a hub of railroad-related activity. "On Bridge Street," the *Salem Evening News* reported, referring to a street slightly southwest of the Bensons' home, "is a large repair shop of the company, comprising five large and numerous smaller buildings ... [and] a machine shop is also located here." There "250 regular employees" were busily occupied "repairing 300 passenger cars and 3500 freight cars" each year; the noise level near the Eastern Railroad Car Shop marked the Bensons' new neighborhood as a direct heir to the noisy "Knocker's Hole" where blacks had once lived in eighteenth-century Salem.[18] Also nearby was Salem's Gas Company facility, where fumes from the coal-fed processing of gas added to the atmospheric assault on this industrial neighborhood in the outer reaches of northeastern Salem.[19] The rent at 9 Rice Street, however, was quite low, only $6.50 a month in 1881. This was likely the primary appeal for the Bensons and Wentworths, who could afford to live there in adjoining houses, a feat that might have been more difficult to accomplish elsewhere in the city.[20]

Even as he moved his home away from other blacks in Salem (those few that remained there after the exodus of more than half of the community), Benson also began to exhibit his further alienation from his black townsfolk. As an active seafarer, Benson had always spent most of his time away from Salem and the people he knew there. Still, Benson always showed a palpable sense of personal attachment and connection to Salem's black community in the journal entries he composed in the 1860s. He referred to church services in Salem's black meeting house. He also hinted at the interpersonal connections he and his family had established with individual black in his home ashore, such as his house-mate Susan Seymour.[21] By the 1870s and 1880s, however, Benson made fewer and fewer personal references to Salem in his journal notebooks. Scattered newspaper clippings do appear, including a short piece on Salem's St. Peter's Church and a lengthy obituary of Abraham Williams, a black mariner from Salem who died in 1880 at about one hundred years of age.[22] But with few exceptions, when Benson wrote about Salem in his journals he restricted his comments to his immediate family and his residence at "No.9 Rice Street." None of Benson's journals from the 1870s or 1880s mention a single black Salemite by name, with the exception of his wife and children. They never allude to the city's larger black community, or to Benson's place within it. In truth, by this time Benson barely passed any time in Salem at all, except for the scant two or three weeks that lay between the *Glide*'s return to Boston from Zanzibar and her subsequent departure shortly thereafter. Benson still complained of "homesickness," but now he usually meant his actual home itself, and not the larger habitation of black Salem that suffused his earlier journal volumes. Benson was no longer as grounded in his black community ashore as he had once been. The sense of isolation that pervaded so many aspects of his life, including his shipboard existence and his marriage, crept into his relationship with black Salem as well, the consequence of his personal feelings as well as the shrinkage of his circle of black intimates.[23]

THE DIFFICULTIES Benson encountered at sea and ashore were common among contemporary seafarers. William Beadle's incompetencies were not entirely unparalleled during the Age of Sail, as a number of shipmasters were known to display erratic behavior. Some of these men engaged in extreme drunkenness or unwholesome activities with prostitutes or other port women, and some launched into irrational, even violent outbursts. Lengthy feuds between ships' officers like that between Captain Beadle and his first mate Welch also took place aboard other vessels and may have occurred with even greater frequency than they were reported in official logs or sailors' journals. There is also ample evidence of conflicts between foremast hands on long sailing voyages like the *Glide*'s or even longer journeys like those of whaling vessels. Captain Beadle's use of force as a disciplinary measure was entirely in keeping with seafaring norms in an era when seafaring culture granted shipmasters absolute power to rule as they saw fit, up to and including meting out physical punishment. Benson's personal difficulties aboard the *Glide* pale in comparison to tales of black cooks and stewards who experienced frequent and open racial enmity from white sailors, and floggings or beatings from ship captains. In one extreme case, a black cook was shot by a captain for displaying an improper attitude toward shipboard superiors, an impropriety Benson would never have committed but also a punishment he thankfully never faced.[24]

Benson's marital difficulties also fit common patterns of his era. Karen Lystra has identified numerous instances of marital strain between nineteenth-century couples, noting that these often stemmed from "the conviction that one spouse did not love the other," much like Benson's contention that his wife had never expressed her love for him. Stress also arose between lovers whenever they were separated for any length of time. While most maritime historians have focused on the economic and communal ramifications of sailors' long absences from home, this aspect of seafaring life certainly had drastic implications for their intimate relationships with their wives or sweethearts. Benson's marriage had been so transformed by his long journeys away from home that later attempts to remain there introduced tension to the household, as he felt "in the way." Many sailors doubtlessly encountered this phenomenon. In fact, for some particularly unlucky men long voyages bred infidelity at home, and rumors of "untrue women" frightened many an insecure and lonely sailor at sea. Ironically, Lystra points out that unhappy couples frequently found that their relationship improved during extended separations, which provided relief from endless squabbling when they were together. For a sailor like Benson, the marital tensions rooted in his long sea voyages might have eased with his return to the sea, as he seemed to realize after he returned to seafaring in 1875.[25]

Benson's most basic internal conflict, the competing lures of home life and sea life, were shared by many sailors, and even by many men who never went to sea. The mariner's dilemma was typical among many nineteenth-century American men, who had a marked aversion to domesticity. Victorian men, nurtured by a masculine culture of virility and competition, often found home life dull and unstimulating. The insulated and feminine environment of the home represented a significant threat to men's independent manhood at a time when this value reigned supreme in society's core definitions of manliness. Under these conditions the all-male workplace was more reassuring and fulfilling for men. When the sailor left home, then, he sought not only adventure in exotic places or freedom on the open seas but also fulfilled cultural imperatives in the same fashion as landlubbers who left home each morning to go to their places of business.[26]

While the conflicts that now characterized Benson's life were not unusual, they did represent great changes for him. Benson's earlier journals never referred to any troubles that approached the severity of those he experienced under Captain Beadle. Captain John McMullan ran a tight ship aboard the *Glide* in the 1860s and neither Benson's journals nor ship's logs indicate any significant technical or disciplinary problems (Beadle's two weakest areas) under McMullan's command. Although Benson wrote in 1864 that one of the mates was "a mean man, in most every thing" and even described a rough-and-tumble on-deck battle between the *Glide*'s mates, his early journals refer only to isolated incidents that in no way parallel the constant chaos aboard Beadle's *Glide*. And when Benson recorded his disagreements with his cooks in earlier years, he described brief inconsequential spats between close friends; these were totally unlike the deteriorated relationships he had with the *Glide*'s cooks later on. Finally, in his early journal volumes Benson clearly identified his proper place as his home ashore, with his loving wife. Later in his career he was much more ambiguous, and he vacillated between his two worlds, Salem and the *Glide*, and often seemed to choose the latter as his true home.[27]

Many of the problems that plagued Benson toward the end of his life, including his changing perceptions and attitudes, his problems aboard the *Glide*, his marital issues, and his increased isolation both at sea and ashore, were especially affecting because of their relation to his advancing years. When Benson set sail in the *Glide* in 1878 he was, at forty-eight years of age, the oldest man aboard the vessel. Captain Beadle was eleven years younger, and given the youth of most nineteenth-century seafarers it is unlikely that any other crewmembers were much older. Also, Benson was a lifelong mariner, a rarity in an era when most sailors went to sea for only a few voyages before finding more permanent shore employment. Perhaps the only man aboard with enough seafaring experience to rival Benson's was Captain Beadle, who had been going to sea since he was a ship's boy in the mid-1850s. Beadle's experience, however, did not mitigate the severity of his deficiencies as a sailor, and so Benson was not only the oldest man aboard but also the canniest seafarer as well.

Benson's age and seafaring acumen lent him a special kind of status, and his behavior demonstrated that he was well aware of this. Benson's journal entries from the 1860s indicate his familiarity with sailing techniques and instruments, as he noted the ship's latitude and longitude, temperature, and any significant course changes in his daily entries. Not once did he mention that he spoke with the *Glide's* officers about these subjects, though. In contrast, his journals of the 1870s and 1880s describe many consultations with the captain and mate, particularly when the vessel was floundering about in East African waters south of Madagascar. Benson also exhibited a greater propensity to advance his own opinions about other matters, as he did in one minor disagreement with the captain regarding the comparative tenderness of "Hen and Cock Turkeys." Benson's increased volubility and willingness to speak up stemmed from his status as an elder aboard the *Glide*, at least in his own estimation. That the vessel's officers paid attention to the words of the steward, who was not technically a sailor according to shipboard etiquette, shows that they too valued his advice and respected his experience.[28]

Benson's age had a strong effect on the tone of his journal entries in these later years. His cantankerous comments about Captain Beadle's eating habits and arguments with the mate differed sharply from his writings a decade earlier. While Benson had always written openly about himself, describing his emotional states and even hinting at sexual behavior, his 1860s references to his shipmates were infrequent and usually limited to specific actions or incidents that involved them. In his later journals, though, Benson was often opinionated and even slighting about his companions. Benson wrote of Captain Beadle's mistakes and infirmities, bemoaned the petty quarrels between the captain and mate, criticized the cook's tobacco smoking and poor reading habits, excoriated any aboard who drank the "confounding rum," and even mocked the "confusion" of inexpert ship's hands when they first tried to set the bark's sails. He also reminisced more in his journal entries, not often about his home but quite a bit more about encounters with old shipmates or seafaring acquaintances. The journals composed by this fifty-year-old seafarer reflected the passage of time since the early 1860s, when a much younger Benson first took pen to paper and commenced keeping his journal.[29]

Benson was not just one of a dying breed of black sailors but one of a dying breed of black Salemites as well. By the time he reached his late forties, Benson had few peers in Salem. By 1880, when he turned fifty, only 24 other black men over the age of forty-five still lived in Salem. His wife

Jenny, then forty-three, was one of only 31 black women over forty years of age in the city. These numbers reflect the remarkable changes that had taken place in black Salem since the Bensons had met and married nearly three decades earlier. In 1853, Charles and Jenny Benson were young adults living in a black community with a median age of twenty-seven years and five months. During the first twenty-five years of their marriage the Bensons lived among many dozens of other blacks in their stage of life. By 1880, however, most of the Bensons' contemporaries had either died or left Salem. In 1850, 107 blacks over age forty lived in Salem, while thirty years later there were only 60 people in that age group. By 1880, Charles and Jenny Benson were part of a shrinking group of older blacks in a city where the average black was thirty-one, and they were living in an area geographically isolated from other blacks. Living in a black community that was barely half the size it had once been, among people who did not remember or had never known most of his friends and acquaintances, it is no wonder that Charles Benson felt alienated and disconnected from the black community that had once sustained him. A half-century after his birth, Benson was getting old. He was wearing down.

As BENSON neared the quarter-century mark of his maritime career, the years and stress of seafaring began to take a toll on his physical health. Like all sailors, Benson had contracted several illnesses at sea earlier in his career, most notably the intestinal disorders that contributed to his retirement from seafaring in 1865. Yet he had always recovered, and even on the 1877–78 voyage he made in his late forties, Benson reported nothing more serious than "my regular cold, that I always get on soundings."[30]

There were worrisome signs, however. Benson's eyes began to "trouble" him on occasion, and his age began to take its toll. One day in mid-1878 he reported:

> Last night I could not sleep. I had a severe pain around my heart, which caused my left breast to swell very much. I also had very curious feelings up & down my left side, also dissiness in my head, & confusion of sounds in my ears, it was past 2 in the morning before I fell into a troubled sleep.

When his mysterious malady vanished without a trace, Benson forgot about it. But several months later he was in agony once more. "My hand is so lame that I can hardly hold my pen," he wrote in early February

1879. "I hurt it in Aden & now the Rhumetism is in it." On the following day he was still experiencing severe pain, stating, "Oh! my hand aches." Soon afterward the throbbing ebbed, and three weeks later he was home again in Salem, many of his aches and pains forgotten in the thrill of coming home.[31]

Benson's rheumatism would prove more persistent than he expected. His decades at sea were having a cumulative effect upon his health, and his ability to recover quickly from illness was waning. In 1880, several months after his fiftieth birthday, Benson began to comment on the deterioration of his body. At first only his teeth hurt; "I have the Tooth Ache like ——— fun," he wrote in July 1880, adding two weeks later, "my teeth torment me day and night." This was something new for Benson, who commented, "I never had so much tooth ache before."[32]

Soon afterward Benson grew apprehensive, and he began to fear the future in a way he had never described before.

> Time passes slowly away. I am looseing Flesh, I cannot sleep well nights. I do not ha[ve] more than two hours sleep at a time, nor have had for over a month. Something more than usual seems to hang around me I cannot tell what, how, but there is a continual something that keeps me restless both day and night. I dread to have the curtain rise, for I feel there is deep sorrow there, yet I long to know the worse. God help me to bare it. Am I getting Old & nervous, silly? or is this a grand reality that is to be? Time will decide.[33]

His dreams were also disturbed. On July 12, 1880, Benson opened his notebook to an empty back page and scribbled, "12 of July dreamed of mothers death," without elaborating on the content of his dream about his mother, Elizabeth Benson, who was then alive and living with his brother George L. W. in Lynn. For a while he put his fears behind him and confined his journal writings to more subjects such as shipboard activities and the weather. Then, on September 3, he became ill again.

"I have not been well to day," Benson wrote on September 3, 1880. "Have been sick at the stomach, have Rheumatism in my Right arm and hand. Have caught cold, somehow. I want to get home." The next day Benson reported that little of interest had occurred aboard the *Glide* but added in a postscript that, "Some scrapeings hurt my port eye." Over the next several weeks his health degenerated rapidly. While his rheumatism abated, Benson's eye condition worsened. Not a day went by without some notation of his pain, as Benson wrote, "My Eye is very bad," "my eyes are painful . . . the nerves of my face tremble & twitch disagreeably," and "My Eye troubles me." His toothache returned as well, accompanied by painful headaches and sleeplessness. In the midst of his agony, Benson departed from his usual journal entry format to write a short note to his wife: "If any thing happens to me, Jennie Remember I die loveing you, be good to the children." Yet his health slowly improved, and by the time the *Glide* reached Boston on September 27 Benson felt much more "chearfull and glad."[34]

Benson spent less than three weeks at home in Salem before beginning his next voyage to Zanzibar, which was ill-omened from the start. First he "lost" his train to Boston and was forced to wait for the next train an hour later. Upon arriving at Boston's Lewis Wharf, where the *Glide* was docked, Benson discovered that his "Cook was sick and could not go"; the replacement cook eventually showed up both late and drunk. When all was finally in order and the *Glide* set sail Benson was still gloomy, for he was worried about Jennie's "poor health" as well as his own. He was also distressed to observe that even the *Glide*'s condition was disintegrating, noting, "the Bark leaks bad." As the voyage progressed Benson's journal entries began to convey a tone of hopelessness, even despair, as his short statements echoed with a constant refrain of "Oh dear." Within only three days of his departure Benson was so downcast that he even stopped writing in his journal. His explanation, written a week later, confirmed his negative state of mind: "some how I had no heart to write . . . & have not got to rights yet."[35]

As the voyage progressed Benson's health problems worsened. In mid-November his rheumatism flared up again, and his left eye, which had never healed properly, began to trouble him. Stormy weather and heavy seas in early December caused him further difficulties with the rheumatism in his arm. Yet by the end of 1880 Benson seemed to have recovered his health and some of his spirit. He wrote more of homesickness than physical sickness for the remainder of December, fretting at the *Glide*'s "slow getting about" but adding, "Well I must grin & *bear* it." His final entry in his 1880 journal volume, dated December 31, gave no hint that he felt especially ill, although it did express a certain foreboding:

this is the last day of the year, how have I spent it? have I done my Best to be good, have I done every thing as well as I could? I am afraid I have failed in many things. I must try to do better next year if I live. I wonder if Jennie thinks of me to night, by by 1880 you brought many Joys, and many sorrows, we will never see you more by by. 79 days from home

On March 1, 1881, three months after composing his farewell to 1880, Charles A. Benson wrote his final journal entry. Rather than adding it to the empty back pages of his 1880 notebook, he found an empty space at the end of his 1878 journal, which he had brought with him in his sea chest. In shaky letters Benson wrote, "This day come in pleasant but cooler then we have had it for some time my health has bin so poor and I have had so many things on my mind I have neg———." Benson never completed his sentence, although he may have intended to explain why he had been neglecting his journal writing. But the deterioration of his handwriting, spelling, and grammar, and the unnatural brevity of this journal entry spoke volumes about his failing health.

Charles Benson never recovered from the illnesses he contracted at sea. He died on July 12, 1881, of rheumatism, an affliction experienced by myriads of sailors whose years of exposure to the elements made them especially susceptible to the disease. His death, only thirteen days before the end of the *Glide*'s nine-month voyage to and from Boston, was the culmination of a maritime life that had begun nearly thirty years earlier. It also underscored the validity of all of the fears and apprehensions Benson had expressed over the previous few years. Benson had felt "dread" and "restlessness" about this voyage, so much so that he had written, "Oh dear! this going to sea, it will kill me."[36] These forebodings, and his singular dream of his mother's death exactly one year before his own, indicate that on some level Charles Benson had some foreknowledge of the death at sea that awaited him.

Benson died as a sailor, and so he was laid to rest at sea and not in a Salem grave. His fate confirmed his pessimistic expectations of prior months and fulfilled a wistful statement he had made three years earlier. "I suppose I must stand it as long as I can work," he had written on December 26, 1878, "& when I can't work I want to 'step out.'" This prediction came fairly close to the truth, for in his final months Benson could not even write in his journal and was probably incapable of performing his steward's duties. He could no longer work and so he "stepped out," only a scant two weeks before he would have returned to his wife and children. Despite the tragic overtones, there was something appropriate about his fate. Charles A. Benson's life was defined by his work. His ideals of masculinity, discipline, hard work, providership, camaraderie, and self-worth were all bound together in his role as steward of the bark *Glide*. When Benson could no longer fill that role, his personal identity was irretrievably compromised. It was at that point that his life ended, not in Salem, the home ashore that he dreamed about, wrote about, but where he ultimately could not live. Instead Benson died where he had lived, aboard the *Glide* on the open sea.

EPILOGUE

"Charles A. Benson of this city steward of the Bark Glide"

THE PASSING of Charles Augustus Benson occurred at the end of a sea voyage and the end of an era. At only fifty-one years old Benson had been the last remnant of a generation of black men who had looked to the sea for their livelihood. He was also one of the only active seafarers who could still remember the long-ago days of Salem's Brazil trade, extinct for a quarter century. The American Age of Sail was drawing rapidly to a close by the time Benson died in 1881. The wooden spars and billowing sails of Benson's day, the "snapping & creaking of ropes & timbers" that had once filled the silences of a bark at rest, were no more. The small, leaky wooden craft that had housed Benson and his shipmates gave way before fleets of behemoths of iron and steel, belching forth smoke from their coal-fed steam engines. New England–born seamen like Benson were a vanished breed by century's end, their berths now occupied by immigrant laborers who faced even worse working conditions and wage levels than their Yankee predecessors, if that were possible. The Atlantic maritime world Benson had known was gone, taking him with it.

In a very real sense, Charles Benson's entire life had taken place against a backdrop of decline and decay. By the time he was born, the older farming culture that molded his rural childhood was already crumbling under the inexorable pressures of capitalist modernization. His was one of the last generations of northern blacks who grew up outside the urban centers that came to dominate northern black culture and consciousness by the midpoint of the nineteenth century, the villages of his youth vanishing into the past. Even after he moved to a larger community in search of new opportunities, Benson could only watch as the occupational and social networks around him deteriorated over the years. The Union itself deteriorated before Benson's very eyes, an inevitable conflict so destructive that he would not even watch it unfold except from a distance. And looming over all of this deterioration, from the end of his family's century-long tenure in Framingham to the end of Salem seafaring to the ultimate disappearance of Salem's black community, was the specter of personal loss. Over the course of his lifetime Benson mourned the death of many of the people closest to him, including one or more of his own children, as well as the withering of his own youthful marriage.

Despite all of these omens of dissolution, Charles Benson never wavered from his conviction that his life and experiences were essentially constructive in nature. Whether he was dedicating himself to building his family, his professional career, or his sense of self, Benson continued to believe that his efforts had purpose. The economic and marital ruin that befell him in Framingham merely strengthened his resolve to succeed in the life he started anew in Salem; the unexpected entanglement caused by Jenny's unplanned pregnancy became a foundation for a lifelong marriage based on love and emotional commitment; his failure to find shore work in Salem provided the impetus for him to begin a long and accomplished association with seafaring that continued to prosper even under unlikely circumstances. Even his death came on his own terms, his departure fulfilling the unconscious prophecy he made years earlier about how he would someday "step out."

Informed of Charles's death upon the return of the *Glide* in July 1881, Jenny Pearl now faced life without a husband, just as Charles's mother had in the 1840s and Charles's first wife, Martha, had after he abandoned her a lifetime ago. Prepared by the decades she had already spent on her own when he was away at sea, Jenny did what she always had—she went on alone. Forced by circumstance to live on as a widow, she continued to hold strong even as her children, the only lasting legacy left her by her husband, died one by one. William Henry D. was the first, dying of disease in 1889 when he was only fourteen. Then Charlie died before the age of forty, and their oldest sister, Fransisca, died sometime before the end of the nineteenth century. Through it all their mother persevered, until the Great Salem Fire of 1914 left her with no home and nowhere to go. Only then did she leave Salem, the city her late husband had so cherished, to live with her sole remaining descendent, Fransisca's daughter Bessie Wentworth. When she died in 1921 at the age of eighty-four, Margaret Jenny Benson had been a widow for forty years. She never remarried.

On one level, Charles Benson was deluding himself when he thought he could transcend the realities of his life by taking an idealized approach. His belief in the supremacy of the Victorian code was never borne out by his experiences. Restricted by the racial constructs of his time to servile jobs of low status, he was never truly given the opportunity to rise above his station. Excluded from conventional avenues of occupational or social mobility due to his race, he could never attain the heights of self-realization promised by the culture in which he had so much faith. Finally, the life of poverty and hard labor to which he was sentenced would take its toll on his health and that of everyone he cared about, leading to suffering and eventually premature death for all except the wife he held most dear.

Yet in the end Benson may have triumphed after all. On August 3, 1881, three weeks after he died at sea, the *Salem Post* published an obituary memorializing him.

> Chas. A. Benson of this city steward of the Bark Glide died July 12th, of rheumatism while on the passage from Alden [*sic*] to Boston, aged 51 years. Mr. Benson was well known in this city having sailed in the employ of Robert Upton and Capt. Bertram for a number of years. He has sailed in the following vessels: Bark Wyman, Capt. John Ashby; Bark Swallow, Capt. Edwin Upton; Barks Elizabeth and Nubia, Capt. John Ashby; Bark Dorchester, Capt. Staniford Perkins and Capt. Cloutman, and for 6 years under Capt. Beadle in the Taria Topan and Glide. He will be well remembered by military organizations as he has on many occasions ministered to the wants of the inner man for them on their excursions. He leaves a host of friends who will hear of his death with grief. Seldom does a man for so long a time fill such a responsible position as did Mr. Benson and leave a record so satisfactory and so pleasing to all who knew him.

Some forty-five years later, a local historian, George Granville Putnam, thought enough of Benson's obituary to include it in his four-volume history of maritime Salem, *Salem Vessels and Their Voyages*. Putnam quoted the piece and added:

> Many a Salem boy, homesick and seasick, will remember kindnesses from him in the shape of some delicacy.... It is with a deep sense of high appreciation of this worthy man that this tribute is here paid in his memory. Walter H. Trumbull, who sailed as a passenger in the *Glide*, said to the writer, "Say something nice about my good friend, Charley Benson." Mr. Benson was steward of the *Glide* on her very first voyage. Truly may it be said of him that "he was faithful to the uttermost."

The *Post*'s obituary and Putnam's later comments could easily be interpreted along racialist lines akin to the patronizing, emasculating vision of nonwhites that had been so prevalent in antebellum Salem. Benson's obituary mentioned nothing of his personal life or his family, naming only the white ship captains and owners he knew. He was lauded not so much for his own skills as for his service of others, presumably whites, to whom he "ministered" in a manner that was adjudged "responsible" and ultimately "satisfactory" and "pleasing" to his white acquaintances. Putnam's addendum that "he was faithful to the uttermost" only enhanced the model of black achievement as that of a service worker who fulfilled his duty with humility and faithfulness. This approach hearkened back to Salem newspapers of the 1850s with their faithful slaves and laudable "Old Darkeys," reflecting turn-of-the-century conceptions linking black racial uplift to hard work in menial or servile occupations.[1]

That is not how Charles Benson would have read his own obituary, however. To Benson, the piece represented the ultimate affirmation of his life and the values that guided his choices. None of Salem's black men and precious few mariners were deemed worthy of a published obituary at the time Benson received his, with most relegated to a cursory line or two of tiny print in the "local events" sections of the city's newspapers. That he received one at all stood as a testimony to his exceptionalism in his chosen professional field. The long list of Benson's vessels and commanding officers likewise attested to the occupational achievements that were so important to him, particularly toward the end of his life. The appearance of Benson's "host of friends" in the obituary further contextualized his life in the midst of a social circle, a phenomenon that he had often missed during his lonely years at sea. And the description of Benson that appeared at the outset, "Chas. A. Benson of this city steward of the bark Glide," may have provided the most perfect possible encapsulation of a life divided between home and work, the shore and the sea, family and duty.

Most important of all, in his summation of Benson's life the obituary writer emphasized precisely those qualities that were most important to Benson himself. His core values were those of hard work, self-control, and pride in a job well done. These were the ideals of Victorian masculinity, of the men who left their homes and families for the workplace in an effort to provide for their loved ones. As a man who judged himself by his "responsible position" and "satisfactory record," Benson would have found something eminently appropriate about the way he ended his days without abandoning the code of values that had guided him. And in the end that ideology did not fail him. He died as he had lived, as Charles A. Benson of Salem, steward of the Bark *Glide*, remembered by those who knew him in exactly the way he thought of himself.

APPENDIX

"Talking about Salem Beverly Lynn &c."

Black and Total Population of Salem, Massachusetts, by Decade

	Black	Total
1850	412	20,264
1860	278	22,252
1870	262	24,117
1880	203	27,563
1890	166	30,801
1900	146	35,956
1910	163	43,697
1920	130	42,529

Black Population of Selected Towns and Massachusetts, by Decade

	Salem	Lynn	Boston	Providence, R.I.	Massachusetts
1850	412	115	1,999	1,499	9,064
1860	278	226	2,261	1,537	9,602
1870	262	371	3,496	2,559	13,947
1880	203	564	5,873	3,582	18,697
1890	166	715	8,125	3,963	22,144
1900	146	n/a	11,591	4,817	31,974
1910	163	700	13,564	5,316	38,055
1920	130	812	16,350	5,655	45,466

Sources: Manuscript schedules and published compendia of the U.S. Census, 1850–1920. Black population figures for Salem are adjusted with supplemental data from *Salem Directory and City Register*, 1837–1921, and Salem crew lists, 1805–75.

NOTES

"*I bare record & My record is true*"

Introduction

1. Charles A. Benson Papers, Peabody Essex Museum (CAB) 1, April 28, 1862.

2. Few black journals exist, as W. Jeffrey Bolster has noted. And out of the hundreds of thousands of seafarers from America's nineteenth-century Age of Sail, only several hundred journals currently reside in libraries and institutions. There may be a great many more journals out there somewhere. See Bolster, "'To Feel Like a Man,'" 1185; Creighton, *Dogwatch and Liberty Days*, 1.

3. Salvatore, *We All Got History*, 21–22.

4. David Katzman, untitled paper presented at "The Growth of African-American Urban Communities," NEH Summer Seminar, Lawrence, Kan., July 18, 1994.

5. Howe, *Making the American Self*, 108–12, 262–63; Whitman quotation from his "Democratic Vistas."

6. Robbins, "Identity, Culture, and Behavior," 1202–5.

Chapter One

1. Family genealogy (through George Benson) in Barry, *History of Framingham*, 63, and Temple, *History of Framingham*, 472; supplementary details in *Vital Records to the Year 1850*, Massachusetts State Archives (VR), for Framingham, Natick, and Sudbury.

2. Population in Barry, *History of Framingham*, 62–63. Some data from Josiah H. Temple, "Framingham," in Drake, *History of Middlesex County*, 1:435–53, and Conklin, *Middlesex County and Its People*, 565–68. In 1800, blacks constituted 1.52 percent of the total population of Massachusetts; see Levesque, *Black Boston*, 78, table I-4.

3. White, *Somewhat More Independent*, 21, 80–113; Berlin, *Many Thousands Gone*, 56–57; Nash and Soderlund, *Freedom by Degrees*, 32–40.

4. Piersen, *Black Yankees*, 25–36; Melish, *Disowning Slavery*, 27–29; see also 16–21 for Melish's points on slaveowners and slave roles in the region. For New England culture, see Henretta, "Families and Farms," 26; Clark, *Roots of Rural Capitalism*, 23–30; Demos, *A Little Commonwealth*, 77–78.

5. VR, Framingham, 239; Barry, *History of Framingham*, 63. Lorenzo Greene points out that "surnames did not become common for Negroes until after slavery had been abolished in New England"; see his *Negro in Colonial New England*, 201. Black names are also discussed in Gutman, *Black Family in Slavery and Freedom*, 185–256; Nash, *Forging Freedom*, 79–88. For slave aspirations in the "charter generation," see Berlin, *Many Thousands Gone*, 47–50.

6. Mather quoted in Melish, *Disowning Slavery*, 32. Framingham's "colored pews" in Temple, *History of Framingham*, 238. For an alternative interpretation of the church's attitude toward slaves, see Berlin, *Many Thousands Gone*, 60.

7. On rural slaves' religious autonomy, see Zilversmit, *First Emancipation*, 24–25; also Piersen, *Black Yankees*, 58–61. For an urban perspective, see White, *Somewhat More Independent*, 88, 95–106, and "Proud Day," 13–31; Reidy, "'Negro Election Day'"; and Melvin H. Wade, "'Shining in Borrowed Plumage,'" in St. George, *Material Life in America*, 171–82.

8. Temple, *History of Framingham*, 195–96, 201–3, 236; Barry, *History of Framingham*, 107–8.

9. Will of John Swift, 1743, Middlesex County Probate #22049, Massachusetts State Archives.

10. Temple, *History of Framingham*, 236–37, 472; Barry, *History of Framingham*, 63.

11. Gary Nash, "Forging Freedom," in Berlin and Hoffman, *Slavery and Freedom*, 3–4; Greene, *Negro in Colonial New England*, 297–300; MacEacheren, "Emancipation of Slavery in Massachusetts," 294, 297–303.

12. VR, Framingham, 239, implies that the marriage, date unknown, took place in a Framingham church. The 1705–6 Massachusetts law banning intermarriage in Greene, *Negro in Colonial New England*, 208–10; for interracial marriage between white women and black slaves in eighteenth-century New England, see Cottrol, *Afro-Yankees*, 21–22. In 1786 the Massachusetts legislature passed an act on the "solemnization of marriage," voiding preexisting intermarriages like that of the Bensons; see Jordan, *White over Black*, 472.

13. T. H. Breen, "Making History," in Hoffman, Sobel, and Teute, *Through a Glass Darkly*, 67–95.

14. Salem in Quarles, *Negro in the American Revolution*, 10; Benson, in Office of the Secretary of State, *Massachusetts Soldiers and Sailors*, 1:968, where he is described as "age, 16 yrs.; stature, 5 ft. 2 in.; complexion, yellow; hair, black; eyes, black" and "reported a Negro." Finally, see Benson, Pension Application, National Archives.

15. Revolutionary War service details in Benson, Pension Application, especially his oath dated June 1820; fiddling, in an obituary of Abel Benson, *Massachusetts Ploughman*, September 25, 1843. Roles of typical "Negro soldiers," in Quarles, *Negro in the American Revolution*, 74–78.

16. Bureau of the Census, *Heads of Families*, National Archives. Quotation from "Declaration by Abel Benson," dated June 13, 1823, included in Benson, Pension Application.

17. Stapp, *Afro-Americans in Antebellum Boston*, 16–17, 288 n. 14–17.

18. Financial information in Benson's pension application; see documents dated 1818 through 1829, including pension-related documents, deed to Henry Benson, mortgage to John Kittridge, and personal statements by Henry Benson and John Kittridge in the pension files.

19. Clark, *Roots of Rural Capitalism*, 21–58.

20. Vital records for Boston, "Marriages, 1807–1828," New York Public Library; *Boston City Directory*, 1821, 261. Black migrants to urban areas often maintained strong ties to rural home and kin; see Trotter, *Great Migration*; Lewis, *In Their Own Interests*, 102–9.

21. Boston population figures quoted in Levesque, *Black Boston*, 82, table I-8, 88, table I-14; Census Office, *Book I of the Fourth Census, 1820*, National Archives, 5* (Boston), 8 (Providence, R.I.), 8* (including numerous cities in Connecticut). For black underenumeration in the census, see Sharpless and Shortridge, "Biased Underenumeration," 409–39. For Boston port information, see Albion, *Rise of New York Port*, 15 and appendices 1–7, 389–98.

22. Horton and Horton, *Black Bostonians*, 3. Curry, *Free Black in Urban America* confirms that in Boston "the proportion of black residents was highest in Southac and Belknap streets (together with their adjoining courts), but thirty-seven percent of those living in the former street and fifty-eight percent in the latter were white" (79). See also Daniels, *In Freedom's Birthplace*, 17; Levesque, *Black Boston*, 32–33, 37.

23. *Boston City Directory*, 1825, 290; see also 190–98. Belknap Street Church in Levesque, *Black Boston*, 263–71; Daniels, *In Freedom's Birthplace*, 21–22; Horton and Horton, *In Hope of Liberty*, 142–43, 151–52. Black schools in Levesque, *Black Boston*, 165–75; Daniels, *In Freedom's Birthplace*, 22–23; Horton and Horton, *Black Bostonians*, 71. Belknap Street would remain a center of black dwellings in Boston for decades; see Gooding, *On the Altar of Freedom*, 16.

24. Bulfinch and Davis quoted in Whitehill, *Boston*, 70–71. Only one (unpublished) history of black Boston during this era comments extensively on the seamier side of black Bostonians' living conditions, Ward, "Nineteenth-Century Boston," 35–36; a milder description is given in Levesque, *Black Boston*, 382–84.

25. Horton and Horton, *Black Bostonians*, 8; Massachusetts Bureau of Statistics of Labor, *Third Annual Report* (Boston, 1872), 513, 516–17; Handlin, *Boston's Immigrants*, 60; Stapp, *Afro-Americans in Antebellum Boston*, 21.

26. The attraction between George Benson and Elizabeth Simpson may have resulted from a mutual commonality of values and experience stretching back to their pre-urban identities and their respective lives in Framingham and Pembroke; see Borchert, *Alley Life in Washington*, 240–41.

27. "Marriages, 1807–1828," p. 15. Details on Elizabeth W. Simpson's life before her marriage to George Benson are spotty. There is no official record of an Elizabeth W. Simpson in Pembroke; however, the Vital Records for the nearby town of Marshfield register the marriage of "Mr. Sylvester Prince of Marshfield & Miss Nancy Simpson of Pembroke" in 1832 (VR, Marshfield, 283). The Princes were a well-known African American family in Marshfield, and it is likely that Nancy Simpson was related to Elizabeth and that the family continued to dwell in Pembroke after Elizabeth's departure.

28. George L. W.'s middle names are unknown. The extended Benson family frequently named newborns after relatives, as in the case of George Benson's nephew Abel, Charles Benson's sons William and George, and Charles's niece Jenny, who was likely named for Charles's wife, Margaret Jenny Francis. If George L. W. was also named after relatives, then the L. may have stood for either Levi or Labin (after one of the child's uncles) and the W. was likely William; but this is all speculative. For Benson addresses, see *Boston City Directory*, 1827, 293; 1828, 302; 1829, 295; 1830, 327.

29. Horton and Horton, *Black Bostonians*, 3, 71; Horton and Horton, *In Hope of Liberty*, 91–92.

30. Horton and Horton, *In Hope of Liberty*, 67–70; Litwack, *North of Slavery*, viii.

31. Quoted in Daniels, *In Freedom's Birthplace*, 26. Hall's address is quoted at greater length in Nell, *Colored Patriots*, 61–64. For more on white racism, see Horton and Horton, *In Hope of Liberty*, 162–66; Horton and Horton, *Black Bostonians*, 4.

32. While he does not speculate about reasons, Peter Knights notes that many of those who migrated from agricultural towns to Boston moved on within a decade or two, frequently returning to their hometowns. See Knights, *Plain People of Boston*, 120; Peter Gottlieb relates this to later generations of black migrants in *Making Their Own Way*, 49–51.

33. I estimate the timing of the move based on George Benson's listings in the *Boston City Directory* for 1828, 1829, and 1830 (but not subsequently) and his listing in Framingham in the manuscripts of Census Office, Fifth Census, National Archives, roll 67, p. 74. The manuscript census for Framingham, compiled in order of physical proximity, listed in George Benson's name as a head of household immediately following his father's.

34. For full text of speech see Webster, "Second Reply."

Chapter Two

1. Levesque, *Black Boston*, chap. 8, esp. 266–71, 289; Horton and Horton, *Black Bostonians*, chap. 4, esp. 43–45; Litwack, *North of Slavery*, chap. 6; Horton and Horton, *In Hope of Liberty*, 126–27. Also Brown, *Life of William J. Brown*, 46.

2. Horton and Horton, *In Hope of Liberty*, 172–76, 224–26; White, "Proud Day," 34–38, 50.

3. Horton and Horton, *In Hope of Liberty*, 224–25. My arguments regarding Charlotte Forten are developed in "'New Guinea at One End, and a View of the Alms-House at the Other,'" 212–14.

4. Palfrey later served in the House of Representatives, where he made several fiery abolitionist speeches; he is even credited in one source for coining the phrase "slave power," a popular shibboleth among antebellum northern political leaders. Winsor, *Memorial History of Boston*, 3:476, 377, 395; for religion among black Bostonians, see Levesque, *Black Boston*, 271, 290–91.

5. Census Office, *Sixth Census*, National Archives, 44; also Census Office, Sixth Census manuscript schedules, National Archives, roll 188, p. 205–10, On segregated education in Massachusetts in the 1830s, see Litwack, *North of Slavery*, 114–15; Horton and Horton, *In Hope of Liberty*, 153; Levesque, *Black Boston*, chap. 5, esp. 171.

6. Vital records for Boston, "Holbrook Deaths Index, 1801–1848," New York Public Library; *Vital Records to the Year 1850*, Massachusetts State Archives, Framingham, 411, Natick, 205.

7. Abel Benson, Middlesex County Probate docket #27309, Massachusetts State Archives.

8. Benson, Pension Application, National Archives.

9. Faler, *Mechanics and Manufacturers*, 94, 99.

10. Vickers, *Farmers and Fishermen*, 3, 55, 99, 112–14, 283.

11. For several of the earliest-known black neighborhoods in Salem, including "Roast Meat Hill," "New Guinea," and others, see Bentley, *Diary*, 2:383; Hawthorne,

"The Custom-House," in *Scarlet Letter*; and Francis H. Lee Papers, quoted in Broadhead, notes for "Brief History," courtesy of the author. Also see Brooks, "Some Localities," 115, 117; Broadhead, "Brief History," 1.

12. The official census tabulation of Salem's 1850 black population cited a total of 324 black residents; when augmented by data from the manuscript census schedules, city directories, and Salem vessel crew lists, the adjusted population figure comes to 412. Official statistical total in Census Office, *Seventh Census*, Book 1, *Population*, 50–51 (population figures for other cities are located elsewhere in that volume). See also Bureau of the Census, *Century of Population Growth*, 82–83, National Archives. Adjustments from Salem census manuscript schedules from Census Office, Seventh Census, 1850, National Archives, roll 312; *Salem Directory*, 1850 and 1851, Salem Crew Lists, National Archives, Waltham, Mass., roll 498. For more on under-enumeration of blacks in the census, see Sharpless and Shortridge, "Biased Under-enumeration," 409–39.

13. Only eight of fifty-four residences contained ten or more blacks in 1850; nearly half of all black homes in Salem that year contained only five or fewer blacks. For the Salem-Boston turnpike, see Hunt, *Pocket Guide to Salem*, 11. There are few published works on black Salem. White, "Salem's Antebellum Black Community," for example, focuses on black education, but without a larger context in terms of the black community. Broadhead's unpublished "Brief History," provides a sketchy historical overview of the black settlement in Salem, with an emphasis on the colonial era.

14. Hunt, *Pocket Guide to Salem*, 17.

15. Davenport, *Homes and Hearths*, 56–60, discusses the almshouse and the many "mildly insane" inmates who had been placed there "for safe-keeping."

16. *Salem Gazette*, July 28, 1863; See also Davenport, *Homes and Hearths*, 22–23; *Salem News*, July 23, 1881.

17. *Salem Register*, August 11, 1853.

18. *Freedom's Journal*, November 9, 1827, 139; Grimke, *Journals*, September 12, 1855, 140; *Salem Gazette*, May 26, 1857, March 20, 1866, February 11, 1868.

19. Horton and Horton, *In Hope of Liberty*, 252–55.

20. Collison, *Shadrach Minkins*, 146–47.

21. Federal censuses; *Salem Directory*, 1850–70; Census of the State of Massachusetts, 1855 and 1865, State Archives; Oden, "*Journal of Charlotte L. Forten*," 124–36; Porter, "Remonds of Salem," 259–95; Oden, "Black Putnams," 240–49; Horton and Horton, *In Hope of Liberty*, 227.

22. Salvatore, *We All Got History*, 103–10.

23. Other black business-owners lived in the midst of the black community, including the Morris family of restaurateurs, the dining-room owner Aaron Moses, and the caterer Edward Cassell, who became famous at the turn of the century for serving a meal to the Prince of Wales (later Edward VII) at Salem. Some Remonds did live closer to the black areas, but only those who lived at their businesses: John Remond lived at his oyster dealership in the middle of town; some of the female Remond barbers lived on Essex Street, which had almost no other black residents; and James Sherman's Derby Square oyster-house was several blocks from the closest black homes.

24. Grimke, *Journals*, 3, 18–22; Winch, *Philadelphia's Black Elite*.

25. In Charles A. Benson Papers, Peabody Essex Museum, vol. 1, all Sunday entries throughout the volume refer to "meeting" and "church."

26. Grimke, *Journals*, 111, 365 (entries for November 18, 1856, and June 22, 1862).

CHAPTER THREE

1. While no birth record exists, Benson gives her birthday and age in Charles A. Benson Papers, Peabody Essex Museum (CAB), 3, March 13, 1878. Various census records and the age listed on her death certificate also confirm the year of Margaret Francis's birth.

2. Since only thirteen other black Salemites were listed as property owners in the 1850 census, this particular branch of the Francis clan was clearly more financially secure and established than most of the town's other blacks; Francis data from Census Office, Seventh Census, 1850, National Archives, roll 312. The history of Black Frank's nickname and a description of his heroism in the face of a deadly 1859 fire is told in the *Salem Gazette*, June 10, 1859.

3. The friendship may have been between the Dailey and Francis women, who spent more time in Salem than did their seafaring husbands. In Charles Benson's second marriage, his wife also would spend many time in Salem than he (see chap. five).

4. In later years, Drew would also work in the catering business; see *Salem Gazette*, March 23, 1858, for mention of Drew's catering a Salem Cadet Assembly.

5. For a discussion of boarders among nineteenth-century urban blacks, see Horton and Horton, *Black Bostonians*, 3, 15–25; see also Modell and Hareven, "Urbanization and the Malleable Household," 467–79.

6. Katzman, *Seven Days a Week*, 81–84. Margaret Francis was probably not a live-in servant, because live-in servants were usually enumerated with the families where they worked.

7. CAB 1, October 3, 1862, CAB 3, March 13, 1878. The Bensons' premarital sex and pregnancy seems to have caused them no social stigma, a common experience in 1850s America, especially among blacks. See Smith and Hindus, "Premarital Pregnancy in America," 537–70; Pleck, *Black Migration*, 186; Borchert, *Alley Life in Washington*, 73.

8. CAB 3, February 27, 1879; *Salem Register*, March 3, 1853. The Bensons' wedding was among the very last duties the elderly town clerk would perform, since Joseph Shed died in early April at the age of seventy; see *Salem Register*, April 14, 1853.

9. Although she was only fifteen years old, Margaret Francis could legally marry Benson; as Michael Grossberg points out, "Both law and social policy protected youthful alliances by conferring legality on any union consummated after the wife reached twelve and her husband fourteen" (Grossberg, *Governing the Hearth*, 107). The age difference between bride and groom, too, was not unusual. Benson's older brother George L. W. also married a much younger woman, ten years his junior.

10. CAB 1, June 4, 1862.

11. Filling out the last category were the city's four black oyster dealers and "victualer" William Morison. The definitions of skilled, semi-skilled, and unskilled occupational categories follow the occupational classification system designed to fit African American urban communities created by James Horton and Lois Horton; see

Black Bostonians, app. A, 129–30. Similar definitions are discussed in Pleck, *Black Migration and Poverty,* app. B, 212–13; Thernstrom, *Other Bostonians,* 289–92; Knights, *Plain People of Boston,* app. E, 149–56; and Katzman, *Before the Ghetto,* app. B, 217–22.

12. Two or more black men were employed in shoemaking, storekeeping, stove polishing, and currying; the town also boasted one black machinist, one gardener, one grocer, one porter, and one "jobber." Ex-mariner Daniel Cooper kept a boarding house, mainly for the young transient black sailors who came to the port; the small size of Salem's black community precluded the establishment of more all-black rooming houses, such as those that abounded in larger cities.

13. See *Salem Register,* May 12, 1853, for an advertisement for the shop of Caroline Remond Putnam and Sarah P. Remond, and *Salem Register,* June 13, 1853 and January 8, 1855, for M. J. Remond and Cecelia Babcock's establishment; also the 1851 *Salem Directory,* 241. See also Oden, *"Journal of Charlotte L. Forten,"* 129–30.

14. Katzman, *Seven Days a Week,* 81, 84.

15. In Boston, for example, 25 percent of all black workers were seamen and 20 wpercent more were laborers in 1850; the proportions in Salem were similar. Yet, out of nearly 2,000 black Bostonians, only 575 listed any occupation whatsoever, suggesting that under-reporting of work (especially by women) was common. See Pleck, *Black Migration and Poverty,* table II-1, 23; Handlin, *Boston's Immigrants,* table XIII, 250–51. Handlin notes that his data were gathered directly from Boston's 1850 federal census manuscript schedules (234). A more thorough examination of occupational patterns in black Boston, adjusted to include other sources of evidence in addition to the census, is Horton and Horton, *Black Bostonians,* 8–11, 138, n. 15. For another New England community, see Warner, *New Haven Negroes,* 17–27.

16. Bolster, *Black Jacks,* 25–28. See also Bolster, "'Every Inch a Man,'" in Creighton and Norling, *Iron Men, Wooden Women,* 138–68; and Bolster, "'To Feel Like a Man.'"

17. *Boston City Directory,* 1826, 304; Albion, *Rise of New York Port,* 15, 123. No records exist to establish the details of Labin Benson's seafaring career; there are few Boston crew lists remaining from this era.

18. Bolster, "To Feel Like a Man," esp. 1189; Putney, *Black Sailors,* 49–102. See Putney, "Pardon Cook, Whaling Master," 47–54, for the story of one black captain of the 1840s and his connections to the famed black family network of early nineteenth-century shipowners and officers, the Cuffes.

19. CAB 3, July 2, 1878.

20. Salem Crew Lists, National Archives, Waltham, Mass. (SCL), 1810, rolls 479–80, 1815, roll 481, 1820, rolls 483–84, 1825, rolls 486–87, 1828, roll 488.

21. SCL, roll 489; see rolls 488–91 for the years 1828–34. Although most ships' crew lists did not explicitly identify ranks among the crew, black cooks and stewards were invariably listed separately from the other sailors, either at the bottom of the crew list or near the top, just after the officers but distinct from ordinary and able seamen.

22. SCL 1830, roll 489, 1840, rolls 493–94, 1850 roll 498, 1854 roll 499. Several of the 1854 sailors voyaged in the company of other blacks; the brig *Hayward,* bound for the west coast of Africa, even sailed with an all-black crew.

23. Albion, Baker, and Labaree, *New England and Sea,* 161.

24. Albion, "From Sails to Spindles," 115.

25. CAB 2, November 21, 1864.

26. On Margaret Benson's 1921 death certificate her father's name is listed as "Joseph Francis." Salem crew lists for the 1820s and 1830s reveal that two black men by that name sailed out of Salem, an older man born in Africa and one twenty years or so younger who was born in Salem. I believe the two were father and son, and that the younger Joseph Francis, who was in his twenties when Margaret Jenny Francis was born in 1837, was her father.

27. Some of Salem's best-known black restaurateurs and victualers of the nineteenth century were sometime seafarers, including Prince Hall, Joseph Morris, and Benson's shipmate of the 1860s, Aaron Moses. It is probable that seafaring connections established by these men were especially helpful in their trade in oysters, wines, and any delicacies requiring imported goods that would arrive via ships inbound from foreign ports-of-call. The link between work as a seafaring cook and the shore food trades was common among black mariners in many port cities.

28. *Salem Register*, July 13, August 24, 1854. For all information regarding Benson's voyages from 1854 to 1864, see the appropriate years and vessels named in SCL, rolls 499–502. Voyage dates are from those inscribed on the crew lists themselves and when so noted have been verified using arrival and departure information listed in the *Salem Register* and the *Salem Gazette*.

29. *Salem Register*, September 14, 1854.

30. Galey, "Salem's Trade with Brazil," 198–201. As Galey notes, Salem traders referred to their Brazilian destinations by province titles rather than specific port city names (200). Thus Salem ships bound for the port of Belem were said to be headed for "Para," Recife was referred to as "Pernambuco," and, in the most unusual change, the city of Sao Luis in the Maranhao province was called "Maranham" by Salemites engaged in the Brazil trade. The Argentine port of Buenos Aires is spelled "Buenos Ayres," as it was on all nineteenth-century Salem crew lists.

31. Ibid., 202–11.

32. Bertram, *John Bertram*, 17–19; Galey, "Salem's Trade with Brazil," 198, 211.

33. The *M. Shepard* was one of the stalwarts of the Brazil trade, making three-month-long runs to and from Para for over a decade. See Galey, "Salem's Trade with Brazil," 207–8.

34. Over a period of nearly three years (from July 1854 to March 1857), Benson spent a total of approximately six months in Salem. The remainder of his time was spent at sea.

35. The *Gem* may have made another few voyages out of Salem during the 1850s, but it certainly did not do so after 1860. After its coal run to Canada, the vessel could have been transferred to coastal shipping and thus disappeared from records for foreign trade.

36. The completion date of the voyage is unknown. No evidence remains to testify to the *Miquelon*'s 1856 return to Salem in either crew lists or newspaper accounts. For all intents and purposes, the vessel vanished from the historical record after leaving Salem on September 11, 1855. Based on the usual length of such voyages, and the fact that Benson is reported to have sailed from Salem on the *M. Shepard* on March 27, 1856, I assume that the *Miquelon* did indeed return to the United States sometime before then.

37. Benson's alter-ego was part of the same pattern of decline. After the false "Benson's" voyage aboard the *Costarelli* ended in 1857 the bark recorded only one more departure out of Salem the following year before it stopped departing from Salem.

38. Bertram, *John Bertram*, 17–19.

39. Passage from the journal of a British naval officer, dated 1799, quoted in Lyne, *Zanzibar in Contemporary Times*, 4. Bennett, *History of the Arab State*; Sheriff, *Slaves, Spices, and Ivory*; Allen, "Sayyids," esp. 15–17, 26–28, 91–92.

40. Lyne, *Zanzibar in Contemporary Times*, 14–33; Allen, "Sayyids," 72–89; Bennett, *History of the Arab State*, 20–25. Sheriff downplays Said's personal role in the transformations occurring in Zanzibar. His view emphasizes instead the inevitable process by which the island became a "compradorial" state, the mere "instrument of British influence." See Sheriff, *Slaves, Spices, and Ivory*, esp. 3–6.

41. Sheriff, *Slaves, Spices, and Ivory*, 1, 78–87, 129. Zanzibar did produce its own gum copal, but it was of a grade inferior to that obtained in Africa.

42. Lyne, *Zanzibar in Contemporary Times*, 245–50; Bennett, *History of the Arab State*, 24–30; Sheriff, *Slaves, Spices, and Ivory*, 49–60, 87.

43. Sheriff, *Slaves, Spices, and Ivory*, 134; Gates-Hunt, "Salem and Zanzibar," 7, 24–25.

44. Evidently young George Lee found little to love in his experiences aboard the *Elizabeth Hall*, for he never again went to sea. Lee took up the study of the law instead, following the example of close family friend Robert Morris, one of Boston's first prominent black attorneys.

45. For the Salem-Zanzibar trade, see Bennett, *History of the Arab State*, esp. 31–32, 47–48; much of Bennett's work focuses on this topic and is considered the standard scholarship on the subject. See his "Americans in Zanzibar: 1825–1845," 239–62; "Americans in Zanzibar: 1845–1865," 31–56.

46. CAB 1, cover, introductory pages, and journal entry dated May 7, 1862.

47. CAB 1, June 15, 1862.

48. Creighton, *Rites and Passages*, 12–14.

Chapter Four

1. Charles A. Benson Papers, Peabody Essex Museum (CAB), 1, May 20, June 4, 1862; CAB 2, November 4, 1864.

2. For steward-related complaints in sailors' journals, see, at Peabody Essex Museum, Moreland, diary, September 10, October 24, 26, November 27, 1861, and the anonymous diary kept aboard the *Rattler*, November 28, 1844; at Mystic Seaport Museum, see Davis, diary, May 13, July 4, August 21, 1858, February 4, 1859, and Fitch, diary, January 6, 30–31, February 3, 5, 1843; at Old Dartmouth Historical Society, see Abbe, diary, November 22, November 25, 1858; see also Busch, "*Whaling Will Never Do for Me*," 22–23.

3. Putnam, *Salem Vessels*, 2:64–65.

4. Creighton, *Dogwatch and Liberty Days*, 35; Bolster, *Black Jacks*; Busch, "*Whaling Will Never Do for Me*," 34–41; Davis diary, October 6, December 28, 1858, March 3, 30, April 12, 1859.

5. CAB 1, May 14, 1862.

6. CAB 1, August 10, 1862.

7. CAB 1, April 29, May 9, 10, June 6, 12–30, 1862.

8. CAB 1, May 3, 17, 29–31, July 15, August 21, September 25, October 14–17, 25, November 1, 13, 1862, November 5, 16, 1864.

9. CAB 1, May 12, July 1, 1862.

10. CAB 1, July 11, 18, October 16, 21, 29–31, 1862; Creighton, *Rites and Passages*, 188–89.

11. CAB 1, August 15, November 19, 1862.

12. CAB 1, August 11, November 16, 26, 1862.

13. CAB 1, July 23, 1862.

14. CAB 1, August 6, October 22, 31, 1862. Benson himself washed the captain's clothes, down to his underwear, when they were at sea, and "put [them] out to sun" to dry them as well.

15. CAB 1, July 22, 1862.

16. CAB 1, July 21, 29, September 30, 1862.

17. CAB 1, October 3, 1862.

18. CAB 1, July 21, August 7, September 1, 2, 30, October 7, 1862. Unlike sailors in the forecastle, stewards did not work on a standard schedule of four (or eight) hours off, four hours on. Instead, they were left to sleep through the night and worked only during daylight hours, when their duties of service, food preparation, and cleaning were performed. See Creighton, "Davy Jones' Locker Room," in Creighton and Norling, *Iron Men, Wooden Women*, 131.

19. CAB 1, September 14, 15, 18, October 5, 1862.

20. CAB 1, August 6, 1862. At sea Benson himself washed the captain's clothes— down to his underwear—and "put [them] out to sun" to dry them as well; see October 22, 1862.

21. CAB 1, July 23, August 6, 8, 10, 11, 30, September 3, 14–15, October 5, November 24, 1862.

22. CAB 1, October 13–14, November 18, 1862.

23. CAB 1, September 1, 3, 1862; CAB 2, November 4, 11, 24, 1864.

24. "Introduction" to Creighton and Norling, *Iron Men, Wooden Women*, ix. Several of the essays in that volume have been helpful to my understanding of seafarers' masculinity and gender constructions, including Creighton, "Davy Jones' Locker Room;" Ruth Wallis Herndon, "Domestic Cost of Seafaring;" Norling, "Ahab's Wife;" Bolster, "'Every Inch a Man'"; Laura Tabili, "'A Maritime Race.'" Creighton, *Rites and Passages* was also helpful, esp. 162–94. Lisa Norling points out that the particular conditions of seafaring made maritime communities especially susceptible to the gender ideology of separate spheres for men and women, with women's place being on land and men's at sea; see Norling, *Captain Ahab*, 265–70.

25. Much has been written about the nineteenth-century middle-class "doctrine of the spheres," concentrating especially on its implications for women. For discussions of its manly ideals and proscriptions, see Rotundo, *American Manhood*, esp. 3, 56, 167–68; several essays in Carnes and Griffith, *Meanings for Manhood*; Kett, *Rites of Passage*; several essays in Mangan and Walvin, *Manliness and Morality*; and Rothman, *Hands and Hearts*, 94.

26. Rotundo, *American Manhood*, 21.

27. In *Two Years before the Mast*, Dana relates how he left Boston in "the tight dress coat, silk cap, and kid gloves of an undergraduate at Cambridge." When he returned, he was "a 'rough-alley'-looking fellow, with duck trousers and red shirt, long hair, and face burned as black as an Indian's." Nonetheless, he was congratulated by an acquaintance on his "appearance of health and strength." In his narrative of a whaling voyage, J. Ross Browne also chronicles his transformation from "boyish" youth at nineteen into an unrecognizable and "altered" man of twenty-one. While Dana and Browne deplored the evils of sea life, they implicitly state that their harsh and brutal seafaring experiences turned untried young boys into men. See Dana, *Two Years before the Mast*, 1, 346–47; Browne, *Etchings of a Whaling Cruise*, 2–3, 482–83.

28. Creighton, *Rites and Passages*, 168–70; Bolster "Every Inch a Man," 153–55; Norling, *Captain Ahab*, 142.

29. CAB 1, May 10, 24, 1862. For sailors' attitudes toward chores defined as "domestic," see Creighton, *Rites and Passages*, 185–87.

30. CAB 1, November 1, 1862.

31. CAB 2, October 29, 1864.

32. Creighton, "Davy Jones' Locker Room," 131; Creighton, *Rites and Passages*, 185–89; Bolster, *Black Jacks*, 167. Bolster points out that cooks and stewards did perform some sailors' tasks "when tacking and wearing ship," and that although they were not expected to know much seamanship, many did; see Bolster, "African-American Seamen," 189–93. Thomas Larkin Turner's comments about the steward of the brig *Palestine* are cited in a multitude of sources as being representative of contemporary whites' attitudes toward black mariners. But Turner, the son of the captain of the *Palestine*, apparently harbored a special ill-will toward the ship's steward, calling him "that red shirted, raged pantalooned, holed-stocking, heeled, laughing shark, bedirted, black faced rascal." His comments appear in his diary kept aboard the *Palestine*, Mystic Seaport Museum, February 13, 16, 1838.

33. While the culture of the sailors' male fellowship scorned the open expression of unmanly attributes, it could still adapt to the necessities of sea life. When "women's work," such as sewing or washing clothes, was called for, seamen turned the task into an affirmation of their personal and communal manhood; see Creighton, *Rites and Passages*, 185–89. Karen Lystra terms this phenomenon "masculine reframing," noting that in the nineteenth century sex-role violations were frequently recast in ways that still fit contemporary gender-role standards; Lystra, *Searching the Heart*, 142–47.

34. Tabili, "A Maritime Race," esp. 173–74, 183–84, 187. Tabili's analysis, chiefly regarding British white males' characterization of colonized peoples, also applies to nineteenth-century America. For more on feminine characterizations of American blacks, see Haller and Haller, *Physician and Sexuality in Victorian America*, 48, 51–54.

35. Turner diary, February 16, 1838.

36. Horton, "Freedom's Yoke" in his *Free People of Color*, 101–4.

37. Jim Cullen, "'I's a Man Now,'" in Clinton and Silber, *Divided Houses*, 76–91; Salvatore, *We All Got History*; several essays in Hine and Jenkins, *A Question of Manhood*. For more on the subject of black military participation, including many passing references to manhood and manliness, see Brown, *Negro in the American*

Rebellion; Quarles, *Negro in the Civil War;* Cornish, *Sable Arm;* McPherson, *Negro's Civil War.*

38. Horton, "Freedom's Yoke," 111.

39. Salvatore, *We All Got History,* esp. 152–233.

40. Benson's close identification with his work, signifying his use of masculine reframing to preserve his place as a man in the nineteenth-century ideology of gender, was typical among sailors of his era.

41. CAB 1, June 15, 1862.

42. CAB 1, June 20–July 1, October 20, 1862.

43. CAB 2, October 31, 1864.

44. Gorn, *Manly Art,* 141, 144–45.

45. See Norling, "Ahab's Wife" (esp. 74, 79) on sailors' wives ashore. Herndon, "Domestic Cost of Seafaring," 57, discuss eighteenth-century sailors, but her conclusions apply equally well to the nineteenth century. Finally, Margaret Creighton suggests that most married sailors were either black men or white officers rather than sailors before the mast; see *Rites and Passages,* 170.

Chapter Five

1. Charles A. Benson Papers, Peabody Essex Museum (CAB), 1, May 11, 1862.

2. CAB 1, first page and May 3–4, 1862.

3. See Creighton, *Dogwatch and Liberty Days,* 69–77; Creighton, *Rites and Passages,* 10–14. Other "epistolary" journals include that of Ambrose Bates, kept aboard the *Milwood,* 1867 (cited in *Rites and Passages,* 12); and Marshall Keith, diaries kept aboard the *Cape Horn Pigeon,* 1866–69, Old Dartmouth Historical Society. Much like Benson, Keith, then second mate on a whaling voyage, was an especially expressive and frank journal-keeper who was unusually open about his sexual dreams and experiences, as well as his emotional state of mind.

4. CAB 1, May 3, 1862.

5. CAB 1, May 7, 1862.

6. CAB 1, May 4, 7, 11, June 4, July 11, August 25, 1862.

7. CAB 1, May 3, 6, 13, 14, 21, June 7, November 1, 1862.

8. CAB 1, May 4, 1862.

9. CAB 1, May 11, 18, June 8, July 6, August 3, September 28, October 19, 1862.

10. Rotundo, *American Manhood,* 110–11; Norling, *Captain Ahab,* 169–70.

11. CAB 1, October 23, 1862; Norling, *Captain Ahab,* 171–72.

12. CAB 1, May 11, 1862.

13. CAB 1, June 7–8, 1862.

14. CAB 1, May 18, 1862.

15. CAB 1, April 28, May 4, 1862.

16. CAB 1, May 4, 20, September 10, 11, 1862.

17. CAB 1, August 11, 1862.

18. CAB 1, October 3, 1862.

19. Rotundo, *American Manhood,* 25–27.

20. October 3, 19, 1862.

21. CAB 1, November 2, 1862.

22. *Salem Directory* for 1855, 1857, and 1859; Bureau of the Census, Eighth Census, National Archives, roll 497, manuscript returns of the Census of the State of Massachusetts, 1865, State Archives, roll 10, Essex County, Salem. Emma J. Benson, born in 1848, appears only in the 1860 and 1865 censuses but is otherwise unidentified; Charles did note on June 24, 1862, that it was "Emmas birthday" and on January 1, 1878, that "this month poor Emma died," without mentioning the year of her death. For more on black fostering of children, see Horton and Horton, *Black Bostonians*, 18–19.

23. CAB 1, November 1, 1862.

24. Bolster, "African-American Seamen," 393–94; see also *Black Jacks*, 169.

25. CAB 1, May 13, 1862.

26. Lystra, *Searching the Heart*, 130–36.

27. CAB 1, June 4, 1862.

28. CAB 1, April 28, May 7, June 15, 1862. It would be prudent to note that at least one middle-class Victorian man used the phrase "my Arm" as a coded reference to his sexual organ in private communications with his lover; see Lystra, *Searching the Heart*, 99. I do not think that Benson had this in mind, though, since he tended to employ other sexual euphemisms.

29. CAB 1, July 22–23, 25, September 23, 1862.

30. CAB 1, October 10, 11, 12, 21, 22, 27, November 4, 11, 15, 1862.

31. It is possible that Benson was unfaithful to his wife at some prior time in his seafaring career, although this is unsubstantiated. Katherine Richardson notes that in 1861 the ship's log reported that the steward of the *Glide* contracted venereal disease while on shore leave (Richardson, "Travels and Tribulations of Charles Benson," 78); it would be erroneous to assume that this was Benson since neither log nor crew list data imply that Benson was aboard the vessel at this time, as he was in fact serving elsewhere during the *Glide's* maiden voyage. However, Benson's own journal entries do provide a subtle suggestion that he may have transgressed on some earlier voyage, namely his repeated overemphasis that in port he "did not see a woman," perhaps implying that he had done so in the past. CAB 1, August 11, 30, 1862, see also Putnam, *Salem Vessels*, 2:64–65.

32. Furthermore, it is unlikely that Benson would have engaged in same-sex activity, which was universally condemned by the nineteenth-century bourgeois mores that guided Benson's thinking and values; for more, see Busch, *"Whaling Will Never Do for Me,"* 147–48.

33. The classic article on nineteenth-century male sexuality and attitudes regarding masturbation is Charles E. Rosenberg, "Sexuality, Class, and Role in Nineteenth-Century America," in Pleck and Pleck, *American Man*, 219–54 (see esp. 223–26 and 236–37). See also Rotundo, *American Manhood*, 120–21; Bennett and Rosario, *Solitary Pleasures*; MacDonald, "Frightful Consequences," 423–31; Haller and Haller, *Physician and Sexuality*, 195–225; and D'Emilio and Freedman, *Intimate Matters*, 68–69.

34. Burg, *American Seafarer*, xiv, 21–31; Burg notes how widespread masturbation was "among boys and young men" (24). Keith, diary kept aboard the *Edith May*, Old Dartmouth Historical Society, March 10, 1868 states, "I done that awfull deed" immediately following a graphic description of a sexual fantasy; I interpret this as masturbation.

35. Mitchell, diary, Mystic Seaport Museum, May 3, July 12, 1863; for more on sailors' relationships with prostitutes and native "wives," see Busch, *"Whaling Will Never Do for Me,"* 142–43; Creighton, *Rites and Passages,* 181–85.

36. Busch, *"Whaling Will Never Do for Me,"* 142.

Chapter Six

1. Charles A. Benson Papers, Peabody Essex Museum (CAB), 1, May 13, 1862.

2. Bolster, "African-American Seamen," 311; Horton and Horton, *In Hope of Liberty,* 110–11; see also Putney, *Black Sailors,* 80–85, for wage descriptions and comparisons with those earned by white sailors.

3. Putnam, *Salem Vessels,* 64–65.

4. Massachusetts Bureau of Statistics of Labor, *Second Annual Report* (Boston, 1871), 200, 403, 419, and Salem costs of living table, 425–33; Massachusetts Bureau of Statistics of Labor, *Third Annual Report* (Boston, 2), 510–20; Salem labor data from 1865 Census of the *State of Massachusetts, State Archives.* For black enlistment and bounties, see Gooding, *On the Altar of Freedom,* xxix–xxx, 17, when Gooding, a New Bedford man, complained about the low enlistment rate among black Bostonians in early 1863.

5. CAB 1, August 23, October 9, 1862.

6. CAB 1, July 29–30, August 4, 8, September 4, 1862. Salem Crew Lists, National Archives, Waltham, Mass. (SCL), roll 502, bark *Glide,* 1862.

7. CAB 1, September 1, 1862. Often short of cash, Benson took salary advances from Captain McMullan when in port, and from the cook John L. Jones. Each lent him as much as twenty-five dollars over time, more than a month's salary for Benson or Jones.

8. CAB 2, November 24, 1864.

9. CAB 1, July 27–August 6, 1862, July 28, 1862.

10. Although there is no reason to question Benson's veracity, there is no record of steward Robert Hill on the *Storm King* on its 1861–62 voyage; see SCL roll 502, bark *Storm King* and bark *William H. Shailer.*

11. *Glide* log, October 2–3, 1861, October 30–November 2, 1861; CAB 1, September 16, 19, 26–30, 1862.

12. William H. Becker, "The Black Church: Manhood and Mission," in Hine and Jenkins, *Question of Manhood,* 327–32.

13. CAB 1, August 6, October 3, October 7, 1862.

14. Jim Cullen, "'I's a Man Now,'" in Hine and Jenkins, *Question of Manhood,* 489–501; Salvatore, *We All Got History.*

15. Darlene Clark Hine and Ernestine Jenkins, "Black Men's History," in Hine and Jenkins, *Question of Manhood,* 46–51; Cullen, "I's a Man Now," 492–93; Horton and Horton, *In Hope of Liberty,* 267–70; Salvatore, *We All Got History,* 110–18.

16. CAB 1, May 30, June 16–17, September 1, October 6, 1862.

17. CAB 1, July 22, August 6, 1862. These references had nothing to do with slavery in the United States, for the British Navy was engaged in a crackdown on Arab slave-trading between East Africa, Zanzibar, and the Middle East at the time.

18. Quarles, *Negro in the Civil War,* xiii.

19. In the 1860 federal census (Bureau of the Census, Eighth Census, National Archives) and the 1865 Massachusetts state census, Johnson was judged a "mulatto." His pension records, however, describe him as being five feet tall, with black hair, black eyes, and a "dark complexion"; see his records in U.S. Veterans Administration, Record Group 15, National Archives, George Johnson IA 800908 and WI 848715 (Georgiana Johnson). The mystery remains unresolved. In contrast to Johnson's unique experience, see Quarles, *Negro in the Civil War*, 29–32.

20. Information regarding black sailors in the U.S. Navy is from the database compiled from the Weekly Returns of Enlistments at Naval Rendezvous by the African American Sailors' Research Project at Howard University, supplied to me courtesy of Joseph P. Reidy. For more on black naval participation in the Civil War, see Valuska, "Negro in the Union Navy."

21. Emilio, *Brave Black Regiment;* Fox, *Record,* is the published diary of one of that regiment's officers and details the action seen by most of the black Salemites who served in the Union army. Military service information for these men is taken from *Salem Directory* volumes 1863–65; the 1865 Census of the State of Massachusetts; roster lists in Fox, *Record,* 114–44, and George F. McKay, "Roster of the Fifty-Fourth Massachusetts Infantry," in Emilio, *Brave Black Regiment,* 339–92. Fletcher's role as meeting secretary appears in Emilio, *Brave Black Regiment,* 12–13; Remond's presence is noted there as well, and see also Gooding, *On the Altar of Freedom,* xxviii, which notes Remond's recruiting efforts as far away as New Bedford, Mass., within a few days of his Boston appearance.

22. Pension application records in Record Group 15. Existing records include John Cassell, Invalid Application 1058256 and Widow Application 639436 (Mercy Morris Cassell); Jacob C. Chase, IA 1372139; George Johnson, IA 800908 and WI 848715 (Georgiana Johnson); John Henry Johnson, IA 868950 and WI 932532 (Maggie Johnson); Simeon J. Wheatland, WA 497328 (Sarah H. Wheatland). William Sherman's pension records, IA 490652 and Navy JO 37756, have vanished somewhere in the National Archives and are unlikely to be found.

23. CAB 1, May 10, 12, 1862.

24. *Salem Gazette,* January 13, 1863.

25. *Salem Gazette,* January 13, February 27, 1863. See also Takaki, *Iron Cages,* 113–16, 125. On white images of black men, see Fredrickson, *Black Image in the White Mind,* 53–55; Blassingame, *Slave Community,* 223–38; Eric Lott, *Love and Theft,* 244 n. 31; Boskin, *Sambo,* 15. For racism among white soldiers, see Quarles, *Negro in the Civil War,* 183–213; Redkey, *Grand Army of Black Men,* esp. 249–48; Salvatore, *We All Got History,* 122–50. For many black soldiers, the key issue was that of pay; for an extended time, black soldiers' pay was set at ten dollars a month, three dollars less than white soldiers received; see Gooding, *On the Altar of Freedom,* 82–83.

26. Dean Rehberger, Introduction to Trowbridge, *Cudjo's Cave,* v–vi, xv–xvi.

27. Trowbridge, *Cudjo's Cave,* 117–18, 137.

28. Ibid., 122.

29. Ibid., 132–33; CAB 2, November 2, 1864.

30. Trowbridge, *Cudjo's Cave,* 500–501. Rehberger analyzes the bourgeois characteristics of the hero, Penn Hapgood, in his Introduction, xxiii–xxx.

31. "Religious Life of the Negro Slave," 479, 680.

32. CAB 2, November 25, 1864.

33. "Religious Life of the Negro Slave," 678.

34. Baker, *Journey Back*, 19–20, 33–34.

35. Major, *Juba to Jive*, 319–20 and Major, *Dictionary of Afro-American Slang*, 85. For the *Chicago Defender* quotation, see Wentworth and Flexner, *Dictionary of American Slang*, 354.

36. National Archives: Census Bureau, manuscript schedules of the Seventh Census (1850), roll 312, "Essex County, Mass.: Salem"; Bureau of the Census, Eighth Census, roll 497, Ninth Census, roll 613, Tenth Census, roll 532. State Archives: Census of the State of Massachusetts, 1855 (roll 12) and 1865 (roll 10), "Essex County: Salem"; *Salem Directory*, 1837–81.

37. CAB 1, May 9–11, June 10, 1862.

38. CAB 2, November 13, 1864.

39. Broadhead, "Negro in Salem," 3.

40. CAB 1, May 25, 1862.

41. Curry, *Free Black in Urban America*, 174–95, esp. 194–95; Levesque, *Black Boston*, 263–313; Horton and Horton, *Black Bostonians*, 39–52; Daniels, *In Freedom's Birthplace*, 21–23; Cottrol, *Afro-Yankees*, 49–50, 57–62.

42. At Peabody *Essex Museum*, Moreland, diary, September 10, October 24, 26, November 27, 1861, and diary kept aboard the *Rattler*, November 28, 1844, at Mystic Seaport Museum (MSM), Davis, diary, May 13, July 4, August 21, 1858; at Old Dartmouth Historical Society, Abbe, diary, November 22, 25, 1858, and Jenney, diary, November 12, 25, 1859; one extended story of a poor steward is recorded in Fitch, diary, MSM, January 6, 30–31, February 3, 5, 1843. See also Briton Cooper Busch's treatment of this story in *"Whaling Will Never Do for Me,"* 22–23.

43. Creighton, *Dogwatch and Liberty Days*, 35. Creighton defines duff as "a boiled flour pudding occasionally made with raisins" (12). Bolster, "African American Seamen," 296.

44. CAB 2, November 1, 28, 29, 1864.

Chapter Seven

1. Putnam, *Salem Vessels*, 2:65–66.

2. Salem Crew Lists, National Archives, Waltham, Mass., roll 502, "1860C–1866," bark *Glide* (1864); Charles A. Benson Papers, Peabody Essex Museum (CAB), 2, November 16, 1864.

3. *Salem Gazette*, October 18, November 11, 1859, June 26, 1866.

4. CAB 2, October 31, November 2, 4, 28, 29, 1864.

5. Bennett, *History of the Arab State*, 78–80; Bennett, "Americans in Zanzibar: 1845–1865," 52–53; Gates-Hunt, "Salem and Zanzibar," 10, 24–25; Sheriff, *Slaves, Spices, and Ivory*, 92–104, 129–37.

6. Putnam, *Salem Vessels*, 2:65–68.

7. CAB 2, November 30, 1864.

8. CAB 2, November 19, 16, 29, 1864.

9. CAB 2, October 30, November 17, 1864; CAB 1, October 22, 27, November 4, 1862.

10. CAB 2, October 29, 1864.

11. CAB 2, November 21, 1864.

12. CAB 1, April 29, May 30, June 3, 6, 11, August 20, 23, October 1–2, 1862.

13. Brooks, *Civil War Medicine*, 113–17.

14. Ibid., 115–16; Duffy, *Healers*, 217–19; Adams, *Doctors in Blue*, 20–26.

15. CAB 1, May 10, June 20, July 14, August 2, October 23, 1862; CAB 2, November 2, 4, 1864; Burton, *Zanzibar*, 1:96–101, 163–69, 322; Adams, *Doctors in Blue*, 21.

16. Warner, *Therapeutic Perspective*, 91–94; Duffy, *Healers*, 91–97.

17. Warner, *Therapeutic Perspective*, 166–68, 226–31.

18. Ibid., 46–51, 98–100; Duffy, *Healers*, 100–103; Haller, *American Medicine*, 79–81.

19. Duffy, *Healers*, 112–19; Haller, *American Medicine*, 104–29; Warner, *Therapeutic Perspective*, 176–82.

20. On laudanum, see Duffy, *Healers*, 232–33; Brooks, *Civil War Medicine*, 65, 116–17; Adams, *Doctors in Blue*, 195–96; "Opium in China." See also "Peppermint."

21. "Opium in China"; Warner, *Therapeutic Perspective*, 137, 139–40.

22. CAB 2, October 30, November 2, 17, 29, December 1, 1864/ On blue pills, see Warner, *Therapeutic Perspective*, 60; William H. Johnson's Civil War Letters.

23. Haller, *American Medicine*, 77–90; Adams, *Doctors in Blue*, 39–40; Duffy, *Healers*, 212–13.

24. CAB 2, October 31, November 1, 3–4, 1864; Warner, *Therapeutic Perspective*, 92–94, 100.

25. CAB 2, November 5, 11, 20, 1864.

26. Brooks, *Civil War Medicine*, 65, 68; Clifford M. Foust, "Rhubarb History"; CAB 2, November 2, 4, December 2, 1864.

27. CAB 2, November 1, 11, 1864.

28. CAB 2, October 31, 1864.

Chapter Eight

1. Crew list for the bark *Glide* (1865), in Salem Crew Lists, National Archives, Waltham, Mass., roll 502, "1860C–1866." Proof of Benson's shore stint from 1865 to 1875 includes laundry lists dated January 1–July 1, 1865, composed by Benson in Salem, in the back pages of his 1864 journal volume; *Glide* crew lists from 1865 through 1870 that lack his name; *Salem Directory* listings in 1866, 1869, 1870, and 1872 that attribute shore work to Benson; and his obituary, which states that Benson spent only six years at the end of his life at sea, corresponding to the period 1875–81. See also the adapted obituary in Putnam, *Salem Vessels*, 2:95, 108–9.

2. Putnam, *Salem Vessels*, 2:66–67.

3. Charles A. Benson Papers, Peabody Essex Museum (CAB), 2, lists in back pages following journal entries.

4. The triumphant parade of the Fifty-fourth is described in Emilio, *Brave Black Regiment*, 318–21; Fox recounts that of the Fifty-fifth in *Record*, 84. Liberty Guard parade noted in *Salem Gazette*, November 24, 1857. For the changes evidenced by returning black Civil War veterans after the war, see Salvatore, *We All Got History*, 150–215, on the new leadership roles taken by Worcester's black veterans, most notably Sergeant Amos Webber of the Massachusetts Fifth Infantry, Company D. See also Reidy et al., "With a Tattoo," courtesy of the authors.

5. *Salem Gazette*, July 12, 1867, November 18, December 28, 1869, March 8, 1870.

6. *New National Era*, March 17, April 7, 28, 1870. For Charles Sumner Wilson, see also *Salem Gazette*, March 8, 1870; Charles Sumner Wilson, file no. 1, in U.S. Adjutant General's Office, Colored Troops Division, roll 1.

7. Fredrickson, *Black Image*, 177–87. For Salem examples, see *Salem Gazette*, January 27, 31, June 1, 9, 1865.

8. Pleck, *Black Migration*, esp. xvi, 9–10, 130–35, 144–46, 157; Trotter, *Great Migration*, 2–21; Kusmer, "The Black Urban Experience in American History" (and commenting essays by James O. Horton and Lawrence W. Levine), in Hine, *State of Afro-American History*, 91–138.

9. Gerber, *Black Ohio;* Kusmer, *Ghetto Takes Shape;* Gregg, *Sparks from the Anvil*, 6–17. See also Lewis, *In Their Own Interests*.

10. Church conflict in *Salem Gazette*, August 14, 1866. For Remond's involvement in the formation of the church, see Broadhead, "Brief History," 3; New York *Freedom's Journal*, March 14, 1828, 201.

11. Horton and Horton, *Black Bostonians*, 25.

12. Salvatore, *We All Got History*, 153–55.

13. Salem's 1865 black population was calculated from Census of the State of Massachusetts, 1865, with additional information from the *Salem Directories* of 1864 and 1866. Ages for some individuals not listed in the 1865 Massachusetts state census were derived from data in census returns for other years, including the federal censuses for 1850, 1860, 1870, and 1880, and the 1855 Massachusetts state census.

14. In 1860 Salem's population was over 22,000; it subsided to a level of about 21,200 by 1865. See Moffatt, *Population History*, 69; Solomon, "Growth of the Population," 87–88.

15. Many southern migrants stayed in Salem for a short time. For a striking example, see the pension application file of John Henry Johnson in U.S. Veterans Administration, Record Group 15, National Archives, IA 868950 and WI 932532 (Maggie Johnson). Johnson was a former slave from Virginia who signed on with the Massachusetts Fifty-fifty Infantry in Salem in 1863 but returned to Virginia immediately after the war. I believe that many of Johnson's fellow migrants from the South who stopped in Salem ended up in Boston's large black community, but I do not have any hard evidence.

16. The information gathered from the federal census returns for 1870 and 1880 been supplemented with data from Salem city directories published during the years before 1870 and after, esp. 1866, 1869, 1874, 1878, and 1881.

17. Thernstrom and Knights, "Men in Motion," 47 n. 36.

18. Pleck, *Black Migration*, 136. For comparisons with transience among white urban residents, see Thernstrom and Knights, "Men in Motion"; Thernstrom, *Other Bostonians*, esp. 222, table 9.1; Knights, *Plain People of Boston*, 103–18.

19. Some of these "arrivals" were newborn children.

20. Boston, which experienced a 68 percent increase in population between 1870 and 1880 (see Pleck, *Black Migration*, 209, table A-1), was the most likely destination for Salem's black out-migrants. Pleck posits that between 11 and 40 black Bostonians hailed from Salem by 1890 (48–49), but I have been unable to verify those figures. Other blacks may have moved to nearby Lynn or, like the Putnams, to Worcester. Thernstrom and Knights propose that people of the late nineteenth century moved

only short distances from their home towns or states ("Men in Motion," 48–49 n. 39); it is likely that this pattern holds for Salem, but I have no specific evidence to support the contention.

21. Hunt, *Pocket Guide to Salem*, 17; Bennett, "Americans in Zanzibar: 1825–1845" and "Americans in Zanzibar: 1845–1865"; Albion, "From Sails to Spindles," 115–16, 136; Galey, "Salem's Trade with Brazil," 198–211; Bertram, *John Bertram*. Salem's trade had centered on gum copal, rubber, cotton goods, and gunpowder; Salem's heavy reliance on cotton and gunpowder proved to be especially disastrous during the Civil War years, when these goods became practically unattainable to private traders. For a discussion of the larger maritime declension in New England during this era, see Albion, Baker, and Labaree, *New England and the Sea*, 161.

22. Black sailors were regularly omitted from official records. Many of them were young and single and so were easily missed; moreover, seamen were frequently at sea during the collection of census data. This fact explains the discrepancies between crew lists and official records, such as census records and city directories; these official records reported only 29 black mariners in Salem in 1850 and 46 in 1855, while crew lists reported 56 and 53, respectively. Even more glaring is the fact that only 5 of the mariners mentioned in official 1850 sources shipped out that year aboard Salem vessels; 24 of them did not (perhaps leaving from Boston or else taking a respite from seafaring). It is intriguing to note that the actual number of Salem's black mariners in 1850, including the 56 men on crew lists and the 24 additional mariners listed in censuses and directories, could have been as high as 80.

23. Two of the three were transplanted Africans who had probably worked their passage to America. In 1880, steward Charles A. Benson was the sole remnant of what had once been a large native-born contingent of black Salemite mariners.

24. As Thernstrom and Knights have observed, "the rate of business mortality" was "notoriously high for small marginal enterprises" at this time ("Men in Motion," 9); the Remonds' experiences show that this high rate was true even for larger, established black businesses. For the Remond family, see Oden, "Black Putnams," 244–45, and Porter, "Remonds of Salem," 288, 291–92. Caroline Remond Putnam spent much of her time abroad in Europe beginning in the 1860s; her sister Maritche Remond finally joined her there for good in 1885.

25. Albion, "From Sails to Spindles," 122–24. By the 1870s these vessels were no longer traveling in and out of Salem but were instead working out of the port of Boston.

26. Katzman, *Before the Ghetto*, 104–5; Foner and Lewis, *Black Workers*, 6–7.

27. *Salem Directory*, 1869; Census of the State of Massachusetts, 1865, State Archives; Bureau of the Census, Ninth Census (1870), National Archives.

28. *Salem Directory* for 1866, 1869. The 1869 *Directory* misspelled the name of Benson's employer, Aaron Moses, stating that Benson was a "Clerk at Atton Mosis, 25 Front street." Moses' name was spelled correctly in his own *Directory* listing and in an illustrated advertisement for his eating establishment, which appeared on page 303.

29. In addition to Benson, a very few black clerks did work in Salem during this era, including Civil war veteran Francis Fletcher, who ended up a house painter by 1869 according to the *Salem Directory* and 1870 federal census, and one other named

Abraham Marbary (or Marbray), who apparently clerked for white employers no later than 1861.

30. *Salem Directory*, 1872.

31. CAB 3, June 30, July 4, 1878.

32. CAB 3, April 28, 1878.

33. CAB 3, December 26, 1878.

34. CAB 4, August 11, 1880.

35. CAB 4, July 28, August 3, 1880.

36. CAB 3, August 7, 1878.

37. CAB 3, December 26, 1878, January 17, 1879; CAB 1, May 13, 1862.

38. CAB 3, December 27, 29, 1878.

39. CAB 3, January 4, 13, 14, 18, 28, February 7, 1879.

40. CAB 3, December 27, 31, 1878; January 8–9, 1879.

41. CAB 3, July 4, 1878.

42. CAB 3, September 11, 1878.

43. CAB 3, April 17, 1878; CAB 4, December 16, 1880.

44. CAB 3, June 29, 1878.

45. CAB 3, October 8, 1878.

46. CAB 3, July 7, December 25, 1878; CAB 4, August 19, November 3, 1880.

Chapter Nine

1. Putnam, *Salem Vessels*, 2:62–129.

2. It is possible but unlikely that Benson was the *Taria Topan*'s cook; although he had not served in that capacity since the 1850s, he did have significant experience as a cook from his earliest voyages.

3. Ibid., 71–73, 106–17; Department of the Interior, National Parks Service, *Salem*, 135.

4. Bennett, *History of the Arab State*, 107–9; Lyne, *Zanzibar*, 71–72.

5. Bennett, *History of the Arab State*, 53–58, 87–88, 91–115; Burton, *Zanzibar*, 1:96–101, 163–69, 322; Sherriff, *Slaves, Spices, and Ivory*, 10, 62–67, 107–9, 137–51, 235.

6. Sherriff, *Slaves, Spices, and Ivory*, 92–104, 129–37; Bennett, *History of the Arab State*, 78–80; Burton, *Zanzibar*, 2:414; Gates-Hunt, "Salem and Zanzibar," 10, 24–25. Also Bennett, "Americans in Zanzibar: 1845–1865," 52–53, notes that Zanzibar's cotton imports fell from 7,000 bales in 1859 to 50 bales in the year ending July 1, 1865.

7. Bennett, "Americans in Zanzibar: 1865–1900," 46–48; Trumbull, "Account of my Trip from Salem to Zanzibar," Peabody Essex Museum, 50, 54–55, 60, 88.

8. Putnam, *Salem Vessels*, 66–71, 118–121; Salem Crew Lists, National Archives, Waltham, Mass., roll 502, 1860C–1866.

9. Putnam, *Salem Vessels*, 71, 119.

10. Charles A. Benson Papers, Peabody Essex Museum, (CAB), 3, March 31, 1878.

11. CAB 3, March 13, April 8–9, 1878.

12. CAB 3, May 5, 1878; see also Roger Wilmut, ed., *Complete Monty Python's Flying Circus* (New York: Pantheon Books, 1989), 1:104.

13. CAB 3, May 10, 1878; CAB 4, July 14, 1880.

14. CAB 3, May 3, 1878.

15. CAB 3, September 2, 1878.

16. CAB 3, July 24, 1878, see also July 25–August 9, 1878.

17. CAB 4, November 9, 1880; see also November 4, 5, 7, 15, 24, 1880.

18. Putnam, *Salem Vessels*, 78, 92, 108–9, 119.

19. CAB 3, October 19, 1878. It is possible that Beadle's removal from command of the *Taria Topan* reflected an attempt to embarrass or shame him into a better performance, a common tactic among shipowners, according to Margaret Creighton; see her *Rites and Passages*, 88–90.

20. CAB 3, December 3, 1878.

21. CAB 3, December 4, 1878.

22. CAB 3, December 7, 1878; see also May 27, November 23, December 26, 1878, February 3–5, 17, 1879.

23. CAB 3, May 30, November 25, 1878.

24. CAB 3, December 10, 1878.

25. CAB 3, November 29, 1878.

26. CAB 3, April 8, July 17–30, October 1–5, November 16–19, December 1, 27, 1878.

27. CAB 3, May 10, September 13, October 20, 1878.

28. CAB 3, May 31, 1878.

29. CAB 3, June 12, 1878.

30. CAB 3, May 31, November 13–14, 23, 29, December 9, 12, 1878.

Chapter Ten

1. Charles A. Benson Papers, Peabody Essex Museum (CAB), 3, February 7, 1879.

2. In Benson's era and subsequent periods, blacks seeking middle-class respectability have encountered difficulties not only from whites but from some segments of the African American population; lower- and middle-class differentiation within the black community has been receiving increased scholarly study. The earliest research was published by the black sociologist E. Franklin Frazier in his *Black Bourgeoisie* in 1957; subsequent works include Landry, *New Black Middle Class* and Pattillo-McCoy, *Black Picket Fences*. A recent work focusing on one community at the turn of the twentieth century is Feldman, *Sense of Place*.

3. CAB 3, January 29, 1879.

4. CAB 3, July 21, October 12, 1878.

5. Benson does not name the cook in his journal entries, and no crew lists exist to identify the man.

6. CAB 4, June 27, 30, July 8, 1880.

7. CAB 3, July 9, 1878.

8. CAB 4, October 14, 1880.

9. CAB 3, July 12 and June 27, 1878.

10. CAB 4, July 1, 1880.

11. CAB 3, December 26, 29, 1878.

12. CAB 3, June 8, 1878.

13. CAB 3, August 15, 1878; CAB 4, December 22, 1880.

14. In 1878, First Mate Welch in particular snarled at Benson on several occasions, usually regarding some facet of Benson's relationship with Captain Beadle; see CAB 3, December 12, 1878.

15. Benson's comments about George Morris's backward ideas include a reference to his ignorance of "Politicks," but Benson's own political views are unknown. Other blacks were passionately committed to the Republican Party during the postbellum years; see in Salvatore, *We All Got History*. Benson's written record of this period is empty of even a single reference to contemporary American political figures, white or black, or any major events of the time.

16. CAB 3, July 7, 1878.

17. *Salem Directory*, 1878–81; Bureau of the Census, Tenth Census, National Archives. The many residential changes the Bensons made over the years were hardly uncommon among city dwellers of their era; Thernstrom and Knights point out that "in Boston in the 1880's . . . hardly half" of the city's families "lived at the same address for at least a year." In other cities, such as Chicago and New York, the population's movements may have been even more "fluid and volatile." See *Men in Motion*, 19–20.

18. Gillespie, *Illustrated history of Salem and environs*, 49.

19. This facility is described in full in ibid., 32.

20. According to "Report of the Social Conditions of the Working-Man," compiled in 1876, the average annual rent paid by Essex County men was $105.10 (the average for the entire state of Massachusetts was even higher, at a level of $109.07). The yearly rent the Bensons paid in 1880, at $6.50 a month, was only $78.00, far lower than the Essex County average. It is likely that a major reason for this low rent was the undesirable nature of the neighborhood and environment surrounding Rice Street. See Massachusetts Bureau of Statistics of Labor, *Seventh Annual Report*, 1876, 26; CAB 3, back cover.

21. CAB 1, September 10, 1862.

22. CAB 4, enclosed clippings.

23. CAB 4, August 14, 1880.

24. Creighton, *Rites and Passages*, 87, 108–15, 121–26; Busch, *Whaling Will Never Do for Me*, 18–31, 34–39, 41.

25. Lystra, *Searching the Heart*, 193–94, 212–13; Creighton, *Rites and Passages*, 179–85.

26. Rotundo, *American Manhood*, 176.

27. CAB 1, August 23, October 9, 1862; CAB 2, November 16, 1864.

28. CAB 4, August 26, 1880.

29. CAB 4, June 27, July 9, October 30, 1880; reminiscences in CAB 3, April 24, December 27, 1878; CAB 4, July 12, 1880.

30. CAB 3, April 24, 1878.

31. CAB 3, May 9, 1878, February 12–14, 1879.

32. CAB 4, July 20, August 8, 1880.

33. CAB 4, August 18, 1880.

34. CAB 4, September 3–27, 1880.

35. CAB 4, October 14–16, 25, 1880.

36. CAB 3, August 4, 1878.

Epilogue

1. Putnam, *Salem Vessels*, 2:95. For other examples of contemporary racialist thought in Salem, see Massachusetts Bureau of Statistics of Labor *Social and Industrial Condition of the Negro*, 319; Davenport, *Homes and Hearths*, 9; Silsbee, *Half Century in Salem*, 27, 94–96, 100. See also Boskin, *Sambo*, 100–108, 123–29; Boime, *Art of Exclusion*, 153–219. Boime's analysis of Augustus Saint-Gaudens's Boston Common *Memorial to Robert Gould Shaw*, often seen as a monument to black "valor and devotion" (erroneously so, in Boime's view), is especially trenchant; see 199–219.

BIBLIOGRAPHY

"My Books & papers I find I have a goodly number"

PRIMARY SOURCES

City Directories

New York Public Library. *Boston City Directory*. Boston: [various publishers], 1821, 1825, 1827–1830.

Peabody Essex Museum, Salem, Mass. *Salem Directory and City Register*. Salem: [various publishers], 1837–1921.

Town Records

Danvers Public Library, Danvers, Mass. Danvers Town Records, 1853.

Framingham City Hall, Framingham, Mass. Framingham Town Records, 1820–55.

Natick Public Library, Natick, Mass. Natick Town Records, 1840–53.

Salem City Hall, Salem, Mass. Salem Birth, Death, and Marriage Records, 1837–1920.

Vital Records

Massachusetts State Archives, Boston, Mass. *Vital Records to the Year 1850* (VR) for Massachusetts towns of Danvers, Framingham, Marshfield, Natick, Pembroke, Salem, Shirley, Sudbury.

New York Public Library. Vital records for Boston, Mass., 1630–1849. Vol. 15. "Holbrook Deaths Index, 1801–1848" (typed), microfiche 489; "Marriages, 1807–1828," microfiche 151.

Newspapers

American Antiquarian Society, Worcester Mass., and Beinecke Library, Yale University, New Haven, Conn. *Salem Gazette*, 1850–80. *Salem Register*, 1850–80.

Framingham [Mass.] Historical Society. *Massachusetts Ploughman*, 1843.

Library of Congress, Washington, D. C. *New National Era*, 1870. *New York Freedom's Journal*, 1827, 1828, 1839.

Peabody Essex Museum, Salem, Mass. *Salem Evening News*, 1897.

Federal and State Government Documents

Massachusetts. Bureau of Statistics of Labor. Annual Reports. Boston, 1872–1905.

———. *The Social and Industrial Condition of the Negro in Massachusetts (Thirty-Fourth Annual Report of the Bureau of Statistics of Labor)*. Boston: Bureau of Labor, 1904.

Massachusetts State Archives, Boston, Mass. Census of the State of Massachusetts,

1855 and 1865, manuscript returns. Massachusetts birth records, marriage records, death records. Middlesex County Probate Dockets.

U.S. Adjutant General's Office. Colored Troops Division. Record Groups 94 and 149. *Selected Documents Relating to Blacks Nominated for Appointment to the United States Military Academy during the Nineteenth Century, 1870–1887* [microfilm].

U.S. National Archives and Records Service, Waltham, Mass. Records of the Collectors of Customs for the Collection District of Salem and Beverly, Mass. Salem Crew Lists, 1805–75 (SCL).

U.S. National Archives and Records Service, Washington, D.C.

    Benson, Abel. Pension Application no. W23574. In *Revolutionary War Pension and Bounty Land Warrant Application Files*, roll 221. Washington, D.C.: U.S. Government Printing Office, [various dates].

    U.S. Census Office. Fourth Census of the United States, manuscript schedules, Middlesex County, Mass., 1820 [microfilm].

    ———. *Book I of the Fourth Census, 1820.* Washington, D.C., 1821.

    ———. Fifth Census of the United States, manuscript schedules, Middlesex County, Mass., 1830 [microfilm].

    ———. Sixth Census of the United States, manuscript schedules, Middlesex County, Mass., 1840 [microfilm].

    ———. *Sixth Census or Enumeration of the Inhabitants of the United States as Corrected at the Department of State in 1840.* Washington, D.C., 1841.

    ———. Seventh Census of the United States, manuscript schedules, Essex and Middlesex Counties, Mass., 1850 [microfilm].

    ———. *Seventh Census of the United States.* Book I, *Population.* Washington, D.C., 1853.

    U.S. Department of Commerce and Labor, Bureau of the Census. *A Century of Population Growth: From the First Census of the United States to the Twelfth, 1790–1900.* Washington, D.C., 1909.

    ———. *Heads of Families at the First Census of the United States, Taken in the Year 1790.* Washington, D.C., 1908.

    ———. *Negro Population in the United States, 1790–1915.* Washington, D.C., 1918. Reprint, New York: Arno Press, 1968.

    ———. Eighth Census of the United States, manuscript schedules, Essex County, Mass., 1860 [microfilm].

    ———. Ninth Census of the United States, manuscript schedules, Essex County, Mass., 1870 [microfilm].

    ———. Tenth Census of the United States, manuscript schedules, Essex County, Mass., 1880 [microfilm].

    ———. *Compendium of the Eleventh Census of the United States.* Washington, D.C., 1892.

    ———. Twelfth Census of the United States, manuscript schedules, Essex County, Mass., 1900 [microfilm].

    ———. Thirteenth Census of the United States, manuscript schedules, Essex County, Mass. [microfilm].

    ———. *Thirteenth Census of the United States: Abstract of the Census.* Washington, D.C., 1913.

————. Fourteenth Census of the United States, manuscript schedules, Essex
County, Mass., 1920 [microfilm].

————. *Fourteenth Census of the United States: 1920.* Washington, D.C., 1921.

U.S. Veterans Administration. *Revolutionary War Pension and Bounty Land Warrant
Application Files* [microfilm].

————. Record Group 15, Civil War Pension Files.

Manuscripts

Mystic Seaport Museum, Blunt-White Library, Mystic, Conn.

Davis, Henry L. Diary kept aboard *South America,* Log 532.

Fitch, Silas. Diary kept aboard *Charles Phelps,* Log 142.

Mitchell, Harry B. Diary kept aboard *Fairy,* Log 5.

Townshend, William H. Diary kept aboard *Imaum,* Log 579.

Turner, Thomas Larkin. Diary kept aboard *Palestine,* Coll. 95 vol. 14.

Weir, Robert. Diary kept aboard *Clara Bell,* Log 164.

Nicholson Whaling Collection, Providence, R. I. Marshall Keith. Diary kept aboard
Brewster, Log 95.

Old Dartmouth Historical Society, Whaling Museum Library, New Bedford, Mass.

Abbe, William A. Diary kept aboard *Atkins Adams,* Log 485.

Jenney, Edward N. Diary kept aboard *Alfred Gibbs,* Log 998.

Keith, Marshall. Diaries kept aboard *Cape Horn Pigeon,* Log 371 and *Edith May,*
Log 372.

Peabody Essex Museum, Phillips Library, Salem, Mass.

John Battis Diary.

Diary kept aboard *Chaledony.*

Diary kept aboard *Rattler.*

Diary kept aboard *William Schroder.*

Charles A. Benson Papers (CAB). Vol. 1 (1862); vol. 2 (1864–65); vol. 3 (1878–79);
vol. 4 (1880–81).

John Bertram Papers, bark *Glide,* Box 3, Folder 5.

Cook, Caleb. Zanzibar Notebook, Family Manuscripts, 1861.

Emmerton, Ephraim Augustus. Diary kept aboard *Sophronia,* 1848.

Harrington, A. Diary kept aboard *La Grange,* 1849.

Haskell, Edward. Diary kept aboard *Tarquin,* 1862.

Huntington, William. Diary kept aboard clipper ship *Contest,* 1863.

Logs of the bark *Glide,* 1861–80.

Log of the bark *Taria Topan,* 1878–79.

Miles, D. L. Diary kept aboard bark *Brothers,* 1866.

Moreland, Francis. Diary kept aboard *Sooloo,* 1861.

Salem, Massachusetts, Crew Lists, typescripts, 1800–1815.

Taylor, William C. Diaries kept aboard *Angelina,* 1862 and *Northern Belle,* 1861 and
1863.

Trumbull, Edward. "Account of my Trip from Salem to Zanzibar," bark *Taria
Topan,* 1886–87, MSS 105.

SECONDARY SOURCES

Adams, George Worthington. *Doctors in Blue: The Medical History of the Union Army in the Civil War.* New York: Henry Schuman, 1952.

Albion, Robert Greenhalgh. "From Sails to Spindles: Essex County in Transition." *Essex Institute Historical Collections* 95, 2 (April 1959): 115–36.

———. *The Rise of New York Port [1815–1860].* Boston: Northeastern University Press, 1984.

Albion, Robert Greenhalgh, William A. Baker, and Benjamin W. Labaree. *New England and the Sea.* Middletown, Conn.: Wesleyan University Press, for Mystic Seaport Museum, 1972.

Allen, Calvin H. Jr. "Sayyids, Shets, and Sultans: Politics and Trade in Masqat under the Al Bu Sa'Id, 1785–1914." Ph.D. diss., University of Washington, 1978.

Andrews, William L. *To Tell a Free Story: The First Century of African-American Autobiography.* Urbana: University of Illinois Press, 1986.

Baker, Houston. *The Journey Back: Issues in Black Literature and Criticism.* Chicago: University of Chicago Press, 1980.

Barry, William. *A History of Framingham, Massachusetts.* Boston: J. Munroe & Co., 1847.

Bennett, Paula, and Vernon A. Rosario, eds. *Solitary Pleasures: The Historical, Literary, and Artistic Discourses of Autoeroticism.* New York: Routledge Press, 1995.

Bennett, Norman R. "Americans in Zanzibar: 1825–1845." *Essex Institute Historical Collections* 95 (July 1959): 239–62.

———. "Americans in Zanzibar: 1845–1865." *Essex Institute Historical Collections* 97 (January 1961): 31–56.

———. "Americans in Zanzibar: 1865–1915." *Essex Institute Historical Collections* 98 (January 1962): 36–61.

———. *A History of the Arab State of Zanzibar.* New York: Harper & Row, 1978.

Bentley, William. *The Diary of William Bentley.* Gloucester, Mass.: Peter Smith, 1962.

Berlin, Ira. *Many Thousands Gone: The First Two Centuries of Slavery in North America.* Cambridge: Harvard University Press, 1998.

———. "Time, Space, and the Evolution of Afro-American Society on British Mainland North America." *American Historical Review* 85 (1980) 44–56.

Berlin, Ira, and Ronald Hoffman, eds. *Slavery and Freedom in the Age of the American Revolution.* Urbana: University of Illinois Press, 1986.

Berlin, Ira, Joseph P. Reidy, and Leslie Rowland. *The Black Military Experience.* Series 2. Vol. 1 of *Freedom: A Documentary History of Emancipation, 1861–1867.* New York: Cambridge University Press, 1982.

Bertram, John. *John Bertram of Salem, Massachusetts.* Edited by Rosamond de Laittre. Santa Barbara, Calif.: Rosamond de Laittre, 1964.

Blassingame, John. *The Slave Community: Plantation Life in the Antebellum South.* New York: Oxford University Press, 1979.

Boime, Albert. *The Art of Exclusion: Representing Blacks in the Nineteenth Century.* Washington, D.C.: Smithsonian Institution Press, 1990.

Bolster, W. Jeffrey. "African-American Seamen: Race, Seafaring Work, and Atlantic Maritime Culture, 1750–1860." Ph.D. diss., Johns Hopkins University, 1991.

———. *Black Jacks: African-American Seamen in the Age of Sail.* Cambridge: Harvard University Press, 1997.

———. "To Feel Like a Man: Black Seamen in the Northern States, 1800–1860." *Journal of American History* 76 (March 1990): 1173–99.

Borchert, James. *Alley Life in Washington: Family, Community, Religion, and Folklife in the City, 1850–1970.* Urbana: University of Illinois Press, 1980.

Boskin, Joseph. *Sambo: The Rise and Demise of an American Jester.* New York: Oxford University Press, 1986.

Broadhead, Eleanor. "A Brief History of the Negro in Salem." Paper prepared for the Committee on Racial Understanding for the Confrontation on Racism, April 11–12, 1969. Courtesy of Phillips Library, Peabody Essex Museum, Salem, Mass.

Brooks, H. M. "Some Localities About Salem." *Essex Institute Historical Collections* 31 (1895): 115–17.

Brooks, Stewart M. *Civil War Medicine.* Springfield, Illinois: C. C. Thomas, 1966.

Brown, William J. *The Life of William J. Brown, of Providence, R.I.: With Personal Recollections of Incidents in Rhode Island.* 1883. Reprint, Freeport, N.Y.: Books for Libraries Press, 1971.

Brown, William Wells. *The Negro in the American Rebellion, His Heroism and His Fidelity.* 1867. Reprint, New York: Johnson Reprint Corporation, 1969.

Browne, J. Ross. *Etchings of a Whaling Cruise.* Cambridge, Mass.: Harvard University Press, 1968.

Bruss, Elizabeth. *Autobiographical Acts.* Baltimore: Johns Hopkins University Press, 1976.

Burg, B. R. *An American Seafarer in the Age of Sail: The Erotic Diaries of Philip C. Van Buskirk, 1851–1870.* New Haven: Yale University Press, 1994.

Burton, Richard F. *Zanzibar: City, Island, and Coast.* 2 vols. 1872. Reprint, New York: Johnston Reprint Corporation, 1967.

Busch, Briton Cooper. *"Whaling Will Never Do for Me": The American Whaleman in the Nineteenth Century.* Lexington: University Press of Kentucky, 1994.

Carnes, Mark C. *Secret Ritual and Manhood in Victorian America.* New Haven: Yale University Press, 1989.

Carnes, Mark C., and Clyde Griffith, eds. *Meanings for Manhood: Constructions of Masculinity in Victorian America.* Chicago: University of Chicago Press, 1990.

Clinton, Catherine, and Nina Silber, eds. *Divided Houses: Gender and the Civil War.* New York: Oxford University Press, 1992.

Clark, Christopher. *The Roots of Rural Capitalism: Western Massachusetts, 1780–1860.* Ithaca: Cornell University Press, 1990.

Collison, Gary Lee. *Shadrach Minkins: From Fugitive Slave to Citizen.* Cambridge: Harvard University Press, 1997.

Conklin, Edward P. *Middlesex County and Its People: A History.* 4 vols. New York: Lewis Historical Publishing Co., 1927.

Cornish, Dudley Taylor. *The Sable Arm: Negro Troops in the Union Army, 1861–1865.* New York: Longmans, Green, 1956.

Cottrol, Robert J. *The Afro-Yankees: Providence's Black Community in the Antebellum Era.* Westport, Conn.: Greenwood Press, 1982.

Creighton, Margaret. *Dogwatch and Liberty Days: Seafaring Life in the Nineteenth Century.* Salem: Peabody Museum, 1982.

———. *Rites and Passages: The Experience of American Whaling, 1830–1870.* New York: Cambridge University Press, 1995.

Creighton, Margaret, and Lisa Norling, eds. *Iron Men, Wooden Women: Gender and Seafaring in the Atlantic World, 1700–1920.* Baltimore: Johns Hopkins University Press, 1996.

Curry, Leonard P. *The Free Black in Urban America: The Shadow of the Dream.* Chicago: University of Chicago Press, 1981.

Dana, Richard Henry. *Two Years Before the Mast: A Personal Narrative of Life at Sea.* Garden City, N.Y.: 1959.

Daniels, John. *In Freedom's Birthplace: A Study of the Boston Negroes.* 1914. Reprint, New York: Negro Universities Press, 1968.

Davenport, George F. *Homes and Hearths of Salem.* Salem, 1891.

D'Emilio, John, and Estelle B. Freedman. *Intimate Matters: A History of Sexuality in America.* New York: Harper & Row, 1988.

Demos, John. *A Little Commonwealth: Family Life in Plymouth County.* New York: Oxford University Press, 1970.

Drake, Samuel Adams. *History of Middlesex County, Massachusetts.* 2 vols. Boston: Estes & Lauriat, 1880.

Duffy, John. *The Healers: A History of American Medicine.* Urbana: University of Illinois Press, 1979.

Dumas, David W. "The Naming of Children in New England, 1780–1850." *New England Historical and Genealogical Register* 132 (1978): 196–209.

Early, Gerald, ed. *Lure and Loathing: Essays on Race, Identity, and the Ambivalence of Assimilation.* New York: Viking, 1993.

Emilio, Luis F. *A Brave Black Regiment: A History of the Fifty-Fourth Regiment of Massachusetts Volunteer Infantry, 1863–1865.* New York: Johnson Reprint Corporation, 1968.

Faler, Paul G. *Mechanics and Manufacturers in the Early Industrial Revolution: Lynn, Massachusetts, 1780–1860.* Albany: State University of New York Press, 1981.

Feldman, Lynne B. *A Sense of Place: Birmingham's Black Middle-Class Community, 1890–1930.* Tuscaloosa: University of Alabama Press, 1999.

Flexner, Stuart Burg. *I Hear America Talking: An Illustrated History of American Words and Phrases.* New York: Van Nostrand Reinhold, 1976.

Foner, Philip S., and Ronald L. Lewis, eds. *The Black Worker: A Documentary History from Colonial Times to the Present.* 8 vols. Philadelphia: Temple University Press, 1978–84.

———. *Black Workers: A Documentary History from Colonial Times to the Present.* Philadelphia: Temple University Press, 1989.

Foust, Clifford M. "Rhubarb: The Wondrous Drug." The Rhubarb Compendium. Chapter 3, "Rhubarb History." Retrieved June 2001 from <http://www.rhubarbinfo.com/rhubarbhistory.htm>.

Fox, Charles Bernard. *Record of the Service of the Fifty-fifth Regiment of Massachusetts Volunteer Infantry.* Reprint, Salem, N.H.: Ayer Co., 1991.

Frazier, E. Franklin. *Black Bourgeoisie*. 1957. Reprint, New York: The Free Press, 1997.

Fredrickson, George M. *The Black Image in the White Mind: The Debate on Afro-American Character and Destiny, 1817–1914*. New York: Harper & Row, 1971.

Furstenburg, Frank F. Jr., Theodore Hershberg, and John Modell. "The Origins of the Female-Headed Black Family: The Impact of the Urban Experience." *Journal of Interdisciplinary History*, 6, 2 (autumn 1975): 211–34.

Galey, John H. "Salem's Trade with Brazil, 1801–1870." *Essex Institute Historical Collections* 107, 2 (April 1971): 198–219.

Gates-Hunt, Richard H. "Salem and Zanzibar: A Special Relationship." *Essex Institute Historical Collections* 117, 1 (January 1981): 1–26.

Gerber, David. *Black Ohio and the Color Line, 1860–1915*. Urbana: University of Illinois Press, 1976.

Gillespie, Charles Bancroft. *Illustrated history of Salem and environs: Issued as the souvenir edition of the Salem Evening News and describing and illustrating Salem, Massachusetts and immediate vicinity from first settlement to present day*. Compiled by C. B. Gillespie. Salem, Mass.: Salem Evening News, 1897.

Goldberg, Susan, and Barbara A. DeVitto. *Born Too Soon: Preterm Birth and Early Development*. San Francisco: W.H. Freeman, 1983.

Gooding, James Henry. *On the Altar of Freedom: A Black Soldier's Civil War Letters from the Front*. Edited by Virginia M. Adams. Amherst: University of Massachusetts Press, 1991.

Gorn, Elliott J. *The Manly Art: Bare-Knuckle Prize Fighting in America*. Ithaca, N.Y.: Cornell University Press, 1986.

Gottlieb, Peter. *Making Their Own Way: Southern Blacks' Migration to Pittsburgh, 1916–1930*. Urbana: University of Illinois Press, 1987.

Greene, Lorenzo Johnston. *The Negro in Colonial New England*. Port Washington, N.Y.: Atheneum, 1966.

Gregg, Robert. *Sparks from the Anvil of Oppression: Philadelphia's African Methodists and Southern Migrants, 1890–1940*. Philadelphia: Temple University Press, 1993.

Grimke, Charlotte Forten. *The Journals of Charlotte Forten Grimke*. Edited by Brenda Stevenson. New York: Oxford University Press, 1988.

Griswold, Robert L. *Family and Divorce in California, 1850–1890: Victorian Illusions and Everyday Realities*. Albany: State University of New York Press, 1982.

Grossberg, Michael. *Governing the Hearth: Law and the Family in Nineteenth-Century America*. Chapel Hill: University of North Carolina Press, 1985.

Gutman, Herbert. *The Black Family in Slavery and Freedom, 1750–1925*. New York: Pantheon Books, 1976.

Hall, Gwendolyn Midlo. *Africans in Colonial Louisiana: The Development of Afro-Creole Culture in the Eighteenth Century*. Baton Rouge: Louisiana State University Press, 1992.

Haller, John S. Jr. *American Medicine in Transition, 1840–1910*. Urbana: University of Illinois Press, 1981.

Haller, John S. Jr., and Robin M. Haller. *The Physician and Sexuality in Victorian America*. Urbana: University of Illinois Press, 1974.

Handlin, Oscar. *Boston's Immigrants [1790–1880]: A Study in Acculturation.* Cambridge: Harvard University Press, Belknap Press, 1959.

Hareven, Tamara K., and Maris A. Vinovskis, eds. *Family and Population in Nineteenth-Century America.* Princeton: Princeton University Press, 1978.

Hawes, Joseph, and Elizabeth I. Nybakken, eds. *American Families: A Research Guide and Historical Handbook.* Westport, Conn.: Greenwood Press, 1991.

Hawthorne, Nathaniel. *The Scarlet Letter.* 1850. Reprint, New York: Norton, 1988.

Henretta, James. "Families and Farms: *Mentalité* in Pre-Industrial America," *William and Mary Quarterly,* 3d ser., 35 (January 1978): 3–32.

Hershberg, Theodore. "Free Blacks in Antebellum Philadelphia: A Study of Ex-Slaves, Freeborn, and Socioeconomic Decline." *Journal of Social History* 5 (1972): 183–209.

Hine, Darlene Clark, ed. *The State of Afro-American History: Past, Present, and Future.* Baton Rouge: Louisiana State University Press, 1986.

Hine, Darlene Clark, and Earnestine Jenkins, eds. *A Question of Manhood: A Reader in U.S. Black Men's History and Masculinity.* Vol. 1, *"Manhood Rights": The Construction of Black Male History and Manhood, 1750–1870.* Bloomington: Indiana University Press, 1999.

Hoffman, Ronald, Mechal Sobel, and Fredrika J. Teute, eds. *Through a Glass Darkly: Reflections on Personal Identity in Early America.* Chapel Hill: University of North Carolina Press, 1997.

Horton, James O. *Free People of Color: Inside the African American Community.* Washington, D.C.: Smithsonian Institution Press, 1993.

Horton, James O., and Lois E. Horton. *Black Bostonians: Family Life and Community Struggle in the Antebellum North.* New York: Holmes and Meier, 1979.

———. *In Hope of Liberty: Culture, Community and Protest Among Northern Free Blacks, 1700–1860.* New York: Oxford University Press, 1997.

Howe, Daniel Walker. *Making the American Self: Jonathan Edwards to Abraham Lincoln.* Cambridge: Harvard University Press, 1997.

Hunt, Thomas F. *Pocket Guide to Salem, Massachusetts: 1883.*

Hurd, D. Hamilton, ed. *The History of Essex County, Massachusetts.* 2 vols. Philadelphia: J. W. Lewis & Co., 1888.

Jordan, Winthrop D. *White over Black: American Attitudes Toward the Negro, 1550–1812.* Chapel Hill: University of North Carolina Press, 1968.

Katzman, David M. *Before the Ghetto: Black Detroit in the Nineteenth Century.* Urbana: University of Illinois Press, 1973.

———. *Seven Days a Week: Women and Domestic Service in Industrializing America.* Urbana: University of Illinois Press, 1981.

Kett, Joseph F. *Rites of Passage: Adolescence in America 1790 to the Present.* New York: Basic Books, 1977.

Knights, Peter R. *The Plain People of Boston, 1830–1860: A Study in City Growth.* New York: Oxford University Press, 1971.

Kusmer, Kenneth L. *A Ghetto Takes Shape: Black Cleveland, 1870–1930.* Urbana: University of Illinois Press, 1976.

Lammermeier, Paul J. "The Urban Black Family of the Nineteenth Century: A Study of Black Family Structure in the Ohio Valley, 1850–1880." *Journal of Marriage and the Family* 35 (August 1973): 440–56.

Landry, Bart. *The New Black Middle Class.* Berkeley: University of California Press, 1987.

Lane, Roger. *Roots of Violence in Black Philadelphia, 1860–1900.* Cambridge: Harvard University Press, 1986.

Levesque, George. *Black Boston: African American Life and Culture in Urban America, 1750–1860.* New York: Garland Press, 1994.

Levine, Lawrence. *Black Culture and Black Consciousness: Afro-American Folk Thought from Slavery to Freedom.* New York: Oxford University Press, 1977.

Lewis, Earl. *In Their Own Interests: Race, Class, Power in Twentieth-Century Norfolk.* Berkeley: University of California Press, 1991.

Litwack, Leon. *North of Slavery: The Negro in the Free States, 1790–1860.* Chicago: University of Chicago Press, 1961.

Lott, Eric. *Love and Theft: Blackface Minstrelsy and the American Working Class.* New York: Oxford University Press, 1993.

Lyne, Robert Nunez. *Zanzibar in Contemporary Times: A Short History of the Southern East in the Nineteenth Century.* London, 1905. Reprint, New York: Negro Universities Press, 1969.

Lystra, Karen. *Searching the Heart: Women, Men, and Romantic Love in Nineteenth-Century America.* New York: Oxford University Press, 1989.

MacDonald, Robert H. "The Frightful Consequences of Onanism: Notes on the History of a Delusion." *Journal of the History of Ideas* 28 (1967): 423–31.

MacEacheren, Elaine. "Emancipation of Slavery in Massachusetts: A Reexamination, 1770–1790." *Journal of Negro History* 55 (1970): 289–306.

Major, Clarence. *Dictionary of Afro-American Slang.* New York: International Publishers, 1970.

———, ed. *Juba to Jive: A Dictionary of Afro-American Slang.* New York: Viking, 1994.

Mangan, J. A., and James Walvin, eds. *Manliness and Morality: Middle-Class Masculinity in Britain and America, 1800–1940.* New York: St. Martin's Press, 1987.

McPherson, James M. *The Negro's Civil War: How American Negroes Felt and Acted during the War for the Union.* New York: Pantheon Books, 1965.

Melish, Joanne Pope. *Disowning Slavery: Gradual Emancipation and "Race" in New England, 1780–1860.* Ithaca: Cornell University Press, 1998.

Modell, John, and Tamara Hareven. "Urbanization and the Malleable Household: An Examination of Boarding and Lodging in American Families." *Journal of Marriage and the Family* 35 (August 1973): 467–79.

Moffatt, Riley. *Population History of Eastern United States Cities and Towns, 1790–1870.* Metuchen, N.J.: Scarecrow Press, 1992.

Morgan, Edmund. *American Slavery, American Freedom: The Ordeal of Colonial Virginia.* New York: Norton, 1975.

Nash, Gary. *Forging Freedom: The Formation of Philadelphia's Black Community, 1720–1840.* Cambridge: Harvard University Press, 1988.

———. *Red, White, and Black: The Peoples of Early America.* Englewood Cliffs, N.J.: Prentice-Hall, 1974.

Nash, Gary, and Jean R. Soderlund. *Freedom by Degrees: Emancipation in Pennsylvania and its Aftermath.* New York: Oxford University Press, 1991.

Nell, William C. *The Colored Patriots of the American Revolution.* 1855. Reprint, New York: Arno Press, 1969.

Norling, Lisa. *Captain Ahab Had a Wife: New England Women and the Whalefishery, 1720–1870.* Chapel Hill: University of North Carolina Press, 2000.

Oden, Gloria C. "The Black Putnams of Charlotte Forten's Journal." *Essex Institute Historical Collections* 126, 4 (October 1990): 237–53.

———. "*The Journal of Charlotte L. Forten:* The Salem-Philadelphia Years (1854–1862) Reexamined." *Essex Institute Historical Collections* 119, 2 (April 1983): 124–36.

Office of the Secretary of State of the Commonwealth of Massachusetts. *Massachusetts Soldiers and Sailors of the Revolutionary War.* Boston: Wright & Potter, State Printers, 1896.

"Opium in China (1700–1860)." The Opiates. The Schaffer Library of Drug Policy. Retrieved June 2001 from <http://www.druglibrary.org/schaffer/heroin/opiates.htm>.

Pattillo-McCoy, Mary. *Black Picket Fences: Privilege and Peril among the Black Middle Class.* Chicago: University of Chicago Press, 1999.

"Peppermint." Herbal Remedies. Health Encyclopedia. Vitamins-etc.com. Retrieved June 2001 from <http://www.vitamins-etc.com>.

Perley, Sidney. *The History of Salem, Massachusetts.* 3 vols. Salem: S. Perley, 1926.

Phillips, Roderick. *Putting Asunder: A History of Divorce in Western Society.* New York: Cambridge University Press, 1988.

Piersen, William D. *Black Yankees: The Development of an Afro-American Subculture in Eighteenth-Century New England.* Amherst: University of Massachusetts Press, 1988.

Place, C. A. *Charles Bulfinch, Architect and Citizen.* Boston: Houghton Mifflin, 1925.

Pleck, Elizabeth H. *Black Migration and Poverty: Boston, 1865–1900.* New York: Academic Press, 1979.

Pleck, Elizabeth H., and Joseph H. Pleck, eds. *The American Man.* Englewood Cliffs, N.J.: Prentice-Hall, 1980.

Porter, Dorothy Burnett. "The Remonds of Salem, Massachusetts: A Nineteenth-Century Family Revisited." *Proceedings of the American Antiquarian Society* 95, 2 (October 1985): 259–95.

Putnam, George Granville. *Salem Vessels and their Voyages.* 4 vols. Salem: Essex Institute, 1924–30.

Putney, Martha S. *Black Sailors: Afro-American Merchant Seamen and Whalemen Prior to the Civil War.* Westport, Conn.: Greenwood Press, 1987.

———. "Pardon Cook, Whaling Master." *Journal of the Afro-American Historical and Genealogical Society* 4 (summer 1983): 47–54.

Quarles, Benjamin. *The Negro in the American Revolution.* Chapel Hill: University of North Carolina Press, 1961.

———. *The Negro in the Civil War.* 1953. Reprint, New York: Da Capo Press, 1989.

Rampersad, Arnold. "Biography, Autobiography, and Afro-American Culture." *Yale Review* 73 (autumn 1983): 1–16.

Rawick, George. *From Sundown to Sunup: The Making of the Black Community.* Westport, Conn.: Greenwood Press, 1972.

Redkey, Edwin S., ed. *A Grand Army of Black Men: Letters from African-American Soldiers in the Union Army, 1861–1865.* New York: Cambridge University Press, 1993.

Reidy, Joseph P. "'Negro Election Day' and Black Community Life in New England, 1750–1860." *Marxist Perspectives* 1, 1 (fall 1978): 102–17.

Reidy, Joseph P. et al. "With a Tattoo of 'Liberty' on his Right Forearm: Toward a Social History of Black New England Sailors in the Civil War Navy." Paper presented at "Race, Ethnicity, and Power in Maritime America" conference, Mystic Seaport Museum, September 1995.

"Religious Life of the Negro Slave." *Harper's New Monthly Magazine* 27, 160 (September 1863); 161 (October 1863).

Richardson, Katherine W. "The Trials and Tribulations of Charles A. Benson, Steward on the *Glide*, 1861–1881." *Essex Institute Historical Collections* 120, 2 (April 1984): 73–109.

Robbins, Richard H. "Identity, Culture, and Behavior." In *Handbook of Social and Cultural Anthropology*, edited by John J. Honigmann, 1199–222. Chicago: Rand McNally, 1973.

Roediger, David R. "Notes on Working-Class Racism." *New Politics* 2d ser., 7 (summer 1989): 61–66.

———. *The Wages of Whiteness: Race and the Making of the American Working Class.* New York: Verso Press, 1991.

Rosswurm, Steven. *Arms, Country, and Class: The Philadelphia Militia and "Lower Sort" during the American Revolution, 1775–1783.* New Brunswick, N.J.: Rutgers University Press, 1987.

Rothman, Ellen K. *Hands and Hearts: A History of Courtship in America.* New York: Basic Books, 1984.

Rotundo, E. Anthony. *American Manhood: Transformations in Masculinity from the Revolution to the Modern Era.* New York: Basic Books, 1993.

Rowe, G. S. "Black Offenders, Criminal Courts, and Philadelphia Society in the Later Eighteenth Century." *Journal of Social History* 22 (summer 1989): 685–712.

St. George, Robert Blair, ed. *Material Life in America, 1600–1860.* Boston: Northeastern University Press, 1987.

Salvatore, Nick. *We All Got History: The Memory Books of Amos Webber.* New York: Times Books, 1996.

Searle, John. *Expression and Meaning: Studies in the Theory of Speech Acts.* New York: Cambridge University Press, 1979.

Sensbach, John F. "Charting a Course in Early African-American History." *William and Mary Quarterly*, 3d ser., 50 (April 1993): 394–405.

Sharpless, John B., and Ray M. Shortridge. "Biased Underenumeration in Census Manuscripts: Methodological Implications." *Journal of Urban History*, 1, 4 (August 1975): 409–39.

Sheriff, Abdul. *Slaves, Spices, and Ivory in Zanzibar: Integration of an East African Commercial Empire into the World Economy, 1770–1873.* Athens: Ohio University Press, 1987.

Sherman, Stuart C. *The Voice of the Whaleman, with an Account of the Nicholson Whaling Collection.* Providence: Providence Public Library, 1965.

Silsbee, Marianne C. D. *A Half Century in Salem.* Boston: Houghton-Mifflin, 1887.

Smith, Daniel Scott, and Michael S. Hindus. "Premarital Pregnancy in America,

1640–1971: An Overview and Interpretation." *Journal of Interdisciplinary History* 4 (spring 1975): 537–70.

Sobel, Mechal. *The World They Made Together: Black and White Values in Eighteenth-Century Virginia*. Princeton: Princeton University Press, 1987.

Sokolow, Michael. "'New Guinea at One End, and a View of the Alms-House at the Other': The Decline of Black Salem, 1850–1920." *New England Quarterly* 71 (June 1998): 204–28.

Solomon, Barbara N. "The Growth of the Population in Essex County, 1850–1860." *Essex Institute Historical Collections* 95, 2 (April 1959): 82–103.

Stapp, Carol Buchalter. *Afro-Americans in Antebellum Boston: An Analysis of Probate Records*. New York: Garland Press, 1993.

Stowe, Steven. Review of Sobel, *The World They Made Together*. *Journal of American History* 75 (December, 1988), 899–900.

Takaki, Ronald T. *Iron Cages: Race and Culture in Nineteenth-Century America*. New York: Knopf, 1979.

Temple, Josiah Howard. *A History of Framingham, Massachusetts, Early Known as Danforth's Farms, 1640–1880*. Framingham, Mass.: Town of Framingham, 1887.

Thernstrom, Stephan. *The Other Bostonians: Poverty and Progress in the American Metropolis, 1880–1970*. Cambridge: Harvard University Press, 1973.

Thernstrom, Stephan, and Peter R. Knights. "Men in Motion: Some Data and Speculation about Urban Population Mobility in Nineteenth-Century America." *Institute of Government and Public Affairs*, no. MR-143. Los Angeles: University of California Press, for the Institute of Government and Public Affairs, 1970.

Trotter, Joe William, ed. *The Great Migration in Historical Perspective*. Bloomington: Indiana University Press, 1991.

Trowbridge, John Townshend. *Cudjo's Cave*. 1863. Reprint, Tuscaloosa: University of Alabama Press, 2001.

U.S. Department of the Interior. National Parks Service. *Salem: Maritime Salem in the Age of Sail*. National Park Handbook no. 126. Washington, D.C.: U.S. Government Printing Office, 1987.

Valuska, David Lawrence. "The Negro in the Union Navy, 1861–1865." Ph.D. diss., Lehigh University, 1973.

Van Deburg, William L. *Slavery and Race in American Popular Culture*. Madison: University of Wisconsin Press, 1984.

Vickers, Daniel. *Farmers and Fishermen: Two Centuries of Work in Essex County, Massachusetts, 1630–1850*. Chapel Hill: University of North Carolina Press, 1994.

———. Keynote address at "Race, Ethnicity and Power in Maritime America" conference. Mystic Seaport Museum, Mystic, Conn., September 17, 1995.

Ward, David. "Nineteenth-Century Boston: A Study in the Role of Antecedent and Adjacent Conditions in the Spatial Aspects of Urban Growth." Ph.D. diss., University of Wisconsin, 1963.

Warner, John Harley. *The Therapeutic Perspective: Medical Practice, Knowledge, and Identity in America, 1820–1885*. Cambridge: Harvard University Press, 1986.

Warner, Robert Austin. *New Haven Negroes: A Social History*. New York: Arno Press, 1969.

Webster, Daniel. "The Second Reply to Hayne (January 26–27, 1830)." Dartmouth

College Archives. Retrieved May 2001 from <http://www.dartmouth.edu/
~dwebster/speeches/hayne-speech.html>.

Wentworth, Harold, and Stuart Burg Flexner, eds. *Dictionary of American Slang*, 2d
ed. New York: Crowell, 1975.

White, Shane. *Somewhat More Independent: The End of Slavery in New York City, 1770–
1810*. Athens: University of Georgia Press, 1991.

White, Arthur O. "Salem's Antebellum Black Community: Seedbed of the School Integration Movement." *Essex Institute of Historical Collections* 108, 2 (April 1972):
99–118.

White, Shane. "'It Was a Proud Day': African Americans, Festivals, and Parades in
the North, 1741–1834." *Journal of American History* 81, 1 (June 1994): 13–51.

Whitehill, Walter Muir. *Boston: A Topographical History*. Cambridge: Harvard University Press, Belknap Press, 1968.

Whitman, Walt. "Democratic Vistas." In *Prose Works* (par. 69). 1892. Project Bartleby.
Retrieved May 2001 from http://www.bartleby.com/229/20023.html

"William H. Johnson's Civil War Letters." Manuscript Collections. University South
Caroliniana Society. South Caroliniana Library, University of South Carolina.
Retrieved June 2001 from <http://www.sc.edu/library/socar/uscs/1995/
whjohn95.html>.

Winch, Julie. *Philadelphia's Black Elite: Activism, Accommodation, and the Struggle for
Autonomy*. Philadelphia: Temple University Press, 1988.

Winsor, Justin. *The Memorial History of Boston, Including Suffolk County, Massachusetts,
1630–1880*. 4 vols. Boston: J.R. Osgood & Co., 1881.

Zack, Naomi. *Race and Mixed Race*. Philadelphia: Temple University Press, 1993.

Zilversmit, Arthur. *The First Emancipation: The Abolition of Slavery in the North*.
Chicago: University of Chicago Press, 1967.

"Well! there it is, & here we are!"

Note: Page numbers of illustrations are in italics.

HIGHSMITH #45230